2004

VIET NAM
a transition tiger?

VIET NAM

a transition tiger?

Brian Van Arkadie & Raymond Mallon

Asia Pacific Press at
The Australian National University

© Asia Pacific Press 2003

Published by Asia Pacific Press at The Australian National University. This work is copyright. Apart from those uses which may be permitted under the *Copyright Act 1968* as amended, no part may be reproduced by any process without written permission from the publisher. The views expressed in this book are those of the author and not necessarily of the publisher.

National Library of Australia Cataloguing-in-Publication

Van Arkadie, Brian.
Viet Nam—a transition tiger?

Bibliography.
Includes index.
ISBN 0 7315 3750 5.

1. Vietnam - Economic conditions - 1975- . 2. Vietnam - Economic policy - 1975- . I. Mallon, Raymond. II. Title.

338.9597

Edited by Matthew May, Asia Pacific Press
Production by Asia Pacific Press
Cover designed by Annie Di Nallo Design
Printed in Australia by Paragon Printers

959.704
V 217

939.13

CONTENTS

TABLES

SYMBOLS USED IN TABLES

n.a.   not applicable
..   not available
-       zero
.   insignificant

ABBREVIATIONS

ADB	Asian Development Bank
AFTA	ASEAN Free Trade Area
ASEAN	Association of Southeast Asian Nations
CBR	crude birth rate
CDF	Comprehensive Development Framework
CIEM	Central Institute of Economic Management
CIS	Commonwealth of Independent States
CMEA	Council for Mutual Economic Assistance
CPI	Consumer Price Index
CPV	Communist Party of Vietnam
CSCER	Central Steering Commitee for Enterprise Reform
DAC	development assistance community
EPZ	export processing zone
ESAP	Enhanced Structural Adjustment Program
EU	European Union
FDI	foreign direct investment
GDP	gross domestic product
GNP	gross national product
GSO	General Statistical Office
HDI	Human Development Index
HRD	human resource development
IFPRI	International Food Policy Research Institute
IMF	International Monetary Fund
IRRI	International Rice Research Institute
LSMS	Living Standards Measurement Study
MARD	Ministry of Agriculture and Rural Development
MFI	multilateral financial institutions
MOFI	Ministry of Finance
MOJ	Ministry of Justice
MOLISA	Ministry of Labour, Invalids and Social Affairs
MPI	Ministry of Planning and Investment
NIC	newly industrialised country
ODA	official development assistance
OECD	Organisation for Economic Cooperation and Development

PIP	Public Investment Program
PSA	Provincial Seed Agency
SAC	Structural Adjustment Credit
SBVN	State Bank of Viet Nam
SGELI	Steering Group for Enterprise Law Implementation
SOE	state-owned enterprise
UK	United Kingdom
UN	United Nations
UNDP	United Nations Development Programme
US	United States
USSR	Union of Soviet Socialist Republics
VAT	value-added tax
VCCI	Vietnam Chamber of Commerce and Industry
VLSS	Vietnam Living Standards Survey

PREFACE

This volume is a by-product of the work done by the two authors in Viet Nam over the past 15 years. Over that period we have worked with many different government agencies in Viet Nam and for a large number of donors. We have had the opportunity to discuss developments in Viet Nam with many knowledgeable observers—Vietnamese scholars and government officials, domestic and foreign business people, foreign academics, NGO representatives, the staff of donor agencies, diplomats and others. Given the help we have received from so many, it is difficult and a little invidious to acknowledge only a few. Nevertheless, there are a few people who have been particularly helpful and particularly deserve our thanks.

Early in our work in Hanoi, we were both very lucky to work with Vu Tat Boi, then with the office of the Council of Ministers, and the able team of young Vietnamese he assembled to staff and advise the UN Management Development Programme. Under that project, we both participated in a program to select and train twenty-seven young Vietnamese for overseas postgraduate training in subjects relevant to the economic reform process. From those two groups of young people, we made many friends whom we keep meeting in increasingly high-level positions in government, business, academia and donor agencies.

Le Dang Doanh and his colleagues, national and international, at the Central Institute of Economic Management also have provided us with valuable insights and challenged our thinking and interpretations on numerous occasions. Pham Chin Lan from the Vietnamese Chamber of Commerce and Industry was an important source of ideas on business issues.

Many individuals from the offices of government; ministries of planning and investment, finance, agriculture and rural development, and foreign affairs; and provincial peoples' committees have assisted us, both professionally and at a personal level, making Viet Nam a stimulating and productive work environment. In particular, we gained valuable insights working on projects headed by former planning ministers, Do Quoc Sam and Tranh Xuan Gia.

We have also learnt much from discussions with the international community during our work, sometimes learning most when we agreed least. The two Adams—Adam Fforde and Adam McCarty—have been a continuing source of stimulus. Among aid officials during the early 1990s, David Dollar of the World Bank provided valuable insights to all those working on economic reform in Viet Nam, while in more recent years, J.P. Verbiest, previously the Asian Development Bank (ADB) resident representative, and Robert Glofcheski of the UNDP office in Hanoi, have proved stimulating colleagues. Two successive Swedish ambassadors, Borje Lljunggren and Gus Edgren, were also most helpful in generating lively exchanges of ideas. A number of domestic and foreign lawyers and business experts (too many to name) helped stimulate our thinking about law and economic development.

We also thank the development agencies that have funded much of our work in Viet Nam, including the Asian Development Bank, United Nations Development Programme and World Bank, from the multilateral agencies, and the Australian Agency for International Development (AusAID), GTZ, SIDA, DANIDA, NORAD, and the Netherlands DGIS amongst the bilateral agencies. If in the text we have occasionally bitten the hands that have fed us, we have no doubt it will be taken in good spirit.

In preparing the text for publication we received help from Richard Jones in Hanoi, who volunteered his time and energy to check the manuscript, and Matthew May, of Asia Pacific Press, who has taken on the daunting tasking of preparing the manuscript for publication. We also thank those readers who took the time to provide valuable comments on earlier drafts of this manuscript.

Ray Mallon would particularly like to offer his personal thanks to To Hanh Trinh and her family for their insights into Viet Nam. Brian Van Arkadie would like to offer personal thanks also to Ray and his family, and to Goran Andersson, of the Swedish Institute of Public Administration (SIPU), for offering encouragement and hospitality.

Needless to say, as this volume offers personal judgments and interpretations on a number of complex and sometimes contentious issues, none of those thanked should be held responsible for any of the contents, although they surely can claim credit if our efforts prove useful.

Brian Van Arkadie and Raymond Mallon
March 2003

1

VIET NAM'S DEVELOPMENT EXPERIENCE

Since the late 1980s Viet Nam has been remarkably successful in achieving rapid economic growth and reducing poverty. While per capita income levels are still far behind most other East Asian economies, economic growth rates and rates of poverty reduction during the 1990s were amongst the highest in the world.

In addressing that experience this book is intended to make two contributions. First, a comprehensive review of developments in the economy and the evolution of economic policy since the mid 1980s is presented. Second, and more ambitiously, an effort has been made to interpret and explain some key factors driving Vietnamese economic growth.

The latter task is not easy. Viet Nam is a large, diverse and populous country, with a turbulent modern history. During the period covered, Viet Nam has implemented its own version of economic reform (*Doi Moi*, or 'economic renewal') which has been profound enough in its effects to justify identifying Viet Nam as an economy 'in transition'. It has, however, retained a stated commitment to developing a Marxist-Leninist state and has been criticised by many international commentators for the slow pace of reform of an apparently cumbersome administrative and regulatory apparatus.

The high growth rates and reductions in poverty achieved by Viet Nam during the 1990s took the international community by surprise.[1] Throughout the 1990s, many international advisors warned that Vietnamese development targets were overambitious. During the last 15 years, Viet Nam was repeatedly warned that it was at a critical turning point in the reform process, and that concerted efforts were urgently needed to accelerate and 'deepen' its reforms to avert economic stagnation. And yet the Vietnamese economy has performed well, frequently exceeding 'overambitious' targets.[2] In the face of many dire warnings about the consequences of failure to implement all aspects of proposed reform packages, Viet Nam continued with a selective ('step-by-step') approach to reform, in some areas acting decisively, in others moving with a high degree of caution.

During the period covered, the dominant paradigm informing international policy advice was what has been called the 'Washington consensus', associated with the Bretton Woods institutions—the World Bank and International Monetary Fund (IMF). The central themes of the 'consensus' are an emphasis on the virtues of greatly extending the play of free markets, reducing the economic intervention of the state, and maintaining macroeconomic stability. Many of the components of this consensus would be accepted by most economists. Opinions vary, however, about the role of the state, the institutional requirements to make markets work for the common good, and the interventions required to ensure that the benefits of growth are equitably distributed.

While advocates of the Washington consensus are quite ready to claim that the Vietnamese experience validates their paradigm, this volume argues that Viet Nam's quite remarkable development progress is not so readily subsumed within the more orthodox versions of that framework. Basically, according to the tenets of orthodoxy that call for minimum state intervention, the Vietnamese economy should not have performed as well as it has, given continuing extensive state intervention in economic activity.

In seeking to understand the factors that have contributed to Viet Nam's success, the intention is to contribute to a broader literature on the economic performance of East Asia in recent decades which has explored the wide range of institutional and policy experience of the region.[3]

There have always been voices in the mainstream economic literature which have resisted the more simplistic versions of the 'Washington consensus'. Interestingly, in recent years some vocal criticisms have come from economists associated with the World Bank.[4]

The diversity of views reflects the international reality that the development profession and development institutions have still much to learn about economic development processes. Douglass North asks

How do we account for the persistence of poverty in the midst of plenty? If we know the sources of plenty, why don't poor countries simply adopt policies that make for plenty? The answer is straightforward. We just don't know how to get there. We must create incentives for people to invest in more efficient technology, increase their skills, and organize efficient markets. Such incentives are embodied in institutions. Thus we must understand the nature of institutions and how they evolve (2000:n.p.)

Attempts to understand the Vietnamese reality should reduce the dangers of offering irrelevant or counterproductive advice. Lessons also may be derived from this experience that could be useful for other developing and transitional economies. There should, however, be no expectation that a blueprint for reform will be provided, to be applied mechanically elsewhere, as a recurring theme of this study is that successful policy is built on pragmatic responses to specific national circumstances.

While the focus is on more recent developments, the book includes a description of the Vietnamese economic reform (*Doi Moi*) processes from its antecedents in the early 1980s, through to 2001. The authors discuss both the impact of policies on economic performance, and the impact of economic experience on policy formulation.

This introductory chapter introduces some of the questions that motivate this study.

DOI MOI IN AN INTERNATIONAL CONTEXT

The book aims to describe what Viet Nam has achieved in terms of socioeconomic development, especially in terms of the level and distribution of economic growth, during the period of transition. The main narrative depicts events in Viet Nam, but some attempts are also made to compare and contrast Viet Nam's performance with two main benchmarks: East Asian economies during their periods of accelerated growth; and other reforming centrally planned economies.

Viet Nam as a developing East Asian economy: falling behind and catching up

An obvious point of comparison is with the remarkable success the East Asian economies have had during recent decades in greatly increasing per capita incomes and reducing poverty. In the final four decades of the twentieth century, Hong Kong, South Korea, Singapore and Taiwan were transformed from poor underdeveloped economies to modern and relatively affluent economies through growth rates that were among the highest recorded in the history of world development. More recently, dramatic transformations have also been taking place in Malaysia, Thailand and China. Figure 1.1 provides a historical perspective of Viet Nam's economic performance relative to selected Asian economies.

Data from Maddison (2001) show that, at the end of World War II, per capita income in Viet Nam was well above that of China, around 85 per cent that of South Korea, and 80 per cent that of Thailand and Indonesia, but only 62 per cent that of the Philippines (see Figure 1.1). Military struggle during most of the 1950s, 1960s and early 1970s, meant that the economy stagnated and Viet Nam's relative position deteriorated. Of the countries listed in Table 1.1, since 1950 Viet Nam's per capita income has only increased relative to that of the Philippines.

Figure 1.1 **Viet Nam's per capita income as a proportion of selected Asian economies' per capita income, 1950–98 (per cent)**

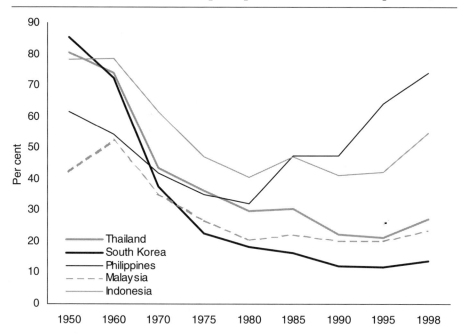

Source: Maddison, A., 2001. *The World Economy: a millennial perspective*, Organisation for Economic Cooperation and Development, Paris.

The relative level of Viet Nam's per capita income declined sharply compared to the successful East Asian economies during the four decades 1950–90, but there was a reversal in this decline in relative position in the final decade of the century (Table 1.2).

The protracted military struggle was the primary cause of decline until the mid 1970s. Military conflicts in Cambodia and with China, and a dysfunctional economic policy regime compounded the decline during the later 1970s and early 1980s. The subsequent reversal of the relative decline is the main theme of this volume.

The timing of the revival in Viet Nam's economic fortunes coincided with the introduction of *Doi Moi*. The central importance of *Doi Moi* is accepted by all commentators on the Vietnamese economy.[5] However, although the shift

Table 1.1	Per capita incomes in selected Asian countries, 1950–98[a]								
	1950	1960	1970	1975	1980	1985	1990	1995	1998
Viet Nam	658	799	735	710	758	929	1,040	1,403	1,677
Thailand	817	1,078	1,694	1,959	2,554	3,054	4,645	6,620	6,205
South Korea	770	1,105	1,954	3,162	4,114	5,670	8,704	11,873	12,152
Philippines	1,070	1,475	1,761	2,028	2,369	1,964	2,199	2,185	2,268
Malaysia	1,559	1,530	2,079	2,648	3,657	4,157	5,131	6,943	7,100
Indonesia	840	1,019	1,194	1,505	1,870	1,972	2,516	3,329	3,070
China	439	673	783	874	1,067	1,522	1,858	2,653	3,177

Note: [a] 1990 international Geary–Khamis dollars
Source: Maddison, A., 2001. *The World Economy: a millennial perspective*, Organisation for Economic Cooperation and Development, Paris.

Table 1.2	Per capita income in Viet Nam, 1950–98[a] (per cent of incomes in selected Asian countries)								
	1950	1960	1970	1975	1980	1985	1990	1995	1998
Thailand	80.5	74.1	43.4	36.2	29.7	30.4	22.4	21.2	27.0
South Korea	85.5	72.3	37.6	22.5	18.4	16.4	11.9	11.8	13.8
Philippines	61.5	54.2	41.7	35.0	32.0	47.3	47.3	64.2	73.9
Malaysia	42.2	52.2	35.4	26.8	20.7	22.3	20.3	20.2	23.6
Indonesia	78.3	78.4	61.6	47.2	40.5	47.1	41.3	42.1	54.6
China	149.9	118.7	93.9	81.2	71.0	61.0	56.0	52.9	52.8

Note: [a] 1990 international Geary–Khamis dollars.
Source: Derived from Maddison, A., 2001. *The World Economy: a millennial perspective*, Organisation for Economic Cooperation and Development, Paris.

in the policy regime explains the timing of the economic revival, it does not explain the sustained strength of the subsequent growth performance.

How was it possible for Viet Nam to shift swiftly from being an inward-looking stagnant economy to such a successful process of assimilation? The answer to this question is partly a matter of policy reform, but also reflects underlying institutional and human resource capabilities.

Viet Nam as a reforming centrally planned economy: a transition success

Comparisons with other transition economies are much more flattering for Viet Nam. Viet Nam has outperformed other transition economies, except for China (Figure 1.2). Moreover, it has done this while maintaining macroeconomic and social stability, and while continuing to improve key human development indicators such as life expectancy and educational and health data. While Viet Nam halved its incidence of poverty, the incidence of poverty in the Commonwealth of Independent States (CIS) increased from 1 in 25 persons to 1 in 5 persons in the decade to 1998 (World Bank 2002:xiii). For most CIS countries, the economic decline in the early stages of reform was far worse than the impact of the Great Depression on developed countries in the 1930s (see World Bank 2002:5).

Substantial changes in the economic system were implemented in Viet Nam at the end of the 1980s without a decline in economic activity. The economy grew despite the sudden collapse of Soviet aid and trade, a continuing US-led boycott that blocked the provision of financial assistance from the multilateral financial institutions. In contrast, deep economic contractions and social dislocation generally accompanied reform in the European centrally planned economies.

Why did Viet Nam perform so much better than other Council for Mutual Economic Assistance (CMEA) economies?[6] A theme developed in this study is that the nature of the system subject to reform was in certain critical respects different from other centrally planned CMEA economies.

Understanding the characteristics of the system subject to reform is critically important to any interpretation of an economic reform process. In the Vietnamese case this is not easy, as the working of the pre-reform system was somewhat obscure.

A key argument of the study is that, despite the adoption of the vocabulary of central planning, the Vietnamese economy was never effectively subjected

Figure 1.2 **GDP growth in selected transition economies, 1980–2000 (per cent per annum)**

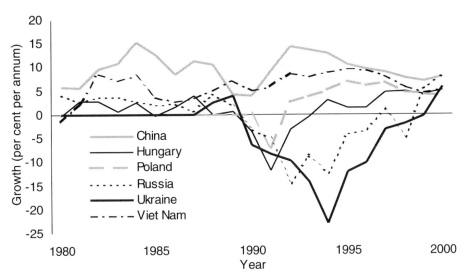

Source: Data from World Bank, 2002. *World Development Indicators*, World Bank, Washington, DC.

to the same level of centralised control as in the former USSR and Eastern European centrally planned economies. Indeed, it could be argued that success during the prolonged military conflicts was largely built around effective decentralisation of day-to-day management decisions and encouraging local initiatives.

Other important features were the relative importance of the rural sector, the dominant role of household units in agriculture production, and the limited development of heavy industry at the beginning of the reform process. The economy was technically less advanced than Eastern Europe and the CIS economies, but demonstrated greater resilience in the face of change and dislocation in the macroeconomy. Soviet-style industrialisation had been limited, so there was not the same inheritance of large scale, inflexible industrial dinosaurs, which has posed such difficult challenges to reform in the former Soviet Union.

The degree of institutional stability maintained during the transition process was also crucially important. Instead of the 'root and branch' destruction of old institutions as a prelude to the installation of new mechanisms, many reforms were directed at making existing institutions work better, while gradually introducing new market institutions. The step-by-step approach to reform was based on continuity in the political system, which operates through building and maintaining consensus on economic and institutional reforms.

Of course, Viet Nam also had one fortuitous advantage: its geographical location. Adjacent to the region which was in the midst of a sustained boom (until the crisis of 1997), there was a spill-over of capital and entrepreneurial energy from dynamic neighbours. This was aided by growing political stability in Cambodia, and improving relations between China and Viet Nam. Demographic transition also contributed positively to growth in this period.

LEARNING FROM THE VIETNAMESE EXPERIENCE

In surveying the Vietnamese experience of successful economic growth, it is not easy to separate the influence of exogenous factors from the impact of policy. Powerful exogenous factors that supported the expansion of the Vietnamese economy have included Viet Nam's regional location and the trajectory of the regional economy, the timing of natural resource (oil) exploitation, the entrepreneurial vitality of the Vietnamese, access to a sizeable and dynamic emigrant community, and the onset of peace. Yet the acceleration of growth also began with strongly negative exogenous factors, such as the economic consequences of the demise of the Soviet Union and the CMEA and the effects of the US embargo.

Part of the problem is sorting out the impact of the systemic reforms introduced under the aegis of *Doi Moi* from such exogenous effects. The balance of the argument will be that the *Doi Moi* reforms were a necessary, but not sufficient, ingredient in the Vietnamese success story (that is, that the degree of success may not be readily replicable in different environments). Nevertheless, it can be reasonably argued that certain lessons can be drawn about effective policymaking.

Another set of difficulties relates to the interpretation of the timing and sequencing of policy impacts. The introduction of the *Doi Moi* reforms began in the second half of the 1980s, and the acceleration in growth began in the early 1990s, suggesting a strong causal relationship. However, that leaves open the issue of how far the foundations of Viet Nam's performance in the 1990s were laid in the pre-reform period. Should aspects of policy in the pre-*Doi Moi* be interpreted as important inputs into the later successes, or should that period be seen simply as an era of mistaken policy, which failed to realise inherent potential and held back the achievement of growth? This account argues that, despite many mistakes, some important building blocks of later success were laid in the pre-*Doi Moi* period.

A further area for speculation relates to policies that have not been implemented. In donor tutorials, euphemistically entitled 'policy dialogue', there have been areas of persistent nagging, where donors have felt that the Vietnamese policy regime has had failings. The most persistent areas of criticism have related to the reform of state enterprises and the regulatory environment for foreign investment. More recently, issues of public administration, governance and corruption have received increased emphasis.

By and large, the record suggests that the often predicted dire consequences of failure to reform more vigorously in such directions have not yet materialised. Does this imply that donor advice has been misplaced, or that even greater achievements would have resulted from more receptivity to donor tutorials, or even that the negative consequences have been merely postponed? These questions are considered in this book, although it is difficult to provide definitive answers.

NOTES

1. A joint United Nations–Government of Viet Nam study of the economy, produced in 1989 by a team under the leadership of one author of this volume was quite optimistic about the prospects for growth. The same was true for an Asian Development Bank (ADB) report which the other author helped draft the same year. A 1990 World Bank economic report concluded that '[i]f Viet Nam follows through on its reform program, its medium-term prospects are excellent'. However, none of these reports included quantitative projections and, if the attempt had been made, projected growth would undoubtedly have been more modest than the actual achievement.

2. Dollar (2001:1) notes that 'Viet Nam has been one of the fastest growing economies in the world in the 1990s, and yet by many conventional measures it has poor economic policies'.

3. The literature on this is extensive. Examples include Amsden (1989), Ha-Joon Chang (1999), Jomo K.S. (1997), Krugman (1994), Wade (1990) and World Bank (1993a).

4. The most distinguished of these critical voices has been that of Joseph Stiglitz, Nobel Laureate and former Vice President of the World Bank. Another ex-World Bank economist, William Easterly, has also mounted a strong challenge to World Bank orthodoxies. And, in fairness

to the World Bank, its own research programs frequently offer a nuanced view of the range of appropriate policies, as in Nelson and Pack (1999).

[5] But some have argued that it has not been positive. Kolko (1997) argues that market reforms have resulted in peasants losing their land, the emergence of a class society through increasing inequality, and the fact that Vietnamese 'industrial workers are amongst the most exploited in the world'. He argues that Communist efforts to merge a socialist world with a market strategy have resulted in the worst of both worlds.

[6] CMEA was the Council for Mutual Economic Assistance, which included the former USSR, the Eastern European centrally planned countries and Viet Nam, but not China.

2

GEOGRAPHY, RESOURCES AND POPULATION

Viet Nam is the twelfth most populous country in the world, but only fifty-eighth largest in terms of land area (Communist Party of Vietnam 2001b). In terms of land area and population it is a little smaller than Germany. The population density is high and cultivatable land per person is very low. The population is heavily concentrated in the Red River and Mekong River Deltas. There is a long, narrow coastal strip linking the deltas. The two substantial highland areas (the Northern and Central Highlands) are more sparsely populated that the deltas. Viet Nam's population is better educated and has a higher life expectancy than that of most countries with similar average per capita incomes.

GEOGRAPHY AND THE NATURAL RESOURCE BASE

Viet Nam extends 1,650 kilometres from north to south. At its widest point the country stretches 600 kilometres from west to east, and at its narrowest point, only 50 kilometres. Viet Nam is located close to major shipping routes, and relatively prosperous and rapidly expanding East Asian economies. It has a very long coast line (about 3,000 kilometres) providing opportunities for fishing and tourism (and smuggling), and also ensuring that most areas of the country are not far from access to transport to foreign markets. While natural resources have played an important role in recent economic development, the country is not particularly well endowed with agricultural, forest, energy, or mineral resources.

Map 2.1   **Main regions of Viet Nam**

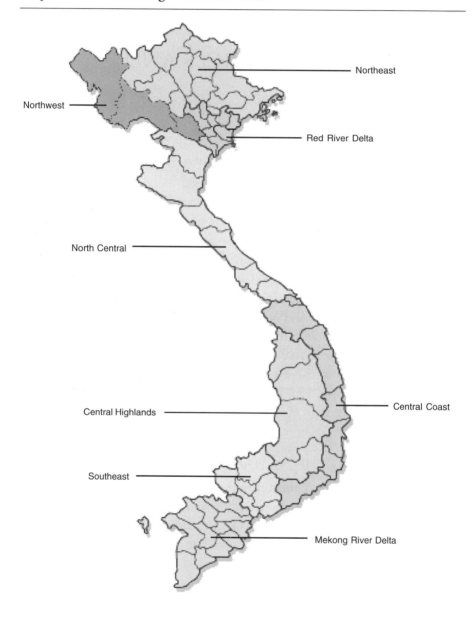

Source: Adapted from World Bank, n.d. Map of Vietnam, World Bank, Hanoi. Available online at http://www.worldbank.org.vn/wbivn/map/map001.htm.

The country's location and length results in great variations in climate, ranging from tropical to temperate, and allows for a diversity of flora and fauna. The southern and central areas are tropical and humid. The northern areas are also humid, but temperatures are much more variable with average temperatures ranging from around 30 degrees in July to 16–18 degrees in January. Average temperatures in the south range from 26 to 28 degrees throughout the year. Typhoons are experienced in most parts of the country, but are most severe in the central provinces. Rainfall variability is very high in the North and Central provinces, contributing to variability in agricultural output and incomes. Rainfall is more reliable in the southern areas, but all parts of the country suffer from frequent natural calamities.

Vietnam has rich biological diversity in its forests, rivers and oceans. A great variety of crops, cultivars and domesticated animals are used in its agricultural systems. Some 275 different animal, 826 bird, and 180 reptile species are found in Viet Nam. Wild animals include elephants, dapple deer, leopards, tigers, bears, wild buffalo, samba deer, mountain goats, monkeys, goats, bobcats, foxes and squirrels. Three out of the seven new species of wild animals identified during the twentieth century were found in Viet Nam's forests. More than 1,000 medicinal plant species have already been identified. An indication of the richness of Viet Nam's biodiversity is shown in Table 2.1.

On the other hand, habitat loss and hunting have resulted in 16 different primate species, 4 large mammals, and 25 bird species being threatened (World Bank 2000:105). Five large water bird species have become extinct in the

Table 2.1 **Biodiversity in Viet Nam**

	Number of species in Viet Nam (SV)	Number of species in the world (SW)	SV/SW (per cent)
Mammals	275	4,000	6.8
Birds	800	9,040	8.8
Reptiles	180	6,300	2.9
Amphibians	80	4,148	2.0
Fish	2,470	19,000	13.0
Plants	7,000[a]	220,000	3.2

Note: [a] It has been estimated that another 5,000 species have still not been formally identified.
Source: Biodiversity Information Management System On-Line, http://www.geoanalytics.com/bims/vm.htm.

Mekong Delta in the last 30 years. Wetlands in the two main deltas are under threat because of high population pressures, and increased economic incentives to exploit these areas.

Agriculture, forestry and fishery resources and the environment

The long north–south axis, and mix of coastal and upland areas, provides scope for Viet Nam to grow a wide variety of tropical and temperate crops and forests. The relatively small ratio of cultivatable land per person greatly influences agricultural technology and the rural economy. The high variability in rainfall and frequent typhoons are important influences on rural social and economic systems. Poorly developed physical infrastructure constrains market access in many locations, especially in the mountainous areas.

The most productive agricultural land is found in the Mekong and Red River deltas, the two most densely populated rural areas. Cropped land per capita is low by international and regional standards—0.09 hectares per person, compared with 0.16 in India and 0.30 in Thailand—but is comparable with Sri Lanka (0.10 hectares) and Bangladesh (0.07 hectares).

The Mekong River Delta accounted for 38 per cent of total value added in the agricultural sector in 1999 (with 12 per cent of the land area), while the Red River Delta accounted for 19 per cent (with only 4.5 per cent of the total land area) (General Statistics Office 2000b). Most of the population (especially the Kinh majority) is concentrated in the two main deltas and a narrow section of the east and southeast coast. Only a small portion of the highland areas bordering Laos and China are suitable for cropping, and population densities

Table 2.2 **Key rural indicators in selected Asian economies**

Country	Rural population (% of total in 2000)	Agricultural output (% of GDP in 2000)	Arable land (ha/capita in 1999)
Viet Nam	80.3	24.6	.09
Bangladesh	78.8	24.3	.07
China	65.7	15.9	.11
India	71.6	25.3	.16
Indonesia	58.8	16.9	.15
Malaysia	42.7	8.6	.35
Philippines	41.4	15.9	.13
Sri Lanka	76.4	19.4	.10
Thailand	78.4	9.1	.30

Source: Asian Development Bank, 2001. *Key Indicators 2001*, Asian Development Bank, Manila.

in these areas are low, with higher proportions of ethnic minority groups. Despite the low ratio of cultivable agriculture land, Viet Nam has emerged as a leading agricultural exporter, and has also substantially diversified agriculture exports in recent years.

Vietnam's forests are concentrated in the upland regions, with about 40 per cent found in the central highlands. Forests are an important economic resource, providing firewood, protein, income and materials for shelter. Until recently, most of the population in mountainous areas lived near forests and earned part of their livelihood through the harvest and sale of bamboo, firewood, medicine, fruit, fodder and game from forests. Some 2,300 forest plant species are harvested for food, medicine, construction, textiles and water proofing (World Bank 2000).

Forest resources are, however, being depleted. Population growth and economic development are increasing pressures to clear forests and to expand agriculture into highland areas and other environmentally fragile areas. Between 1943 and 1997, five million hectares of Vietnamese forests were converted to other uses. Forest cover fell from 43 per cent of the country's total land area in 1945, to just 28 per cent by 1997. Large areas were destroyed during the war with the United States as a result of bombing and deliberate attempts to reduce forest cover by spraying chemical poisons.

Underlying causes of continuing deforestation include poorly controlled logging, rural poverty resulting in burning of forests for farming and foraging for food for fuel, and inappropriate land tenure arrangements. While the government has adopted programs to reduce poverty, better manage forests, and reforest barren hill lands in an attempt to reverse the decline in forest cover, the pursuit of other objectives (for example, promoting accelerated growth of industrial crops for export) has placed increasing pressures on the natural environment.

Inland fishing and marine products are important sources of protein and income for many communities. Almost three million people are directly employed in the sector; nearly 10 per cent of the population derives their main income from fisheries, and fish consumption provides about half of national protein consumption. Exports of aquatic products have been important contributors to rapid export growth. The total area of natural inland water bodies (lakes and rivers) is estimated to be about 4,200 km², and there are additional ponds and seasonal flooded areas of 6,000 km². In addition, a number of reservoirs are used for fishing. Concerns are growing, however, about over-fishing, unsustainable fishing practices, the impacts of industrial pollution, and the sustainability of shrimp farming in former mangrove swamps. With rising demand for water, deforestation and weaknesses in watershed management, and poor irrigation and drainage infrastructure, there are concerns that water quality is deteriorating in many areas.

Energy, minerals and water

Another important contributor to rapid export growth during the late 1980s and 1990s was the development of the country's oil resources. New oil and gas resources continue to be found and developed (mostly offshore from Vung Tau in the south), and will be significant contributors to economic growth and budget revenue for at least the medium term. While many areas are still to be explored, most experts estimate that reserves are substantially less than oil rich Southeast Asian nations such as Brunei, Indonesia and Malaysia on a per capita basis. Coal and hydropower development (especially in the north) has also contributed significantly to economic growth.

While the country is known to possess a wide range of other minerals, commercial exploration is hampered by uncertainty about property rights. Lead, zinc, antimony, pyrite, manganese, limestone, marble, salt and precious stones are also currently being exploited. Studies suggest commercial potential to develop bauxite, phosphates (mostly from apatite), lead, gold, tin, graphite, iron ore, manganese, chrome and asbestos.

Viet Nam is endowed with river systems that have potential for hydro-power development, estimated at about 18,000 megawatts. Some 3,700 megawatts' capacity has already been developed.

POPULATION AND DEMOGRAPHIC TRANSITION

The population of Viet Nam was estimated at 78.7 million in 2001 (General Statistics Office 2000a). The crude birth rate fell from 45 per thousand (1955–59), to 38 (1970–74), to 31 (1985–89), and then to 19.9 per thousand in the 1999 Census (General Statistics Office 2000a). Declining fertility reflects widespread adoption of family planning practices. The government has maintained a population policy that discouraging families of more than two children, but without draconian controls. The decline in the birth rate must also have been associated with success of health policies that increased life expectancy at birth, and with the achievement of high educational enrolments.

While distinct regional differences in fertility persist, with much higher rates in the highland areas than in the delta and urban areas, a substantial decline in fertility is recorded for all regions.[1] The estimated rate of population growth fell from 2.1 per cent per annum during 1979–89 to about 1.7 per cent per annum from 1989 to 1999. The population growth rate has continued to fall, and the General Statistics Office (2000a) now estimates the rate at 1.35 per cent in 2001, with a fertility rate of 2.3 children per woman. Life expectancy has continued to increase during *Doi Moi* from an already relatively high 67 years in 1992 to an estimated 68.6 years in 1999.

Thus, Viet Nam has experienced a rapid demographic transition (McNicholl 2002). Relatively low mortality rates and declining fertility rates have resulted in a clear transition in the population's age profile. At the time of the 1989 Census the profile was a pyramid, with each five year cohort larger than the next older group.[2] By 1999, this profile had changed in a crucial fashion, with a 5–9 year old cohort smaller than the 10–14 group, and the 0–4 cohort showing an even sharper drop in size. Viet Nam is now experiencing a 'demographic bonus',[3] in which a declining population growth rate is reducing the burdens on the education system, increasing the proportion of income earners and making it easier to achieve increases in per capita income, which in turn is associated with a further decline in birth rates.

The country is predominantly rural. Only 19.5 per cent of the population resided in urban areas in 1990.[4] At that time, Viet Nam's economic structure was characteristic of a low-income developing economy. In terms of the sources of livelihood for the population, the country was (and is) still predominantly agricultural. Of the total estimated active labour force in 1992 of 31.8 million, 23.0 million (72 per cent) were engaged in agriculture and little more than one-tenth in industry. In 1990, agriculture and fisheries still accounted for two-fifths (39 per cent) of GDP. Some 80 per cent of the population still live in rural areas.[5]

OVERVIEW OF THE REGIONS

The Red River Delta, with a population of 17.2 million in 2001, is the most densely populated region. It includes the national capital Hanoi and the port city of Hai Phong (the second and third largest cities in Viet Nam). The combined population of Hanoi and Hai Phong is less than half that of Ho Chi Minh City.[6] More than one in five Vietnamese live in the Red River Delta.

Figure 2.1   **Viet Nam population pyramid, 1989 and 1999**

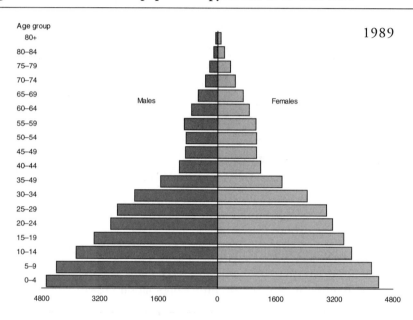

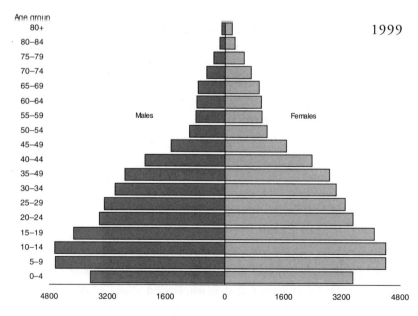

Source: General Statistics Office, 2000. *Statistical Yearbook 2001*, General Statistics Office, Hanoi.

Figure 2.2 **Age dependency ratio in selected Asian countries, 1986–2000**

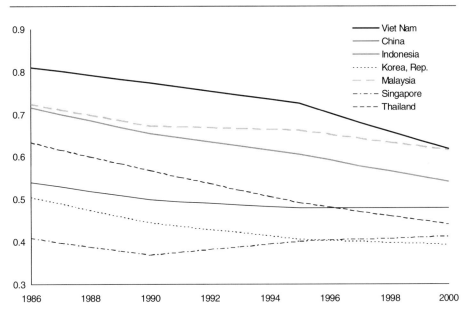

Note: The age dependency ratio is the ratio of dependants (people younger than 15 and older than 65) to the working-age population (those aged 15–64).
Source: World Bank, 2002. *World Development Indicators*, World Bank, Washington, DC.

Table 2.3 **Population distribution by region, 1995–2001 (per cent of total)**

	1995	1997	1998	1999	2000	2001
Red River Delta	22.4	22.2	22.1	22.0	21.9	21.9
Northeast	11.7	11.6	11.6	11.6	11.5	11.5
Northwest	2.9	2.9	2.9	2.9	2.9	2.9
North Central Coast	13.3	13.2	13.2	13.1	13.0	12.9
South Central Coast	8.6	8.6	8.6	8.5	8.5	8.5
Central Highlands	4.7	5.0	5.2	5.3	5.5	5.5
Southeast	14.9	15.1	15.2	15.4	15.5	15.7
Mekong River Delta	21.6	21.3	21.2	21.1	21.1	21.0

Source: General Statistics Office, 2001. *Statistical Year Book 2001*, General Statistics Office, Hanoi.

With particularly high population densities and productive land, yields per hectare are higher here than anywhere else in the country. This region is one of the three focal economic zones identified as areas for concentrated development. Hanoi, by virtue of its status as capital, attracts public and service sector investment, but is also becoming an important industrial centre. The Hanoi/ Hai Phong industrial region is second most important location for foreign invested projects after the Ho Chi Minh City/Dong Nai area.

The Northeast and Northwest regions (the Northern Uplands) have a population of 11.3 million. It is one of the regions of concentrated poverty, where weak infrastructure and limited agricultural land limit development prospects. It has experienced a low rate of agricultural growth and lower than average overall growth. Areas near Hanoi could, however, benefit from Hanoi's growth, particularly if investments are made to ensure good access. The area could also benefit from increased tourism and economic links with Yunnan province in China.

Another problematic region is North Central Coast. This region includes some of the more inhospitable areas of Viet Nam, with frequent typhoons and infertile land. As a result, the incidence of poverty is high. The region is politically important as the link between the two more developed parts of Viet Nam and has had an historical importance as the home area of key figures in Viet Nam's independence movement. The region has a population of about 10.2 million people. Like the Northern Uplands, it is a region of concentrated poverty and has experienced the lowest growth rate of all the regions in the *Doi Moi* period.

Further down the coast, the South Central Coast region (6.7 million people) has higher income levels than its northern neighbour and a growth rate of GDP and proportion of GDP generated from industry close to the national average. This region includes Da Nang, the fourth largest city and third port of Viet Nam, and a centre of one of the three focal economic zones. This area has so far been the weakest of the three focal economic zones as a magnet for foreign investment.

Inland from the South Central Coast region, where the land mass of Viet Nam widens, are the Central Highlands. This is the least densely populated of Viet Nam's regions; with the second largest land mass of all the regions (5,612 thousand hectares), it has only 4.3 million people (2001). While it contains large mountain and forest areas which are either of low potential for agricultural development or deserve protection on environmental grounds, and remote areas whose location and poor access has been a barrier to development, there are also considerable areas of high-potential underdeveloped land adaptable, for example, to high value tree crop development. As a result, it has attracted a high rate of migration and has been the centre of the dynamic growth of coffee production. This region has experienced the highest rate of rural growth and is an important host to rural–rural migrants. In 1989–99 the population of the Central Highlands grew at 4.87 per cent per annum, compared with the national average of 1.70 per cent. The share of the Central Highlands in agricultural value-added has increased sharply and, despite the net migration to this area, agricultural value-added per person in this region has also increased much faster than in the rest of the country.

The southern part of the country includes the Mekong River Delta region and the Southeast region. The Mekong River Delta is the second most populous of the regions, with over 16 million people, although it is less densely populated than the Red River Delta. It has an unrealised potential for agricultural growth both at the intensive margin (increasing productivity per hectare) and at the extensive margin (bringing more land into irrigated cultivation). It is in the Mekong that further expansion in staple food production can be most readily achieved,[7] and this could be associated with movement of labour into the region. Social and economic infrastructure is not as developed as in the Red River Delta, suggesting the need for substantial investment in rural infrastructure to take advantage of the region's potential. There is also a need to invest in road improvements to link rural areas with regional growth centres (notably the town of Can Tho) and with Ho Chi Minh City.

With a population almost as large as the Red River Delta, but a larger land area, the Mekong Delta is the main producer of a marketable food surplus for domestic consumption and export. The Red River Delta also produces a modest surplus. The rest of the country produces close to or below food self-sufficiency. Maize and cassava are the two main food staples after rice and are also mainly grown in the deltas.

The Southeast region includes Ho Chi Minh City and Dong Nai, the most dynamic centres of commercial and industrial development in Viet Nam, and the most attractive to foreign investors. Ho Chi Minh City, with about 5.4 million people (in 2001), is almost twice as populous as Hanoi. In designating the area as a focal economic zone, government is doing no more than recognising

Table 2.4   **Gross regional product per capita by major region, 1995–2000 (ratio of national average)**

	1995	1996	1997	1998	1999	2000
Red River Delta	97	97	98	98	98	99
Northeast	55	54	55	55	55	57
Northwest	40	39	39	42	41	40
North Central Coast	58	56	57	56	55	55
South Central Coast	73	73	73	73	73	73
Central Highlands	61	59	57	58	58	57
Southeast	233	236	234	234	232	228
Mekong River Delta	84	83	83	82	83	83

Source: General Statistics Office, 2002. *Viet Nam Economy in the Years of Reform*, Statistical Publishing House, Hanoi.

Table 2.5   **Share of GDP by region, 1995–2000 (per cent of total)**

	1995	1996	1997	1998	1999	2000
Red River Delta	19.53	19.14	18.86	19.30	18.86	18.59
Northeast	8.09	7.95	7.88	7.91	7.75	7.78
Northwest	1.30	1.26	1.27	1.24	1.15	1.15
North Central Coast	8.02	7.69	7.53	7.38	7.16	7.04
South Central Coast	6.27	6.24	6.31	6.43	6.25	6.25
Central Highlands	2.26	2.30	2.18	2.44	2.43	1.98
Southeast	36.44	37.11	37.76	36.96	38.67	39.99
Mekong River Delta	18.08	18.30	18.21	18.33	17.73	17.22

Source: General Statistics Office, 2002. *Viet Nam's Economy in the Years of Reform*, Statistical Publishing House, Hanoi.

the reality of the strong growth of Ho Chi Minh City, which is spilling over into neighbouring areas. Although already a large city, Ho Chi Minh City still falls short of being an East Asian mega-city,[8] but it is likely to become so within the next twenty years, with all the attendant problems and investment requirements that implies.

REGIONAL DISTRIBUTION OF ECONOMIC ACTIVITY

Some 42 per cent of the population are concentrated in the two deltas. The two main deltas account for more that 55 per cent of agricultural output. The Southeast (including Ho Chi Minh City and Dong Nai) and the Red River Delta dominate industrial output (60 per cent of total industrial output). By

Table 2.6 **Agriculture value-added by region, 1995–2000**

	1995	1997	1998	1999	2000
Percentage of total					
Red River Delta	20.1	19.6	19.6	19.0	18.6
Northeast	8.0	7.9	7.8	7.7	7.7
Northwest	1.9	1.9	1.8	1.9	1.9
North Central Coast	9.0	9.1	8.6	8.6	8.7
South Central Coast	6.1	5.9	5.9	5.7	5.5
Central Highlands	5.9	7.4	7.3	8.6	10.2
Southeast	11.1	11.3	10.8	11.1	11.2
Mekong River Delta	38.0	37.0	38.3	37.4	36.2
'000 dong/person (constant 1994 prices)					
Red River Delta	1,027	1,096	1,162	1,200	1,226
Northeast	780	847	884	920	961
Northwest	759	801	796	881	914
North Central Coast	772	855	857	916	967
South Central Coast	806	854	908	934	929
Central Highlands	1,425	1,818	1,840	2,240	2,702
Southeast	855	935	930	999	1,039
Mekong River Delta	2,012	2,161	2,369	2,457	2,485
Whole country	1,143	1,245	1,313	1,389	1,444

Source: General Statistics Office, 2000. *Statistical Year Book 2000*, General Statistics Office, Hanoi; General Statistics Office, 2001. *Statistical Year Book 2001*, General Statistics Office, Hanoi.

far the highest per capita incomes are in the Southeast, more than twice the national average. Per capita incomes in the Red River Delta are the same as the national average, but incomes in the Mekong Delta are about 83 per cent of the national average. The poorest area is the Northwest (about 40 per cent of the national average).

While the two deltas dominate agricultural output, the share of the deltas in total agricultural output has recently declined. This reflects the more rapid industrialisation and urbanisation of these areas, and the rapid development of industrial crops in upland areas, especially in the Central Highlands. The Central Highlands share of agricultural value-added increased from 5.9 to 10.2 per cent between 1995 and 2000 due to a rapid expansion in the output of coffee and other industrial crops. The Central Highlands region has the highest per capita value-added in agricultural output in Viet Nam followed by the Mekong River Delta.

Table 2.7 **Industrial value-added by domestic enterprises by region, 1995–2001 (per cent of total)**

	1995	1997	1998	1999	2000	2001
Red River Delta	19.8	19.6	19.7	20.0	20.0	20.3
Northeast	7.4	7.6	7.3	7.0	7.0	7.1
Northwest	0.4	0.4	0.5	0.4	0.4	0.4
North Central Coast	4.6	4.3	4.3	4.3	4.5	4.2
South Central Coast	5.9	6.2	6.3	6.5	6.7	6.7
Central Highlands	1.5	1.4	1.4	1.4	1.4	1.3
Southeast	38.9	38.9	38.7	39.0	39.3	39.5
Mekong River Delta	14.6	14.0	13.8	13.5	13.0	12.9
Not allocated to a province	6.9	7.6	8.0	7.9	7.8	7.7

Sources: General Statistics Office, 2000. *Statistical Year Book 2000*, General Statistics Office, Hanoi; General Statistics Office, 2001. *Statistical Year Book 2001*, General Statistics Office, Hanoi.

Table 2.8 **Total industrial value-added by region, 1995–2000**

	1995	1997	1998	1999	2000	2001
Percentage of total						
Red River Delta	17.7	18.4	19.1	19.6	20.4	20.2
Northeast	6.0	5.8	5.6	5.4	5.4	5.4
Northwest	0.3	0.3	0.3	0.3	0.3	0.3
North Central Coast	3.6	3.3	3.2	3.1	3.6	3.8
South Central Coast	4.8	4.8	4.8	4.8	4.9	5.0
Central Highlands	1.2	1.1	1.0	1.0	1.0	0.9
Southeast	49.4	50.3	50.5	50.9	50.2	50.0
Mekong River Delta	11.8	10.6	10.2	9.7	9.3	9.5
Not allocated to a province	5.2	5.4	5.4	5.2	5.0	5.0
'000/person (constant 1994 prices)						
Red River Delta	1,134	1,495	1,725	1,960	2,369	2,650
Northeast	736	906	963	1,027	1,192	1,357
Northwest	155	184	224	223	237	249
North Central Coast	387	449	489	526	709	837
South Central Coast	801	1,018	1,114	1,237	1,476	1,688
Central Highlands	362	390	390	409	452	458
Southeast	4,777	6,031	6,650	7,292	8,252	9,163
Mekong River Delta	788	901	962	1,016	1,131	1,305
Whole country	1,435	1,809	2,004	2,203	2,555	2,877

Sources: General Statistics Office, 2000. *Statistical Year Book 2000*, General Statistics Office, Hanoi; General Statistics Office, 2001. *Statistical Year Book 2001*, General Statistics Office, Hanoi.

Some commentators, focusing on Ho Chi Minh City with its higher income and more developed services, conclude that all the south of Viet Nam is more developed economically than the north. The southeast (which includes the major industrial centres of Ho Chi Minh City, Dong Nai and Vung Tau) does have a considerably higher GDP per capita and accounts for nearly half the country's industrial output. On the other hand, per capita incomes in the Mekong Delta in the south are lower than in the northern Red River Delta. It is the gap between the larger urban centres (including Ho Chi Minh City, Dong Nai, Hanoi and Hai Phong) and rural areas that is more pronounced.

Nearly 40 per cent of industrial output from domestic enterprises comes from the southeast and 20 per cent from the Red River Delta. The Mekong River Delta accounts for a further 13 per cent (Table 2.6).

Most foreign investment in industry has been concentrated in the southeast and the Red River Delta. When industrial output from enterprises with foreign investment is included, almost 50 per cent of total industrial output is from the southeast and 20 per cent from the Red River Delta. The share of total industrial output in the southeast has remained largely unchanged over the last seven years. Output in the Red River Delta has increased marginally, while that in the Mekong River Delta has fallen.

NOTES

1 Even a stable proportion of urban population in the total population would imply some rural–urban migration, as fertility rates have fallen faster in urban areas than in the countryside (in 1989 the crude birth rate in urban areas was 24.1 compared to 33.6 in rural areas). The corresponding crude death rates were 5.1 and 7.9, suggesting a significant difference in the urban and rural natural rates of population increase (General Statistics Office 1994). A 1994 survey indicates that the differences in fertility persist (General Statistics Office 1995).

2 Except for the male cohort of 45–54 at that time, which had been severely depleted by war deaths.

3 A term used to denote 'the radical declines in death and birth rates associated with societal modernization' (Boom and Williamson 1998:419–56). They argue that a demographic bonus has contributed to the stellar economic performance in East Asia in recent decades.

4 Alternative definitions might result in a significantly higher figure. The Viet Nam Urban Sector Strategy Study (*Final Report November 1995*) noted that the Vietnamese definition of urban residence did not conform to international practice, as rural areas within cities and

municipalities were excluded from the urban totals; the study team estimated that, using the more inclusive definition about 8 per cent more of the population resided in urban areas (resulting in a total of 28.1 per cent).

5   The estimate in the Table is from an ADB source that allows regional comparisons. The GSO estimates that about 76 per cent of the population were living in rural areas in 2000.

6   Based on the 1999 Census, the urban populations of the three provinces were Hanoi 1.552 million, Hai Phong 0.572 million and Ho Chi Minh City 4.245 million. However, as the urban–rural distinction is necessarily somewhat arbitrary and the peri-urban rural areas are very much part of the urban economies, the total provincial populations may be more revealing of relative size. The total provincial population in 1999 was estimated to be Hanoi 2.685 million, Hai Phong 1.691 million and Ho Chi Minh City 5.222 million.

7   At least in terms of the eventual production possibilities. There are still difficult water management and infrastructure constraints to be resolved.

8   In 2001, Tokyo had a population of about 26.4 million, Shanghai, 12.9 million; Jakarta, 11.0 million; Osaka, 11.0 million; Manila, 10.9 million; Beijing, 10.8 million; and Seoul, 9.9 million in 2000 (see McNicholl 2002:20).

3

ECONOMIC PERFORMANCE AND KEY ISSUES

A HISTORICAL OVERVIEW OF MACROECONOMIC DATA

Table 3.1 highlights Viet Nam's economic turnaround from the late 1980s in terms of growth, food production, stability, resource mobilisation, and opening up of the economy to trade and foreign investment. This was achieved while maintaining progress in social development. This strong performance took place in an international context where median growth in per capita incomes in developing countries fell to zero over 1980–98 (compared with 2.5 per cent per year from 1960–79) (Easterly 2001).

Following an initial economic recovery immediately after formal reunification in 1976, annual economic growth averaged only 0.4 per cent in the five years to 1980. With population increasing by about 2.3 per cent each year, per capita income declined. Prices increased by an average of more than 20 per cent each year.

Economic growth performance improved during the early 1980s, but macroeconomic imbalances increased and inflation accelerated. As the government sought to stabilise the economy in the early years of reform, growth rates declined. Average inflation remained high, but had been greatly reduced by the end of the 1980s. The 1990s were marked by accelerating growth and price stability.

When *Doi Moi* was introduced at the Sixth Party Congress at the end of 1986, Viet Nam was facing a major economic crisis. The annual rate of inflation

Table 3.1 **Average annual indicators of growth and inflation, 1976–80 to 1996–2001 (per cent)**

	Inflation (CPI)	GDP	Agriculture	Services	Industry
1976–80	21.2	0.4	1.9	-0.1	3.3
1981–85	74.2	6.4	5.3	4.7	9.3
1986–90	298.7	3.9	3.7	8.7	4.7
1991–95	23.5	8.2	4.3	9.5	12.6
1996–2001[a]	3.4	7.0	3.9	7.3	12.2

Note: [a] 2001 data is based on end-year government estimates. Services before 1986 only included trade.
Sources: General Statistics Office, various issues. *Statistical Yearbook*, Statistical Publishing House, Hanoi.

Figure 3.1 **GDP growth by sector, 1997–2001 (per cent change)**

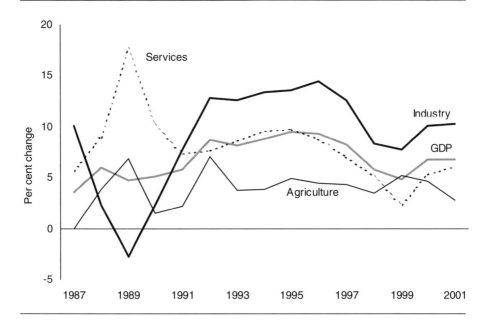

was over 700 per cent, exports were less than half of imports, there was virtually no foreign direct investment (FDI), and only limited official development assistance. When the Seventh Party Congress met in 1991, economic growth had begun to accelerate, the value of exports had quadrupled, and inflation had been brought down to 67 per cent. From the early 1990s, the picture improved markedly, with stable macroeconomic conditions and a dramatic acceleration in growth of income and employment. Trends in economic growth and changes in key indicators since *Doi Moi* are summarised in Table 3.2.

The transition has been accompanied by changes in the structure of major components of GDP. The share of agriculture fell from 44 per cent of GDP (current prices) in 1986 to 24 per cent in 2001, while the share of industry increased from 26 to 38 per cent. The share of services also increased as indicated in the Table 3.3.

More surprising, at least for most external observers of the Vietnamese economy, was the fact that the share of the state in economic output increased from 22 per cent in 1986 to 40 per cent in 1996, before declining marginally in more recent years. Possible explanations for this trend are discussed throughout this report.

WHAT NEEDS TO BE EXPLAINED?

At the end of the 1980s, the economy was stagnating, economic survival for most segments of the population involved a difficult struggle, infrastructure still showed the damage of the generation of warfare, and the nation's economic future seemed quite uncertain. By the turn of the century, there had been a substantial reduction in poverty, a fast-growing middle class enjoyed levels of consumption unimaginable a decade earlier, infrastructure had not only been rehabilitated, but in critical respects had been expanded and, perhaps most important, there was a widely held perception, both among Vietnamese and external observers, that the economy was firmly set on the path of economic development. This breakthrough is not only evident in the economic numbers, but for observers of the economy was palpable in all aspects of economic life.

This dramatic change in economic fortunes raises two questions. The first, and easiest to answer, is what determined the timing of the up-turn of the economy? The answer to that question is straightforward—the *Doi Moi* economic reforms described throughout this volume sparked the turn-around

Table 3.2   **Indicators of economic developments, 1986–2001**

Indicator	Sixth Party Congress 1986	Seventh Party Congress 1991	Eighth Party Congress 1996	Ninth Party Congress 2001[a]
Economic growth (%)	3.4	6.0	9.3	6.8
CPI (%, year to Dec.)	775	67	4.5	0.8
Illiteracy rate (% of population)	10.7	9.2	7.7	6.5
Income per capita (US$)	180	228	339	410
Food grain production (kg of paddy/person)	301	323	385	433
Budget surplus (% of GDP)	–6.2	–3.8	–0.7	–3.5
Budget revenue (% of GDP)	14.0	13.5	23.6	21.8
Gross domestic savings (% of GDP)	n.a.	13.2	16.7	24.0
Current account (% of GDP)	–2.7	–2.0	–11.1	1.5
Gross domestic investment (% of GDP)	n.a.	15.1	27.9	26.1
FDI inflows—US$ million	-	229	1,838	1,200
ODA inflows—US$ million	147	229	939	1,700
Exports—US$ million	494	2042	7,330	15,027
Imports—US$ million	1,121	2,105	10,481	16,162
Trade (% of GDP)	25.1	63.7	100.0	n.a.

Note: [a] Preliminary estimates.
Sources: General Statistics Office, various issues. *Statistical Yearbook*, Statistical Publishing House, Hanoi. International Monetary Fund, various issues. *Vietnam: recent economic developments*, International Monetary Fund, Washington, DC.

Table 3.3   **Structural changes in the economy, 1986–2001 (per cent of GDP at current prices)**

	Sixth Party Congress 1986	Seventh Party Congress 1991	Eighth Party Congress 1996	Ninth Party Congress 2001
Agriculture	43.8	40.5	27.8	23.6
Industry and construction	25.7	23.8	29.7	37.8
Services	30.5	35.7	42.5	38.6
Total	100.0	100.0	100.0	100.0
State	33.1	33.2	40.0	38.6
Non-state	66.9	66.8	60.0	61.4

Sources: General Statistics Office, various issues. *Statistical Year Book*, Statistical Publishing House.

in the economy. The implications of that process for the economic growth performance are clear enough. From the point of view of conventional economic interpretations, the easy part of the story to understand is the impact of market liberalisation and macroeconomic stabilisation. Viet Nam implemented 'sound' economic policies, and reaped the promised rewards. This could be seen as a vindication of the 'Washington consensus' and, indeed, has been presented as such.[1]

There is, however, a more difficult question to be addressed. While the change in the economic policy regime determined the timing and direction of the change in economic performance, it does not in itself explain the pace and sustained character of the subsequent growth. While bad policies can result in economic stagnation and good policies can encourage and accommodate growth, policy is only part of the story. Many countries have implemented ambitious reform programs without stimulating the same level of sustained response. The other part of the story is to explain why, in this case, the economy responded so energetically to the opportunities offered by the new policy environment and why that initial response set the economy on a path of sustained growth.

INSTITUTIONS, HUMAN CAPITAL AND ENTREPRENEURSHIP

This chapter does not claim to offer a definitive answer to the second question, but on the basis of the authors' observations, some clues are offered. Interestingly, it is easier to eliminate some possible explanations than to provide all the answers.

For example, the initial sharp acceleration in growth is not explained by any sharp increase in capital formation. True, investment increased significantly, but the increase in the productivity of given levels of investment was more important than acceleration in the rate of capital formation.

Nor is Viet Nam's performance to be explained by the flow of external aid (although the flow of ideas and exchange of experience were important). The story told here demonstrates that the crucial transformation and acceleration in growth took place in a period when external assistance was declining, so that, although it can be reasonably argued that the growth in foreign aid from 1994 on supported investments without which growth would have been constrained in the late 1990s, it is difficult to make a plausible case that foreign aid either initiated the process or determined the liveliness of the response.

The main difficulty in teasing out a credible thesis is that a good part of the explanation of the Vietnamese performance lies in two areas of analysis, which are important, but where evidence is imprecise—the role of institutions and human capital. The pragmatic willingness to adopt market-oriented reforms was combined with an institutional framework and a population which was able to respond to the opportunities provided by the market stimuli.

The description of the role of state institutions in various parts of this study suggests that the effectiveness of the institutional framework is difficult to explain within the orthodoxy of the Washington consensus. The semi-reformed state economic apparatus has done much better than proponents of faster reform predicted. Many state institutions have performed rather well in taking advantage of competitive markets and adjusting to the new economic realities. Of course, the proponents of accelerated market reform and pure models of market institutions argue that if only reform were faster and more complete, growth would have been even faster, and if further reforms are not implemented with some urgency, growth will falter. Alternative judgements are always possible about counter-historical options, although it should be noted that, given the growth performance actually achieved, it would be surprising if alternative arrangements would have achieved much more.

The actual strengths of existing institutions and the particular path to reform chosen were demonstrated not only by the responsiveness of the 'semi-reformed' system to the possibilities of export-led growth in the period 1990–97, but also in responding with speed and effectiveness to the East Asian crisis from 1998 onwards, when pro-active state economic management (reducing barriers to domestic private investment and curtailing lower priority public investments) allowed the government to manage the potential crisis rather well. Indeed, the caution in implementing advice to reform and deregulate[2] the banking and financial system appear to have helped shield the economy from the full consequences of the speculative financial bubble that shook neighbouring economies.

The danger is that, if institutions are judged largely on their conformity to a predetermined and somewhat dogmatic template, then there is likely to be a failure to understand how they work in practice. It is particularly necessary to make that effort of understanding when institutional behaviour and performance does not conform to preconceptions.

In turn, however, institutions performed well because of the use Vietnamese have made of them. The high quality of human capital and its importance is readily observable in Viet Nam in the facility with which so many actors in the economy—from farmers, to businessmen and state officials—have demonstrated entrepreneurial flair in grasping economic opportunities.

ENTREPRENEURSHIP AND INNOVATION IN DEVELOPMENT

There is a long tradition in the study of economic development that places entrepreneurship in the centre of explanations of development. Schumpeter's *The Theory of Economic Development* (1936), published before the First World War, argued that entrepreneurship was the critical factor in explaining how economic systems raised themselves to new levels of performance. And nearly fifty years ago, Hirschman (1958) returned to similar themes in his *Strategy of Economic Development*. More recently, discussions of human and social capital have laid new emphasis on those human factors that determine the capability of societies to take advantage of economic opportunities.

The difficulty in using entrepreneurship as an explanatory variable arises from the fact that, although economists are willing to recognise the crucial importance of human capital in general and entrepreneurship in particular, it is not easy to define what in practice that means, in terms either of making *ex ante* predictions of performance, or in terms of any policy implications. Effective entrepreneurship is recognisable when it occurs but it is not measurable and its appearance is not easily predictable.

However, convincing evidence has been presented of the importance of entrepreneurship and policies supporting it as a key explanatory variable in explaining the 'Asian economic miracle'. In an interesting analysis of the experience of rapid economic growth in East Asia, Nelson and Pack have distinguished two schools of thought in interpreting the performance. One school (assimilation theories) 'stresses the entrepreneurship, innovation and learning, all encouraged by the policy regime, that these economies had to go through...'. The other school (accumulation theories) 'emphasizes physical and human capital accumulation' (Nelson and Pack 1999:418).

Nelson and Pack develop a strong case in support of the assimilation approach. One point they make is that, even if these follower countries were able to borrow techniques developed elsewhere, this did not simply involve importing an existing technology 'off the shelf', but also involved an important element of entrepreneurship in adapting and assimilating the new production techniques.

Another recent study of the sources of economic growth by Parente and Prescott argues in a similar vein that

> [a] necessary precondition for a country to undergo a development miracle is that the country is not exploiting a significant amount of stock of useable knowledge and therefore is poor relative to the industrial leader. The stock of knowledge will be little exploited if barriers to the adoption and efficient use of this stock are high and have been in place for an extended period. In 1965, many countries besides South Korea met this precondition. Most of these countries remain poor relative to the leader because unlike South Korea, they did not adopt new policies that greatly reduced barriers to the efficient use of this knowledge (2000:4).

REMOVING BARRIERS TO ENTREPRENEURSHIP AND INNOVATION

While it is still early days to describe the Vietnamese achievement as an economic miracle, the economic achievement of Viet Nam in the 1990s is consistent with the views of these two sources. Prior to 1986, Viet Nam had gone through an extended period where there were enormous barriers to the adoption and efficient use of the stock of useable knowledge. During the 1970s and 1980s, most of the population had no access to international media, books, education, travel and research, and no contact with foreigners. The state barred most of the population from investing in skills (for example, foreign language training) and travel that may have opened up new opportunities.

The *Doi Moi* reforms removed barriers to the utilisation of the available and potential stock of knowledge, not only in the narrowly technical sense, but also in the broader sense of the possibilities of taking advantage of Vietnamese comparative advantage, particularly in the regional context. A combination of improved incentives, increased competition, and reductions in barriers to the adoption of existing knowledge are crucial to explaining the rapid improvements in economic performance over the last 20 years.

The other underlying institutional factor which must be addressed is that of the energy, liveliness and entrepreneurial skills of the population A pervasive and critical element in explaining the response to market reforms and the success in making imperfect institutions work is undoubtedly the quality of the Vietnamese workforce. It is, of course, characteristic of informal discussion of the economic performance of countries that, after allowance has been made for policy and such quantitative factors as capital formation, most commentators will offer a view about the characteristics of the national population, good or bad.

This is dangerous ground, as such observations can often be little more than *ex post* rationalisation of observed performance based on anecdotal evidence, and is sometimes no more than ethnic prejudice. Indeed, it is striking that the same institutions and national characteristics that are used to explain success in one period can also be drawn on to explain subsequent stagnation (for example, in the recent economic history of Japan and Germany).

Economists sometimes try to avoid such pitfalls by using the concept of investment in human capital, and in turn relating that to an observable and to a degree quantifiable phenomenon. And that is part of the story in Viet Nam. The rapid exploitation of the possibilities of 'catching up' with neighbouring economies through the adoption of existing knowledge was aided by past solid performance in promoting literacy, numeracy and broader human development in the pre-reform period. At the beginning of the reform period, Viet Nam had much higher levels of mass literacy, life expectancy and middle and higher education than most other countries with a similar level of per capita income. And although the large numbers who had received higher education in the former planned economies had received little business training relevant to operating in a market economy, cadres had been well-trained in a number of technical areas.

As Nelson and Pack (1999) argued in their interpretation of the Asian economic miracle, however, formal investments in human capital are not a sufficient explanation of performance—there was an additional element that put the human capital to work effectively. Nelson and Pack accept that investment in human capital played a role, but argue that it played a role in the context of policies and institutions that supported assimilation of technology and export-led growth. Their explanation stops short of explaining why factors conducive to assimilation of technology were to be found more in East Asia than other parts of the world. Interestingly, Nelson and Pack recognise that the impressive performance across a number of Asian newly-industrialised countries was not achieved through any one, homogeneous policy package, but involved a variety of tactics and agile policy adjustments. Even if the answer lies partly in effective policies, it is still intriguing why in East Asia such effective policy skills were exhibited by a number of differing political regimes. Perhaps speculation in that area takes economists into terrain that they are ill-fitted to navigate.

In Viet Nam, when policy changes opened up the possibilities of exporting, the energy and ingenuity with which new exports were developed was striking, despite the fact that for some years external contact had been limited by government restrictions and the US-led aid boycott. Initial successes by pioneers were quickly followed by others seeking to emulate their success. In Hanoi itself this was evident in such areas as the development of silk clothing and embroidery for sale to foreigners and in the rapid development of mini-hotels, after the first private hotel was opened in 1992. In the agricultural sector, change was equally rapid, with the explosive growth of coffee in the Central Highlands and the spread of aquaculture in the Mekong Delta. Not only was entrepreneurial spirit evident in the new private sector, but even within the state-owned sector there were numerous examples of aggressive adaptation to new market possibilities.

Various sorts of exposure produced an outward-looking stance that contributed to the alacrity with which exporting possibilities were sought out and exploited. For example, many families maintained contacts with the Vietnamese Diaspora in Europe, North America and Australia, and these contacts provided access to capital and information. There was also an awareness of developments in neighbouring countries. Even in the pre-reform days, while formal trading links were mostly with the CMEA countries, informal trade across the porous borders, particularly with China and Thailand, was quite active. Once restrictions were relaxed, entrepreneurs near the Chinese border, for example, were able to read Chinese magazines and books, to meet buyers, and later to travel to China to see production processes and customers.

Maximum use was made of the information and trading possibilities arising from the formal trading links with the CMEA and the knowledge gained from contacts with China before the Vietnam–China conflict of the late 1970s. A good deal of effort was made to cater to the tastes of the few Westerners resident in the pre-reform period (hence the appearance of Nordic folk themes in embroidery to be purchased in Hanoi).

Vietnamese entrepreneurs have been willing to invest time and money to acquire and study information, to study production techniques, and to travel to learn about new markets and techniques. Rural entrepreneurs have made sizeable unrecorded investments in terms of forgone agricultural production and/or wages. State enterprises and public agencies have made substantial unrecorded, but critically important, investments in reorganising management and business procedures, in adapting technologies and in providing on-the-job training to workers. Personal investments of time and money have been made by the aspiring middle class in upgrading skills, as evidenced by the dramatic increase in English language and computer skills in the last decade. Small manufacturers studied international design trends and later invested in direct contact with international buyers, and then invested time in travelling to see new designs and learn about new processes and markets. Some of the key impacts of these developments on business are discussed in later chapters.

As a consequence, a good deal of growth was achieved despite relatively modest but increasing levels of recorded capital investment.

NOTES

1   The World Bank report to the United Nations International Conference on Financing for Development in Monterrey argued that progress made by Viet Nam, China, and other strong performing economies as examples of official development assistance success stories even though many of these countries (especially China) experienced significant economic growth, while receiving relatively little assistance (Development Economics Vice Presidency 2002).

2   Some earlier attempts in Viet Nam to rapidly open up entry to new domestic banks led to rapid increases in the number of credit unions and small private banks, most of which subsequently collapsed.

4

PRELUDE TO REFORM: THE ATTEMPTED INTRODUCTION OF CENTRAL PLANNING

A good starting point for understanding the Vietnamese reform process is to examine the history of the system that was the object of reform from the mid 1980s. For the authors of this book, that involves venturing into territory of which they lack direct experience. Interpretations of developments since 1988 in this volume are strongly influenced by direct observations; for the earlier period, the study depends on written sources and discussions with Vietnamese officials involved in the reform process, bolstered by a certain amount of speculation extrapolating from later observation.

PRE-REUNIFICATION

The North

Between 1954 and 1965, North Viet Nam had sought to implement a Soviet approach to industrialisation and planning. During the war with the United States, that basic approach was maintained. Private economic activity was largely forbidden. Most medium and large-scale enterprises were nationalised as the French departed following their defeat in 1954. Remaining non-state enterprises were engaged in handicraft and other household industries that were subsequently organised as cooperatives after 1957. Nationalised enterprises were owned either centrally or through local governments. Agriculture had been collectivised by the end of the 1950s, and was managed through producer cooperatives, with the exception of private plots of land within agricultural cooperatives.

The Vietnamese economy was, on paper, a classic 'command economy'. Nevertheless, even in principle a fully-fledged Soviet command system was never fully operative. For example, the list of commodities allocated under plans was always very limited as compared to the Soviet material balance system. Many central command mechanisms were not implemented in practice.

Indeed, from 1945 until formal reunification of the country in 1976, the North had to concentrate most of its energies on military struggle. There was a heavy commitment of resources directed to military activity initially to fight the war for independence from France (1945–54), and then the war against the United States and the regime it backed in South Viet Nam. During the US war in particular, attention was focused more on the needs of the war economy than the implementation of economic plans.

A period of relative peace during the late 1950s and early 1960s provided some opportunity for development. The initial policy focus (1955–57) was on land reform, and collectivising the agricultural sector and village and handicraft industries. The radical changes during that period resulted in profound social upheaval, one response to which was migration from some northern areas to the south. The Party has since recognised that 'serious mistakes were committed' under the land reform program (Communist Party of Vietnam 1986a:140). Nevertheless, external commentators have noted that 'the period 1954–60 was on of rapid growth for North Vietnamese agriculture and saw a mushrooming of industry as well' (Beresford 1988:130).

Views on economic strategy were strongly influenced by Soviet orthodoxy in that period. The Third Party Congress held in September 1960[1] focused on the building of socialism and the struggle for reunification. That Congress passed resolutions on the main priorities for the First Five-Year Plan (1961 to 1965), which emphasised the development of heavy industry. External commentators have noted that 'rapid industrialisation was also a feature of the period 1959 to 1964' (Beresford 1988:132).[2] Investment in industry has been estimated to have grown at a rate three times that of the agricultural sector from 1960 to 1975 (Vo Dai Luoc 1994:9).

The share of industrial production in national income increased from 18.2 per cent in 1960 to 24.2 per cent in 1974, with most growth occurring prior to 1965 (de Vylder and Fforde 1988:28). This was 'mainly the result of an increase in external assistance for equipment, raw materials and fuel for industry, coupled with a decline in agriculture production' (Vo Dai Luoc 1994:10). That is, the pattern of growth was strongly influenced by aid coming from the Soviet bloc.

State enterprises were to be the main vehicle for state-led growth. The Party and government were directly involved in the management of enterprises producing high priority goods. These enterprises received preferential access to inputs, had to produce regardless of cost, and were heavily subsidised by the state. State enterprises engaged in lower priority activities were set targets, but had less access to official resources. Significant managerial, political and entrepreneurial skills were required to meet targets in such an environment.

During the war period, there were contradictions between the stated objectives of the Party and the realities of war-time economy. In 1970, Party Secretary-General Le Duan published a reportedly influential book where he stressed the need to 'struggle to take small-scale production to large-scale socialist production'.[3] A Party Plenum in January 1971 stressed the need to develop heavy industry and to lay the foundations for large-scale socialist production. The next Party Plenum in early 1972 went further—arguing for trade to be controlled by socialist enterprises, abolishing artisanal and small-scale production organisations, and replacing these with large-scale state organisations.[4]

In practice, however, from 1965 investment priorities were those of a war economy. Emphasis was given to industries directly supporting the war, especially mechanical engineering, iron and steel, coal and electricity. Many centrally managed enterprises were destroyed through bombing or had to operate well below capacity because of the difficulty in obtaining inputs. Scarce resources were directed to either protecting centrally managed state enterprises or moving them to safer areas, resulting in greater deconcentration of production than the commitment to large-scale production implied. Working under difficult war conditions, pragmatic solutions to keep production going over-rode economic planning concepts.

External assistance was required just to sustain output in centrally managed enterprises. Dependence on external assistance increased, rising from about one-quarter of total government budget revenue in the in the early 1960s to almost 70 per cent in the late 1960s according to one source.[5] Under the stress of the war effort, the economy suffered. Paddy production fell from 7.1 million tonnes in 1972 to 5.3 million tonnes in 1975, while labour productivity fell by 11 per cent during the same period (Beresford 1988).

The government's dependence on external financing to cover fiscal and trade deficits, the bureaucratic nature of decision making and dysfunctional economic incentives facing both the agricultural and industrial sectors led external analysts to conclude that, at the time of reunification, the northern economy was facing chronic economic imbalances (Beresford 1988; de Vylder and Ffforde 1988). It should be noted, however, that under conditions of total war such concepts as 'economic incentives' and 'economic balance' are not particularly meaningful. War economy in any system typically involves inflation, suppressed or open, scarcities, introduction of non-market allocation systems and such like. The fact that the war was won suggests that the system delivered economically in some sense.

One difficulty in interpreting that period and subsequent developments is to judge how far apparent weaknesses were also hidden strengths. De Vylder and Fforde have argued that North Viet Nam 'in 1975 was a "weak state"; despite its proven ability to mobilise the Vietnamese people for the bloody struggle to liberate the South' (1998:33). Evidently it was (and remained) true that there was a large gap between the state's pretensions to manage the economy through central planning and implement a Soviet-style industrialisation strategy and the degree to which a logic of autonomous action and initiative operated, even within the state-'controlled' sector.

Subsequent Party documents agreed that there were serious imbalances and distortions with only limited effective planning, but that this was necessary to achieve victory during the war. In criticising the continuation of such distortions after the war, the Party noted that

> the national economy was disrupted by the US aggression after 1964…the Vietnamese State depended on increased aid from the USSR and other socialist countries…the only means of developing production was by supplying the production units—in the first place industry—with all the means of production (equipment, capital, raw materials, foodstuffs, consumer goods). The factories had to produce the goods whatever the cost. Planning only existed for form's sake. The State assigned tasks to production units, gave them the means and was handed over the finished goods. All the enterprises had to do was to balance the State allowances and their own expenses in the way as the administrative organs do. Thus economic management through administrative subsidies came into being (Communist Party of Vietnam 1986b:17).

The development of locally managed state enterprises became an important priority because of the ongoing military conflict, the limited resources available to the government, and the need for regional self-sufficiency. The amount of investment directed to locally managed enterprises increased four-fold during the war years (Vo Dai Luoc 1994). As a consequence '[i]ndustrial production was maintained in the main, while locally-run industry vigorously developed…[and]…regional economies began to take shape' (Communist Party of Vietnam 1986a:194).

The impact of the war thus had a critical impact on the organisation of the economy. The net result was that the state enterprise sector was more decentralised—both geographically and in terms of decision making—than was the case in most centrally planned economies. While the struggle to move to a socialist system remained on the policy agenda, the central government never achieved the same degree of control over economic activity as was achieved in most East European centrally planned economies.[6]

In addition to responding to the immediate requirements of the war-time economy, the acceptance of decentralised decision making was also consistent with a long tradition of relative autonomy of village and local communities in managing their local economies.[7]

Although the outcome may have implied a 'weak state', in the sense that the state was unable to control economic activity to the degree that it claimed, it also implied that the foundations of a 'strong economy' were being laid unintentionally, both in that the gigantism of Soviet-style industrialisation was avoided and that there was a high degree of practical autonomy within local economic units.

The South

In South Viet Nam, post-1954 industrial policies focused on development of agriculture and light industry. The influx of foreign forces during the 1960s stimulated the demand for food processing as well as demand for other light industries such as garments, construction materials and wood products. The service sector recorded very strong growth during this period. Efforts to shift the burden of the war to the government of the Republic of Viet Nam in the later part of the 1960s and early 1970s were associated with increased investment in the assembly of electronic equipment, machinery and motor vehicles. Facilities were also developed for repairing and maintaining military equipment, ships and aircraft (Vo Dai Luoc 1994).

However, as in the North the pattern of economic growth was determined by the peculiar conditions of war. Strong economic growth during the late 1960s and early 1970s was largely the result of externally financed expenditure on consumption goods, and created an imbalance between sectors catering to the demands of the US operation and the indigenous economy.[8] Exports were only sufficient to finance a very small percentage of imports in 1969–70.[9] High levels of public expenditure affected the balance of the economy. The level of economic activity would not have been sustainable under peace-time conditions.

Following the signing of the Paris Peace Accord in January 1973, external financing to Viet Nam fell sharply. This contributed to economic stagnation and increasing unemployment, particularly in urban areas. Social problems, including dislocation of families, the growth of urban slums resulted from rapid urbanisation, the large number of war invalids, drug abuse and prostitution, were prevalent. In rural areas, agricultural output was badly affected by the damage to infrastructure and the environment caused by bombing and chemical spraying (Beresford 1988).

Difficulties were compounded after reunification because, in addition to the departure of segments of the upper and middle classes, the human capacity in the south of Viet Nam was underutilised due to resistance to the post-war changes from some members of the business community, and suspicion from the new administration about the loyalty of important segments of the intellectual, administrative, and skilled worker communities in the south.

On the positive side, the industry and service sectors were much more developed in the south than in the north. Basic economic infrastructure was also much better developed in parts of the south, especially in the commercial centres. Most importantly, there was an established entrepreneurial class with business, managerial and administrative skills that had the potential to play an important role in economic development.

POST-REUNIFICATION

Following reunification, the government initially relied mainly on *ad hoc* measures to direct the economy, concentrating initially on the formidable tasks of reconstruction and rehabilitation of infrastructure, the resettlement of wartime refugees, raising the level of rice output and building administrative capacity.

The integration of two very different economic systems following the defeat of the Government of the Republic of Viet Nam (South Viet Nam) in 1975, and formal reunification of the country in 1976, presented a formidable challenge.[10] This was because institutions differed considerably, and also because both the North and South, previously heavily dependent on external funding, were faced with much reduced access to foreign exchange at the very moment they needed such funds to drive post-war reconstruction and the transition away from the war economy.

The Fourth Party Congress, held in December 1976, acknowledged the limitations of the industrialisation policies in the North prior to 1975, and calls were made in this forum for a greater share of investment resources to be allocated to the agricultural sector. This, however, did not appear to have been reflected in the strategic objectives for economic development identified by the Congress, namely to

- create the material and technical basis for socialism rapidly
- take the economy from small-scale production to large-scale socialist production with a modern industrial and agricultural structure
- give priority to the rational development of heavy industry on the basis of developing agriculture and light industry; the intensification of agricultural production being regarded as the main task of the 1976–80 Five-Year Plan
- redistribute the social workforce to make productive use of unused land, found mostly in the hilly and mountainous regions
- organise the district as an economic agro-industrial unit
- build the national economy taking account of the needs of national defence
- develop simultaneously a flexible central economy and regional economies
- promote rapid technical and scientific development
- transform the South gradually in order to establish an integrated socialist nation
- resolve economic management problems (Communist Party of Vietnam 1986b:10–11).

The 1976–80 Five-Year Plan included ambitious growth targets, which reflected, in part, the euphoria following the reunification of Viet Nam and an assumption that the strict social and economic discipline that had been exercised during the war could be sustained during peace. It was also assumed that the war would be followed by a rapid build-up in foreign aid flows.[11] Inadequate attention was given to past failures and the difficulties of rapid economic integration given the differences in economic systems and resource endowments between the North and South (Asian Development Bank 1989).[12]

In the period immediately following reunification the approach to socialist transformation had been fairly cautious. However, dissatisfaction with the pace of socialist transformation and the rapid growth in private trade, combined with concerns about internal political opposition to socialist transformation in the southern business community, dominated by ethnic Chinese, led to attempts to accelerate the process of transformation to socialism.

In early 1978, many private enterprises in the south, particularly in Cho Lon, where ethnic Chinese dominated trade, were nationalised or closed. This was followed by an increase in the exodus of 'boat people' from Vietnam (Beresford 1988).

The policy of subsidising state enterprises regardless of cost continued after reunification. Indeed, increased subsidies were allocated for these policies to be applied nationwide, covering new enterprises and newly nationalised enterprises in the south of the country (Vo Dai Luoc 1994). The maintenance of this system after reunification has also been recognised by the Party to have been a mistake.

> This system was necessary in war conditions when the State was receiving a large amount of foreign aid. It should have been abandoned when the war was over, when the country, now reunified, was embarking on the stage of socialist construction. But conservative ideas and the tendency to rely on foreign aid delayed the reorganisation of economic management. Effective for the years of war, the old system, became a hindrance to all economic activities (Communist Party of Vietnam 1986b:17).

The emphasis on a rapid transformation to socialism provided Party and government officials with a mandate to interfere in the day-to-day management of enterprises and household businesses. Delineation of responsibility and accountability became increasingly unclear. The lack of accountability included a perception that the state would financially support the enterprise in the event of financial losses.[13] At the same time, commitment to the war effort as an incentive to produce diminished following reunification. These factors contributed to growing ineffectiveness in the state enterprise sector. Despite the increasing number of state enterprises, and the large share of public expenditure allocated to the state enterprise sector, the share of state enterprises in national output actually declined from 27.7 to 19.7 per cent between 1976 and 1980.

A decision was taken by the Second Party Plenum in July 1977 to accelerate the development of state farms throughout the country and to implement agricultural collectivisation in the south (Communist Party of Vietnam 1986a). Ambitious targets were established to transform individual farming enterprises in the south into production cooperatives. It has been argued that local cadres, who were under great pressure to meet these targets, used force rather than persuasion to establish cooperatives and were more interested in reaching the target number of cooperatives than in how successful the cooperatives were in promoting increased production (Vo Nhan Tri 1990).

Despite the stated priority to be given to agricultural development (as a necessary step towards the ultimate objective of developing heavy industry) most development expenditure continued to be directed to the industrial sector.[14]

A policy biased towards industrial development and the concentration of public investment in industry, particularly large-scale heavy industry, meant that the sectors where Viet Nam could be expected to have a comparative advantage were neglected. Pricing policies favouring the industrial sector was effectively a tax to subsidise inefficient industries. The emphasis given to rapidly creating the material and technical basis for socialism and similar targets put pressure on officials to realise targets such as increasing the scale of collectives and state enterprises at the expense of efficiency (and the stated aim of large-scale production).[15] Party cadres were under considerable formal and informal pressure to conform to the perceived requirements for rapid socialist transformation.

The end of the 1970s saw the peak of attempts to create an orthodox Soviet style of centrally planned economy in Vietnam. The failure of those attempts and the willingness of the Vietnamese system to learn the painful lessons of that failure created the conditions for the subsequent period of reform and accelerated growth.

Formal regulations governing state enterprise were promulgated in 1977 and regulations on enterprise unions promulgated in 1978.[16] The regulations recognised state enterprises as independent legal entities, but they had little independence in operations.

> The enterprise was obliged to fulfil the compulsory targets ordered by the State. The State also worked out plans for production, marketing, and pricing as well as salaries and bonuses, distribution and utilisation of its funds. Hence the scope for initiative at the enterprise level was very limited. Industrial cooperative units in general had a greater autonomy in production and marketing than State Enterprises (Le Trang 1989:156).

Control of state enterprises by line ministries and provincial authorities was organised through unions of state enterprises. Most enterprises were required to be members of these unions. Trang defined unions of state enterprises as 'production-business organisations that organise state enterprises in the same business area, manufacturing similar products, using similar technologies or technologies which are related to each other' (1989:157).

The power entrusted to unions of state enterprises was considerable, including the preparation of sector plans and allocation of responsibility to enterprises under the union to realise specific targets within the overall plan. State enterprises were obliged to fulfil quotas and other targets as directed by the unions. Unions were 'also responsible for supplying technical materials to its members and for marketing their products, monitoring their fulfilment of the techno-economic norms and criteria of the branch, and training or re-training managing cadre and technical workers for its members'. This additional administrative layer caused considerable conflict and confusion and 'a few such unions became intermediaries obstructing their member enterprises' operations' (Le Trang 1989:157).

The problems of inappropriate economic policies, distorted incentive structures, and passive resistance to socialist transition were compounded by the cancellation of external assistance, and increased demands for military expenditure following the invasion of Cambodia in late 1978. After strong growth in 1976, economic output stagnated in 1977 and 1978 and actually declined in 1979 and 1980. There was a particularly pronounced decline in output from state-owned industrial enterprises, with production declining by an average 2 per cent per year between 1977 and 1980.

By the late 1970s, Viet Nam was facing a 'major economic crisis, with acute shortages of food, basic consumer goods, and inputs to agriculture and industry, and a growing external debt' (Asian Development Bank 1989:6). The impending economic crisis was recognised in August 1979 at the Sixth Plenum of the Fourth Party Congress. The Party has since bluntly criticised the policies of this period, noting that these policies

…underlined the weakness and inadequacies in economic and social leadership over the previous years, which showed themselves in manifestations of subjectivism, impatience, conservatism, inertia, bureaucracy, lack of realism, irresponsibility (Communist Party of Vietnam 1986b:15).

and that

the decrease in production in the late 1970s and the mistakes made in laying out the economic structure, especially in allocating investments and capital construction in the preceding five years (1976–80), have left us heavy consequences (Communist Party of Vietnam 1987a:10).

The efforts to develop the economy of the unified nation were in principle guided by a system of central planning. The Interim Three-Year Plan (1978), drawn up with assistance from Soviet advisers, was the first formal attempt at planning for the unified nation. It was intended to lay the foundations for a more complete socialist transformation under the First Five-Year Plan, to start in 1981.

The First Five-Year Plan (1981–85) set out to construct a strict central-planning system with state allocations of capital and inputs and even labour being allocated centrally. There were plans for large-scale investment in cement factories, steel mills and hydroelectric power plants. Virtually all consumer goods were strictly rationed. Money and prices did not play a determining role in the allocation of resources; official prices were low and had little influence on production decisions.

The mechanisms of central planning were never properly established. The setting of plan targets in great detail at the centre, without any instruments for effective enforcement, meant that despite the apparent high degree of centralised decision making there was little effective discipline and a high degree of autonomy at the provincial and enterprise level in practice.

Emphasis on quantitative production targets encouraged enterprises to maximise their allocations of capital and inputs and hoard machines, raw materials and labour, thus amplifying imbalances caused by the overambitious aggregate targets.

In fact, the period in which there was a serious effort to introduce orthodox central planning throughout the country was quite brief, which meant that in the south in particular there was too little time for central planning to be institutionalised. The poor performance of the economy in that period set the conditions for the birth of the reform process.

FIRST STEPS TO REFORM: LIMITED DECENTRALISATION, 1979–86

Early intimations of reform can be seen already at the end of the 1970s, when economic difficulties prevented the consolidation of the centralised planning system.

Economic stagnation led to pressures for change. As early as 1979, socioeconomic targets were revised downwards and agreement was reached on the need to decentralise some decision making and to provide improved incentives for increased production. The debate initiated at the Sixth Party Plenum in August 1979 was an important turning point. The Communist Party and society began to question, in a systematic way, fundamental issues about how society and the economy system should operate. The difficult process of experimentation with reform since then has contributed to a transformation of the beliefs within broad sections of society, the Party and government. This, in turn, has substantially changed the informal constraints that play such an important role in influencing economic performance. Consequently, the options available to alter the formal framework for economic and social activity also changed.[17]

De Vylder and Fforde (1988) have described the reform process as being initiated through partial, unofficial relaxation of constraints on private activity and spontaneous moves towards production and trade outside of official channels ('fence-breaking'), leading to eventual Party recognition of the role of the household sector in agriculture, handicrafts, and retail trading. For example, the Council of Ministers issued a decree providing scope for local state enterprises to operate outside the central plan once central plan targets had been realised.[18]

The system of 'full allocation and full delivery', the system where the state provided all the inputs to state enterprises and recovered all profits, was replaced by a system whereby state enterprises could supplement state allocations with loans from the banking system, and some experimentation with alternative approaches to increasing production was allowed.

In January 1981, a contract system was introduced in the agricultural sector,[19] and the government issued a decision providing limited autonomy to state enterprises.[20] The decision reduced the number of mandatory targets that enterprises had to meet, and introduced the 'three plan' system, which gave enterprises rights to operate outside the plan, but only after centrally planned targets had been met. Up to 85 per cent of the profits from activities outside these targets could be retained by the enterprises, and some of this could be allocated to workers as bonuses. A related decision included provisions for salary payments to state enterprise employees to be related to output.[21]

Other reforms included moves to shift official prices closer to market rates in October 1981, and decentralise trade to local enterprises. These reforms were followed by decisions taken at the Fifth Party Congress in 1982 to reorient previous policies that focused on heavy industry and an inward-oriented economy to give greater attention to agriculture, light industry and export-oriented production. While the concept of central planning continued to be defended, more modest targets were established by the Fifth Party Congress.

- Meet the most pressing and essential requirements of everyday life, gradually stabilising and eventually improving the people's material and cultural life. First of all we must solve the problem of food supplies, and make efforts to meet the requirements in clothing, study, medical care, housing transport, child care, and other essential consumer needs.

- Continue building the material and technological infrastructure of socialism, with the emphasis on boosting agriculture, consumer goods production and exports, while at the same time improving the technical basis of the other economic branches, and making preparations for a more vigorous growth of heavy industry in the next stage.

- Complete the socialist transformation in the southern provinces; continue improving the socialist relations of production in the North; and consolidate the socialist relations of production in the whole country.

- Meet national defence requirements and maintain security and order (Communist Party of Vietnam 1986b).

Despite improved economic growth performance, considerable internal policy debate continued during this period and there was considerable uncertainty about future policy directions. Grassroots initiatives towards economic liberalisation interacted with oscillations between policy concessions and periodic clamp-downs on the free (or unofficial) market (de Vylder and Fforde 1988). Considerable uncertainty about what was legal remained. Such an uncertain environment checked the growth of non-state economic activity as it discouraged long-term investments.

While the authorities showed some flexibility in decentralising decisions and accommodating spontaneous changes, there were differing views about the desirability of such pragmatism. Strong private sector growth, sometimes at the expense of state enterprises, combined with inflationary pressures, led to internal pressures for reversal of earlier reforms. In 1983, administrative changes were made to control 'anarchy' in the market. Private enterprise registration procedures, tax policies, and bureaucratic interference discouraged private sector initiatives, particularly in trading. The freedom of state enterprises to trade outside of official channels was reduced and controls were imposed on foreign trade (Asian Development Bank 1989).

While the partial reforms introduced from 1979 to 1982 had an important impact in improving production incentives, the reforms did not adequately address key issues of pricing, financial discipline and reform of the bureaucratic administrative structures. Public sector and trade deficits increased alarmingly.

Inflation accelerated rapidly and growth began to slow from 1985. Government attempts to reduce these imbalances through currency, price and wage reforms were poorly coordinated, and fiscal imbalances and inflation became acute. By 1986, inflation had soared to an annual rate of more than 500 per cent, growth was slowing, and external deficits had increased sharply. This instability led to social pressures for reforms to promote macroeconomic stability. Partial reform had left the economy in a difficult halfway house, with neither the constraints of a tight planning system, nor the policy instruments for managing a decentralised economy, in place.

ACHIEVEMENTS OF THE PRE-REFORM PERIOD

The account above emphasises the many weaknesses of the pre-reform economic system, which necessitated the initiation of economic reforms (*Doi Moi*). It would be a mistake, however, to conclude that the pre-reform period was without significant social achievements, which have contributed to the subsequent economic success.

Contributions from the earlier period are largely ignored in much of the writing on recent economic developments in Viet Nam, which identify *Doi Moi* as the primary explanation of Vietnam's recent economic success. That is quite correct in the sense that the economic boom could not have happened without the *Doi Moi* reforms and the official sanctioning of the market economy that this implied. One can still ask, though, whether programs in the pre-reform period contributed to the subsequent achievement.

There are three main areas in which programs in pre-reform period helped create the conditions for accelerated growth. The first relates to human resource development. In the period before reform, Viet Nam made substantial investments in human capital. The commitment to provision of basic education and health meant that at the beginning of the reform period the country enjoyed much higher levels of basic literacy and health than most countries at a similar income level.[22] Thus, in 1990, Vietnamese per capita income levels (on a purchasing power parity basis) placed Viet Nam on the same income level as the 'low human development' group of countries, but adult literacy rates were 88 per cent compared to an average 48 per cent for the low human development group. At that time, Viet Nam's indicators of basic education were in line with those of much richer countries in the region—in average years of schooling, Viet Nam was ahead of Thailand and Indonesia, and literacy rates were on a par with other countries in the region.

There had also been a substantial investment in higher education, in Vietnamese institutions, similar to that in the Soviet Union and Eastern Europe and in an earlier period in China. The number of students graduating from colleges and universities in the country averaged over 20,000 per annum through the 1980s.[23] While this training was notably weak in areas such as economics, business skills and law (all important in the subsequent reform process), well trained cadres were produced in a number of technical subjects.

Viet Nam also made use in the 1980s of support from the UN system to provide postgraduate training in the region in subjects such as agriculture, and had cooperative programs with the International Rice Research Institute and other research institutions. Also, the OECD countries which maintained support programs (particularly Sweden) provided opportunities for higher level training.

While it is not possible to separate out and measure the returns to the investment in human resources, there can be no question that the high level of literacy and the trained technical cadres were critical inputs into the success of the Vietnamese economic reforms.

Table 4.1   **Comparative indicators of human development, 1990**

	Real GDP/capita (USD, PPP)	Average life expectancy (years)	Mean years schooling for 25+ years	Adult literacy (per cent)	Child[a] mortality (per 1,000 children)
Viet Nam	1,100	62.7	4.6	88	65
Thailand	3,986	66.1	3.8	93	34
Philippines	2,303	64.2	7.4	90	69
Indonesia	2,181	61.5	3.9	82	97
Low human development	1,110	56.5	2.3	49	n.a.
All developing countries	2,170	62.8	3.7	65	104

Note: [a] Child here refers to children under five years old
Source: United Nations Development Programme, 1993. *Human Development Report*, Oxford University Press, New York.

It should also be noted that, somewhat perversely, the disruptions and emigration associated with the war and unification, while having immediate costs with the departure of qualified people, also had strong positive consequences, as the Vietnamese Diaspora has become a source of international business connections, transfer of know-how and remittances.[24]

A second area in which foundations were laid for future growth was in relation to rural institutions. Communist reforms in the rural sector increased the equality of access to land, which meant that, when the reforms were implemented, there was a basis for a positive production response and a wide diffusion of the benefits of growth.

The consequence of these egalitarian developments can be seen if a comparison is made, for example, with Pakistan. Pakistan has enjoyed periods of robust growth in GNP, but the impact of that growth was limited both in terms of poverty alleviation and sustainability by the rigid rural social structure and related poor performance in human resource development.

Also, in fairness, Soviet supported investments in infrastructure provided needed capacity (for example, electric power generation). In the South, considerable investments had been made during the US war in transport, agricultural research, extension and development, which contributed to the later expansion in production.

NOTES

[1] The unified Indochina Communist Party officially met for the first time in Hong Kong in February 1930. The First Party Congress (of the Indochina Communist Party) was held in Macau in March 1935 and focused on building up the Party and the struggle against imperialism. The Second Party Congress was held in the Tuyen Quang jungle during the resistance against the French in 1951. At this Congress the Indochina Communist Party was dissolved and replaced by three national parties. Discussion focused on the struggle against imperial rule.

[2] De Vylder and Fforde (1988:28) also noted that from 1961–65 the industrial sector 'showed impressive rates of growth'.

[3] Le Duan quoted in Communist Party of Vietnam (1986a:215).

[4] Le Duan quoted in Communist Party of Vietnam (1986a:216–17).

[5] Vo Nhan Tri (1990), quoting official government statistics.

[6] See, for example, de Vylder and Fforde (1988), who argue that North Viet Nam was a 'weak state', and Van Arkadie and Vu Tat Boi (1992).

[7] Neil Jamieson's book *Understanding Vietnam* (1993) explores the interplay between individualism, and commitment to family, village and nation in Vietnamese history. The author offers an interpretation of the differences in social structure at the village level in North, Central and South Viet Nam and an interesting interpretation of the paradoxical combination of a tradition of strong local autonomy and individual initiative, with acceptance of a high degree of discipline with respect to the larger social unit at each level of Vietnamese society. However, while the study provides interesting insights into the historical and philosophical origins of modern Viet Nam it is not so insightful about post-unification developments, and stops short of any treatment of the *Doi Moi* period.

[8] See Jamieson (1993) for a telling account of the tensions that emerged as a result of the lucrative returns from serving the needs of the US community and the squeeze on other activities under war-time inflationary conditions.

[9] Beresford (1988) cites an ADB study (ADB 1971) which estimated that imports financed by US aid amounted to about one-third of the total GDP of South Viet Nam in the late 1960s.

[10] One could make some comparisons with the reunification of Germany, but the problems caused by the protracted war, the low level of economic development and the very limited fiscal resources in both the south and the north compounded the difficulties facing the Vietnamese authorities.

[11] A UN report published in June 1976 recommended that US$400 million be raised for immediate rehabilitation and reconstruction needs. In November 1976, however, the US government vetoed Vietnam's application to join the United Nations, despite support for Vietnam's application by the other 14 members of the Security Council. Viet Nam was finally admitted to the United Nations in September 1977.

[12] Vo Dai Luoc (1994:14–15) noted that documents prepared for the Fourth Congress of the Party included 'an indirect acknowledgment of the limitations of the industrial policy conducted from 1961 in North Viet Nam…[but that]…this policy was taken up again by the following Party congress almost without a single alteration…Only after 1980 when all these targets failed to materialize did the 5th National Congress of the Party decide to readjust the industrial policy'.

[13] Often referred to as the 'soft budget constraint', this is a major contributing factor to inefficiency in state enterprises, especially in centrally planned economies (Kornai 1980).

[14] Vo Nhan Tri (1990:76) reports that the share of state investment directed to the agriculture sector increased from 20.0 per cent in 1976 to 23.7 per cent in 1977, and then gradually declined to 19.0 per cent in 1980. Total state investment increased by about one-third in real terms between 1976 and 1978, but then fell by about 9 per cent over the next two years.

15 See, for example, Communist Party of Vietnam (1987a).

16 Decree 93-CP (8/4/77) 'Articles on Industrial State Enterprises', and Resolution 302-CP (1/12/88) 'Articles on Unions of State Enterprises'.

17 The commitment to a form of socialism, however, has continued through this period.

18 Decree 279-CP (2/8/1979) 'On Work to Promote the Production and Circulation of Commodities not under State Management and the Supply of Inputs or Raw Materials and Waste and Low Quality Materials at the Provincial Level'.

19 Directive No. 100 of the Party Central Committee, 13 January 1981, 'On Piece-work Contracts to Employee Groups and Individual Employees Working in Agricultural Cooperatives'.

20 Decision No. 25-CP (21/1/1981) on 'Several Directions and Measures to Enhance the Rights of Industrial State Enterprises to take Initiative in Production and Business and in Self-Financing'.

21 Decision No. 26-CP (21/1/1981) on 'Wage and Bonus Policies for State Enterprises'.

22 One of the costs of reform has been the weakening of some of the institutions of social service provision. For example, the cooperatives had served both an economic and social function and their decline resulted in a weakening in the provision of education (particularly pre-primary) and of basic health care. An alarming piece of evidence of this decline comes from an analysis of infant mortality, partly based on the results of the 1997–98 Vietnam Living Standards Survey, which suggests that, despite a general improvement, there has been an actual deterioration of provision of some services to the bottom quintile of the population and, as a result, an increasing gap between the survival chances of those born into families in that quintile and higher income groups (Nguyen Nguyet Nga and Wagstaff 2002).

23 Official statistics show the number of students studying in colleges and universities peaked at 154,000 in 1980, and numbers graduating peaked at 34,000 in 1983. In 1990, there were 93,000 students in colleges and universities and 19,000 graduating. Subsequently, from 1994, there was a sharp rise in tertiary education, so that by 1998 there were 492,000 students studying and 62,000 graduating (General Statistics Office 2000a).

24 It is an ironic result of migrations resulting from political upheaval that the unusual opportunities provided for migration as borders are opened for refugees, albeit often grudgingly, have so frequently worked to the economic benefit of the migrants, the host country and, in some cases, the country of origin. Examples amongst many include the positive impacts of refugees from Germany in the 1930s, and Asians and Africans who left Uganda in the 1970s.

5

POLITICAL INSTITUTIONS AND ECONOMIC MANAGEMENT

A key characteristic of the Vietnamese reform process has been political continuity. The political and administrative system has adjusted, but not through abrupt change and frequently not through processes which are very transparent and easy to understand, either by foreigners or even most Vietnamese. This chapter briefly describes some of the salient characteristics of the Vietnamese political and administrative system.

The institutional arrangements for economic management, planning and implementation are complex. Unambiguous statements of policy directions are rarely made. This reflects both the transitional nature of the economic system, and the challenges in reconciling commitments to a Marxist-Leninist state with the market-oriented reforms being implemented. The broad thrusts of Viet Nam's long-term development strategy and five-year plans are outlined in the resolutions of the (Communist) Party Congress. The government is responsible for formulating more detailed five-year and longer-term plans (including drafts for the Party Congress),[1] and for preparing detailed annual expenditure plans for submission to the National Assembly. The National Assembly is playing an increasingly active role in reviewing government plans and in monitoring government performance.

THE GOVERNMENT SYSTEM

Since the beginning of the *Doi Moi* process, Viet Nam has implemented a number of significant changes in its administrative structure. Under the 1992 Constitution, the government is charged with the supervision of public sector agencies at all levels and the overall management of the economy. In the alignment of power and authority among the '*troika*' (that is, the party secretary, the president and the prime minister) the prime minister is vested with the power to appoint deputy prime ministers, ministers and leaders of provincial people's committees (that is, the local provincial level administrations). The prime minister also has the power to establish, dissolve, or restructure public agencies. The president, in principle, has the power to recommend to the National Assembly the dismissal of the prime minister and to act as the Commander-in Chief of the armed forces. The president and the prime minister are elected by the National Assembly from among its members. The Party remains the dominant political force in the country despite some modification of its role in the 1992 Constitution.

The government of Viet Nam operates at three local levels: provinces, districts, and communes.[2] There are 61 provincial-level administrative units. Formally there is a unitary system of government, with centralised state authority exercised over local administrations.

Each level of local administration has an executive arm (the People's Committee), and a legislative arm (the People's Council). Although separate bodies, the People's Committees and the People's Councils have overlapping memberships. The People's Committees have both budgetary and administrative responsibilities. They are charged with the mandate to maintain law and order within their jurisdictions, review and approve plans for socioeconomic development within their delegated authority, execute the budget, and undertake duties as assigned by higher levels of administration.

Decision making at all levels is characterised by consensus-seeking as a strong guiding principle, engaging a wide range of actors before decisions are finalised, thus sharing responsibility and reducing the political risks involved in making difficult decisions. This involves 'opinion collecting' (that is, the required reference to concerned parties made in almost every decison making process at different levels). The emphasis on collective leadership and consensus has the merit of maintaining stability and involving many elements of society in decisions, but it is also the root cause of many problems in relation to the slow government response to critical issues.

In implementing decisions, 'coordination' by relevant state bodies is required before action is taken by a designated authority. This is most obvious with respect to the handling of economic issues. For example, fiscal and monetary management in Viet Nam is shared by the State Bank of Vietnam, the Ministry of Finance, and the Ministry of Planning and Investment. Consensus among the three is expected to prevail, but the prime minister has deciding authority in the event of a difference of view. In the management of official development assistance, the same principle applies.

PARTY AND STATE

Viet Nam remains a one-party state, governed by the Communist Party of Viet Nam. Support for the Party, and its legitimacy, stems from its role in defeating the French and the United States and its allies, to establish the modern Vietnamese nation. Until recently, the Party was led by the generation that founded the Party and led the resistance movement. Close personal and family ties helped ensure Party solidarity.[3] Economic difficulties and declining living standards following re-unification began to undermine support for the Party.[4] Reforms introduced under *Doi Moi*, including measures such as providing land use rights to rural households, and relaxing control on private sector, and the resulting improvements in living standards have helped revive public support for the Party.[5]

Official documents are unequivocal about the paramount role of the Party. Official policy is to preserve the political *status quo*, while moving to a market economy with a socialist orientation. Article 2 of the Constitution states that 'the Socialist Republic of Viet Nam is a state of the people, from the people, for the people. All state power belongs to the people, and is based on an alliance between the working class, the peasantry, and the intelligentsia' (Government of Viet Nam 1995). Article 4 defines the Party in language reminiscent of that used in the former East European centrally planned economies.

The Communist Party of Vietnam, the vanguard of the Vietnamese working class, the faithful representative of the rights and interests of the working class, the toiling people, and the whole nation, acting upon the Marxist-Leninist doctrine and Ho Chi Minh's thought, is the force leading the state and Society (Government of Viet Nam 1995).

The actual role of the Party in state management is opaque.[6] Most senior government officials and members of the National Assembly are also Party members.[7] Most ministers and many provincial leaders are members of the Central Committee of the Party. The Prime Minister, President, and Chairman of the National Assembly are now members of the 19-person Politburo.

The most important economic strategies are outlined in the resolutions of the Party Congress. The Party Congress is a meeting of Party delegates from local Party offices throughout the country, usually held every five years since reunification.[8] In between full meetings of the Party Congress, the Central Committee of the Party[9] usually meets 2–3 times a year to discuss particular policy or sector development issues. The Central Committee of the Party elects the Political Bureau (Politburo) that meets on a more frequent basis to consider day-to-day policy management decisions. Within the Politburo, a five-person standing committee is responsible for day-to-day Party management. Policy formulation within the Party uses the resources of Party institutions, government agencies and national research institutes.

THE GROWING IMPORTANCE OF THE NATIONAL ASSEMBLY

Under the existing legal framework, ultimate legislative authority rests with the National Assembly. The National Assembly is increasingly active in reviewing government plans, budgets, and implementation performance, and more assertive in exercising its authority over lawmaking. It plays an active role in scrutinising legislation, which it does with increasing care. Laws tend to be written in fairly broad terms, however, and their interpretation and implementation depends on administrative directives from the prime minister, ministers and provincial administrations.

The 1992 Constitution defines the National Assembly as the highest organ of the state, the highest representative body of the people, and the only organisation with legislative powers, and the power to amend the constitution. The National Assembly is elected every five years and has a broad mandate to oversee all government functions. It usually meets two (or sometimes three) times a year for about 1–2 months per session. Changes were introduced which took effect following the 2002 National Assembly elections which require more continuous activity by some committees of the Assembly. The influence of the National Assembly is expected to continue to increase with the appointment of 125 paid full-time members amongst the 498 members.

As with so many Vietnamese institutions, it is difficult for the outside observer to make a proper judgement about the role of the National Assembly. At one level, it would be easy to believe that it is likely to be toothless, as it is elected through a process carefully orchestrated by the Party and, although it contains non-Party members, members from the private sector, religious figures and representation of ethnic minorities, these are vetted by the Party and would not contain those fundamentally hostile to the regime.

There is substantial evidence, however, that the Assembly is beginning to be seen by the bureaucracy as a significant source of authority and a potential arena for independent criticism of government performance. Thus, in the drafting of important legislation (for example, the 1999 Enterprise Law), the Assembly has played a strong role in amending and influencing the detailed provisions of the legislation. As law reform has taken on greater importance in the overall reform agenda in recent years, the legislative role of the National Assembly has itself grown in importance.

Debates in the Assembly have also raised critical issues related, for example, to the official development assistance program. The Assembly also provides a platform for the articulation of provincial concerns about the balance of national resource allocation.

It is expected that the role of the National Assembly will continue to expand. It is difficult to predict what the effects of such developments will be, but it should be noted that under a one-party system it is possible for a legislature to play an active and somewhat autonomous role in policymaking, particularly in a consensus-based system such as that of Vietnam, not necessarily less real than that of a multi-party body subject to tight party discipline.[10]

THE NATIONAL–PROVINCIAL RELATIONSHIP

An important characteristic of the reform process has been the regional diversity in response to the new opportunities opened up by *Doi Moi*. Some provinces have taken a lead in pursuing new initiatives, sometimes innovating ahead of national policy, while other provinces have been cautious in implementing change.

It may seem surprising that regional diversity and local initiative should be identified as key characteristics of the reform process, given that the Communist administrative system might be expected to be highly centralised and given the common perception that the government remains overcentralised in many ways. For example, the power to approve master development plans, in both particular regions and sectors, remains with the central authority (decided by the prime minister after receiving 'opinions' of line agencies at central level). Despite such appearances, there is in practice a good deal more decentralisation to the provincial level than is suggested by the formal rules.

A significant degree of autonomy is extended to local administrations with regard to disposition of allocated budgets and adoption and implementation of local socioeconomic development plans. Although the formal fiscal system appears to be quite centralised, lower-level authorities in practice have some freedom for manoeuvre by virtue of access to their own sources of funds from various sources: they own property from which they derive income (for example, provincial and district state enterprises); they can charge various fees and levies (for example, for the use of roads and markets), and they are responsible for the collection of some taxes set at national level, of which they retain a share.

As the financial system is sometimes not very transparent, lower-level units may sometimes have access to funds not apparent from formal budgets and not disclosed to the national authorities.

The balance of political and administrative power can also be more decentralised than suggested by the formal lines of command. As in all political systems, autonomy at the local level will depend on the standing and authority of local leaders, and some provincial leaders may have senior Party rank above that of many national level ministers. Also, although civil servants describe themselves as being 'vertically' responsible to central government ministries, they are 'horizontally' responsible to the local authorities with whom they are in day-to-day contact. Most civil servants make careers either in the national government or at the provincial level, with movement back and forth only at a very senior level. Therefore although a provincial official may notionally be part of the 'vertical' structure of the relevant national ministry, and receive training and be in communication with the ministry in Hanoi, immediate accountability will be to provincial authorities.

Provincial and local departments have a dual responsibility to report to the local Peoples' Committee and Assembly, and to the central line ministries.

Responsibility for planning, implementation and operation of facilities is split, although the implications of this will vary from province to province, depending on the importance of the province. Large urban centres under central administration, and a good number of provincial governments, enjoy a high degree of autonomy. For example, they are authorised to license foreign investments up to a certain value, approve certain local socioeconomic development plans, and formulate their own budgets.

Some provincial governments are unenthusiastic about greater financial autonomy, seeing it to their disadvantage where they lack the capacity required to undertake needed development tasks, and therefore would prefer high levels of assistance (and accept the resulting intervention) from the central authorities. With increasing reliance on aid, the leadership of some localities see the need for central supply of counterpart funds in order to be able to access aid. Moreover, donors, while espousing the virtues of decentralising, have often unwittingly strengthened the power of central bodies by channelling aid funding through the national ministries in Hanoi.

GOVERNMENT CAPACITY

Viet Nam has shown a remarkable capacity to adapt its economic policies and institutions as and when needed. In particular, the ongoing *Doi Moi* process has brought about pervasive reforms in the country, both in terms of economic strategy and government.

Nonetheless, there are a number of serious constraints that hinder public sector management. The high degree of centralisation in principle implied in government rules and regulation, combined with the high degree of autonomy exercised by lower level bodies in practice, coupled with weak financial management capability at different administrative levels, erodes the accountability of policymakers, both at central and provincial levels. There is still a general lack of adequate administrative capability, particularly at the provincial level, which limits the prospects for a more effective form of decentralisation.

The policymaking process is often opaque and is not well understood, not only by outsiders but even by those within government. Allocation of responsibilities is often far from clear, and the need to agree through consensus delays decison making. When it comes to implementation, while individual agencies can be quite decisive, cooperation and coordination between line agencies is often difficult to achieve. That said, although inter-agency coordination is typically not very effective, there is often a strong sense of responsibility for carrying out tasks which fall within defined organisational responsibilities.

The perception of some Vietnamese officials at the early stages of the reform process was that, while there were competent professionals (for example, engineers), their professional expertise typically was not matched by capacity for management or policy analysis. When aid from the multilateral financial institutions and many development assistance community members resumed in 1993, experience or knowledge of standard development agency approaches to project appraisal, design, implementation, and evaluation was extremely limited in Viet Nam.[11]

The central planning tradition did leave a useful commitment to defining long-term development objectives in quantitative terms, and setting up monitorable targets against which to assess achievement.[12] But this approach tended to assume that implementation responsibility primarily rested with the state and state agencies, and was not sensitive to the more subtle relationships of the market economy, in which indirect policy instruments are used to stimulate non-state economic actors to contribute to development, and where the specific outcomes (for example, the composition of output) result from decentralised decisions. Therefore the *Doi Moi* process required a continuing process of learning at all levels of government, not just of the formal requirements of reform, but of new approaches to the role of government and understanding of the relationship between government and other actors in the economy.

NOTES

[1] The National Assembly and members of the Provincial People's Councils are elected every five years, as are the members of the Central Committee of the Party. Each newly elected National Assembly than elects state and government leaders.

[2] In Viet Nam the term 'commune' describes the lowest administrative unit, and has neither the ideological or economic significance the term carried in China or the Soviet Union.

[3] Fascinating insights into the early history of the Party and the extent and importance of personal relationships can be found in William Druiker's (2001) biography of Ho Chi Minh. For an official early history of the Party see Communist Party of Vietnam (1986a).

[4] The internal tensions prior to the Sixth Party Congress are apparent in addresses by the Party Secretary-General in the lead up to the Congress (see Truong Chinh 1986) and in the official documents of the Congress (see Communist Party of Vietnam 1987a).

[5] See, for example, RIAS (2001) for more detailed discussion of the evolving role of the Party.

[6] A US State Department briefing on Viet Nam notes that the constitution approved in April 1992 reaffirms 'the central role of the Communist Party in politics and society, and outlining government reorganization and increased economic freedom. Though Viet Nam remains a one-party state, adherence to ideological orthodoxy has become less important than economic development as a national priority' (US Department of State 2000). In contrast, the Heritage Foundation (2001)—which is widely quoted by segments of the international media—was still arguing in 2001 'the bulk of the economy is still centrally planned and dominated by state-owned enterprises'.

[7] At the last elections for the National Assembly, some 85 per cent of elected members were members of the Party and another 14 per cent were members of the Fatherland Front, which is closely linked to the Party. Only 1 per cent of elected members were independent.

[8] According to the Party's official history, the foundation conference of the Communist Party of Viet Nam was held in February 1930 in Hong Kong, the First Party Congress was held in March 1935 in Macau, the Second in Tuyen Quang province in February 1951, and the Third in Hanoi in September 1960. All post re-unification Congress meetings have been in Hanoi; the Fourth in December 1976, the Fifth in March 1982, the Sixth in December 1986, the Seventh in June 1991, the Eighth in June 1996, and the Ninth from 19–22 April 2001. Mid-term meetings can be convened to discuss emerging issues as occurred between the Seventh and Eighth Party Congresses.

[9] About 150 members elected by the Party Congress.

[10] It is interesting to note that, under a parliamentary system of the Westminster type, parliamentary bodies have become of diminishing importance in the day-to-day business of government, as tight party discipline under a multi-party system curtails any independent role (for example, some would argue that the UK parliament has been reduced to little more than fulfilling the functions of an electoral college).

[11] Even now, while substantial progress has been made in acquiring the relevant skills at the national level, there are still great weaknesses at the provincial level.

[12] Hence, the World Bank was able to claim that Viet Nam development planning framework was consistent with key principles of the World Bank's Comprehensive Development Framework (CDF).

6

THE INTRODUCTION OF *DOI MOI*

This chapter sets out some of the main features of the beginning of the reform process in Viet Nam, particularly in the critical reform years of 1986–90. The successful performance of the Vietnamese economy in the crucial period of dynamic growth, 1992–97, was stimulated by policy reforms, including improvements in private property rights, increasing macroeconomic stability, and a continuing shift from state controls to market mechanisms as instruments of economic management.

THE LAUNCH OF *DOI MOI*

By 1986, the then Party Secretary-General recognised the problems resulting from the emphasis given to central planning and large-scale production, stating

> …we have made mistakes due to 'leftist infantilism', idealism, and to the contravention of the objective laws of socio-economic development. These mistakes were manifested in the…[emphasis given to] developing heavy industry on a large scale beyond our practical capacity…[maintaining] the bureaucratically centralised mechanism of economic management based on state subsidies with a huge superstructure which overburdens the infrastructure. As a result, we relied mostly on foreign aid for our subsistence (Truong Chinh 1986:25).

Following the death of Le Duan in April 1986, Truong Chinh[1] was appointed acting Secretary-General of the Party until the Sixth Party Congress in December 1986, when he was replaced by Nguyen Van Linh. At the same time Do Muoi was elected as Prime Minister, replacing Pham Van Dong.

In the lead up to the Sixth Party Congress, the country was facing mounting economic problems. Despite price 'controls' on most goods and services, the annual rate of inflation was over 700 per cent. The value of exports was considerably less then half the total value of imports. Budget resources were strained because of high military expenditure and support provided to loss-making state enterprises. There was virtually no foreign investment, the technology gap between Viet Nam and its neighbours was growing, visits by Vietnamese nationals to market economies were rare and, apart from a limited number of diplomats and aid workers, there very few foreigners from market economies working in Viet Nam (Mallon 1999).

During preparations for the Sixth Party Congress, considerable debate took place about past mistakes and the need for a major renovation (*Doi Moi*) of the Vietnamese economy. This debate reflected a growing concern about the negative effects that the central planning system was having on the wellbeing of the population. The following extracts from a presentation by Party Secretary-General, Truong Chinh, prior to the Sixth Party Congress, provides an indication of public concern about progress in socioeconomic development.

> Our Party's policies must proceed from the interests, desires and level of our people. To evaluate our policies to decide whether they are right or wrong, good or bad, we should see whether the majority of our people enthusiastically approve and are eager to implement those policies or not. We should see whether production has been boosted, our economy has developed, life has become stabilised and gradually improved, national defence and security has become steady and strong or not.

> Since our whole country entered the stage of socialism, not a few cadre and Party members have alienated themselves from the people, forgetting the years and months of hardship and sacrifices...thinking that...in the struggle for socialism the people only have to obey them. Lenin said 'The danger facing a party in power lies in severing ties with the masses'.

> The peasants have a spirit of private ownership. That is true. To advance to socialism, it is necessary to get rid of that spirit. That is also true...Neither can we say that people who still have a spirit of private ownership are not patriotic. Such an allegation cannot win the people's approval, and only alienates us further from the people...they [the people] cannot agree to our imposing on them things contrary to their legitimate interests and compelling them to obey our subjective will.

> ...mistakes due to wishful thinking, impatience, and our failing to respect objective laws of development and even going counter to them. At the same time, we have indulged in conservatism and sluggishness, maintaining for too long the mechanism of bureaucratic centralism based on

state subsidies. As a result, our production capacities were restricted and could not develop, the working people could not in practice fully exercise their right to be master of society…causing endless inflation and price hikes, the people's life was unstable, ethical and spiritual values were eroded, and negative manifestations multiplied.

It is regrettable that even now a number of comrades have not fully realised the deep effect in many respects of that mistake, they fear that by thinking and doing otherwise than state subsidised bureaucratic centralism they would depart from socialism.

Some comrades propose that in the relationship between centralism and democracy at present, priority should be given to centralism. Such an opinion is wrong both in theory and in practice. Democratic centralism is a principle manifesting a well-knit unity. Without giving full play to democracy we cannot firmly maintain centralism. Without giving full play to democracy and ensuring the autonomy of the grassroots, ensuring the legitimate interests of the working people both in agriculture and industry, in production and the circulation of goods, we shall have no or very little marketable goods, and the latter will not circulate normally. In such a situation, can we ensure centralism? If we overemphasise centralism to the point of having no goods, and of bringing circulation to a standstill, will centralism have any meaning? This is precisely the state of bureaucratic centralism in which we have been enmeshed so far; the Resolution of the 8th Plenum of the Party Central Committee has analysed, criticised and reject it (Truong Chinh 1986:8–18).

Another address by Truong Chinh, two months later, illustrates the ongoing debate within the Party about proposed renovation of the economy.

To oppose bureaucratic centralism and the system of state-subsidised economic management is an extremely hard struggle between the new and the old, between the progressive and the backward, between the dynamism of the demand for renewal on the one hand and conservatism and the inertia of habits on the other, between the need to establish the real right to socialist collective mastery of the working people and the individualism of certain people who, in the name of defending socialism, try to keep their own special rights and gains. This struggle is taking place within our Party, within our state bodies and mass organisations, within our people, within each level and each branch of activity, and within everyone of us' (Truong Chinh 1986:8–18).

FIRST STEPS TO IMPLEMENT *DOI MOI*, 1986–89

Doi Moi was launched at the Sixth Party Congress in late 1986, when the country faced economic crisis. Despite state price controls, there was a market inflation rate of more than 700 per cent per year. Total exports at about US$500 million were less than half the total value of imports (US$1,221 million) and per capita trade levels were very low by East Asian standards. Government revenues were low, the fiscal deficit was large and persistent, and some areas were on the verge of famine. There was some private economic activity, but it was mostly black market and therefore risky. There was a growing development gap between Viet Nam and neighbouring economies. Contacts with market economies were very limited and Vietnamese were actively discouraged from personal contact with foreigners

The broad thrust of *Doi Moi* was officially adopted by the Sixth Party Congress in December 1986. This included agreement on the need for policy reforms aimed at reducing macroeconomic instability and accelerating economic growth, and that all economic levers (price, wages, fiscal and monetary policies) were to be used to achieve these objectives. The Sixth Party Congress agreed to abolish the system of bureaucratic centralised management based on state subsidies, and to move to a multi-sector, market-oriented economy with a role for the private sector to compete with the state in non-strategic sectors. Limited investment resources were to be directed towards three main objectives, namely

- the development of agriculture
- the expansion of consumer goods production
- the expansion of trade and foreign investment relations.

The policy directions announced at the end of the Sixth Party Congress in December 1986 represented a marked departure from previous policies and were the culmination of intensive internal debate about the failure of the old system to bring tangible results to the wellbeing of the Vietnamese people. While the Sixth Congress represented a critical turning point in policy direction, however, only limited details were provided about the specific policy reforms that would be implemented to bring about the desired change. The details of *Doi Moi* were discussed in a series of Party plena following the Party Congress, and documents from the Third and Sixth Plena clearly stated the need to move away from central planning towards indicative planning and macroeconomic policy levers (Communist Party of Vietnam 1991a, 1991c).

Just prior to the conclusion of the Sixth Congress, a number of decisions were issued on the family economy[2] and the role of the private, cooperative and state sectors in the agricultural sector.[3] Following the Sixth Congress, there was a gradual relaxation of the administrative constraints to private sector activity and to domestic trade. In early 1987, many of the checkpoints that had been established to limit domestic trade were reduced, and private markets for agricultural goods developed rapidly.[4]

While some commentators focus on the reforms implemented from 1989 onwards, important micro-level reforms were introduced from 1986 that resulted in a strong supply response that greatly improved the environment for the successful implementation of the subsequent macro level reforms.

In mid 1987, substantial price reforms were introduced with the official price of most non-essential consumer goods being raised to close to market prices and the scope of rationing being substantially reduced. At the same time there was a substantial devaluation of Viet Nam's currency, the Dong.

A key change was the different emphasis given to the role of government in the industrialisation process. The state was to concentrate on 'building the necessary premises for the acceleration of socialist industrialisation in the subsequent stage' (Communist Party of Vietnam 1987b). This was an important change of focus, as noted by Luoc (1994:23), who states that '…while industrialisation was reaffirmed as a necessary task, the basic content of industrial policy was confined to creating the premises for industrialisation at a subsequent stage'.

The Council of Ministers issued regulations[5] which clarified

- the difference between state ownership of property allocated to the enterprise, and the right of enterprise management to use and directly manage this property
- the relationship between the enterprise and government agencies
- the rights of enterprises regarding planning and decisions relating to procurement, sales, pricing, financial accounting, employment and salaries
- rights regarding commercial relations between enterprises.

During 1987 and 1988, the government rationalised and reduced the number of line ministries, state committees and other central government agencies.

A Foreign Investment Law was passed by the National Assembly in December 1987, and enacted in September 1988. It took a couple of years for substantial foreign investment inflows to result but by 1992 inflows were becoming an important source of investment.

A Law on Land was also passed by the December 1987 session of the National Assembly and was enacted in 1988. While state ownership of land was retained, private land-use rights were recognised by the state. Although it was an important step towards the introduction of property rights, this law did not allow for the transfer of land-use rights—despite the existence of an active informal market for land-use rights (World Bank 1993b).

Reforms introduced during 1988 provided greatly improved incentive structures, including steps towards clarifying property rights. A Communist Party resolution, issued in April 1988,[6] provided for a much greater role for individuals and private enterprise in the agriculture sector. Farmers were given long-term rights to land, centrally planned targets were abolished, and farmers could no longer be coerced into joining cooperatives, and were allowed to sell their produce on the open market.

The Party Resolution No.10, passed in 1988, introduced a critically important reform, greatly enhancing the rights of rural families, and diminishing the legal authority of village cooperatives. While there were initially mixed opinions from external commentators about the impact of Resolution No. 10,[7] the Party Secretary-General argued that this was a turning point in agricultural development (Do Muoi 1993). Indeed, some argue that it was one of the key turning points in the whole reform process. Providing farmers with property rights (albeit limited in extent), combined with price and trade reforms, contributed to sustained growth in agriculture from 1988. Strong agricultural growth in 1989 (6.9 per cent) was important in offsetting the worst impacts of the tight monetary policies that were introduced that year to control inflation—industrial output fell by 4.0 per cent in 1989.

A month earlier, the Council of Ministers had issued a series of decrees clarifying the rights of the non-state sector to engage in industrial production.[8] These policy guidelines were reinforced by a Politburo Resolution in July 1988.[9] These policy guidelines recognised the important potential contribution of the non-state sector in industrial production, and explicitly stated that the state recognises and protects the rights of the non-state sector to the ownership and inheritance of property and lawful earnings of non-state enterprises.

Despite these developments, the World Bank argued in 1990 that

> there has as yet been no clear elucidation of property rights, nor is there at present a legal framework to guarantee and enforce these rights. Consequently, there is considerable uncertainty about what actually is permissible and what will be permissible in the future, and that uncertainty retards productive investment (World Bank 1990:55–56).

Undoubtedly there was uncertainty—given development over the previous decade it would have been unrealistic to expect otherwise. Uncertainty could only be expected to diminish after the evolving market institutions, including the legal system, actually developed a track record of underpinning these rights over an extended period of time.[10]

Strong growth in the private sector's share of retail trade showed that the private sector had adequate confidence that an institutional basis existed to enforce basic contracts and to protect property rights in relation to the goods being traded. That is, even before formal legal changes to institutions were made, changes were gradually occurring in informal institutions that substantially affected the way economic business was being conducted. This does not imply that the institutions were perfect. There was an implicit recognition in the national policy agenda that more formal institutions would need to be developed to encourage longer-term private investment in productive capacity.

THE IMPORTANCE OF THE TRANSITIONAL PERIOD

The microeconomic reforms introduced in 1987 and 1988 were important in generating strong supply responses that directly contributed to reducing inflationary pressures, and in contributing to an improved economic climate in which it was politically easier to introduce the tighter macroeconomic policies required for sustained reductions in macroeconomic imbalances.

The earlier experience gained from the experimentation with reform since 1979 was important in changing beliefs and norms of behaviour that facilitated subsequent adjustment. Without the earlier reforms, the adjustment costs associated with the subsequent macroeconomic reforms would have been substantially greater.

The reform process was inherently experimental and gradual. Reform, when it came, involved an incremental process, which can be interpreted as a learning process, with the leadership responding to successes and failures of policies in practice, and also as the outcome of an ongoing debate within the political system regarding economic strategy. The fact that the centrally planned economy never worked effectively in its own terms made the process of *Doi Moi* easier than reform of centrally planned systems that had operated as working systems over long periods.

For the southern provinces in particular the experiment with central planning was quite brief. From 1976, attempts were made to integrate the southern market economy into the planning system of the north, but central planning was only applied in the south with full vigour between 1977 and 1980. The private sector, although illegal, was never fully suppressed.[11] Even in the north, control over the economy exercised by planners was in practice reduced

Table 6.1   **Some milestones in the Vietnamese reform process, 1986–98**

Year	Major reform measures	Policy and legal changes
1986	Decisions issued to develop the family economy; renovate management of state farms; facilitate the private economy and business in agriculture, forestry and fisheries, and to reorganise and renovate agricultural cooperatives.	The Sixth Party Congress announces *Doi Moi* as official Party policy in November.
1987	Law on Foreign Investment issued. Central treasury established	Land Law establishes private use of allocated land in agriculture.
1988	Land Law creates long-term land-use rights for agricultural uses. Party Resolution No.10 recognises households as the basic unit of agriculture production. Central banking functions separated from commercial banking. Foreign exchange controls liberalised.	Industry policy introduced encouraging private investment in industrial development Devaluation of exchange rates. Restrictions on foreign trading enterprises and state monopoly of foreign trade relaxed. Law on Import and Export Duties issued.
1989	Most direct production subsidies and price control removed—end of 'two price' system. Ordinance on Economic Contracts establishes rights for legal entities to enter into contracts. Producers allowed to sell their export output to any licensed foreign trade company	Quotas removed on all but 10 export and 14 import commodities (subsequently reduced to 7 export and 12 import commodities). Foreign exchange rate system unified. Bank interest rates made positive in real terms. Budget export subsidies removed
1990	Law on Private Enterprises established legal basis for establishment of sole proprietorships. Law on Companies established basis for limited liability and joint-stock companies. Tax reforms, including introduction of special sales tax, turnover tax and profit tax.	Law on Foreign Investment. Liberalised Law on State Bank of Viet Nam (SBVN) and National Law on Banks, Cooperative Credit Institutions and Financial Institutions enacted, prohibiting SBVN from commercial banking and empowering it as central bank
1991	Ordinance on civil contracts issued. Criteria set for establishing state enterprises; all state enterprises required to re-register. Major rationalisation of state enterprises undertaken. Private companies allowed to engage directly in international trade.	Foreign exchange trading floors opened at SBVN. Regulation on establishing export processing zones (EPZs) promulgated. Agriculture Bank of Viet Nam allowed to lend to households.
1992	New constitution reaffirms leading role of the Communist Party, but also recognises private property rights in a	Trade agreement signed with the European Union for quota allocated garment exports to the European Union and granting tariff

	state managed, market oriented, multi-sector economy, with socialist orientations.Pilot equitisation program for state enterprises introduced.	preferences on selected imports from the European Union. Foreign investment law amended to reduce bias against 100 per cent foreign owned enterprises and to introduce build-operate-transfer (BOT) options.
1993	Amended Land Law makes agricultural land-use rights transferable and useable as collateral. Bankruptcy Law and Law on environmental protection approved. First Donor Conference facilitates rapid increase in access to official development assistance.	Export shipment licensing relaxed—six-monthly licences issued for 22 export commodities. 90-day duty suspension system for inputs into export production introduced.
1994	Economic courts established. Labour code establishes protection of employer and employee rights, regulation of contracts, social insurance and sets up arbitration mechanism.Law on Promotion of Domestic Investment specifies incentives for domestic investors.	Import permits for all but 15 products eliminated.Inter-bank foreign exchange market introduced. Pilot work on creation of general corporations as groupings of SOE initiated. Export shipment licensing requirements lifted for all commodities except rice, timber and petroleum.
1995	Law on State-owned Enterprises consolidates previous legislative initiatives on state enterprises. Civil Code enacted deepening foundation for market economy, including some legal protection for industrial property rights. Government launches Public Administration Reform program and reduces number of ministries.	Import permits on a shipment basis no longer required for many consumer and producer goods. All export quotas lifted except for those on rice. Range of goods subject to management by import quota reduced to seven. Viet Nam joins ASEAN and commits to AFTA.Number of turnover tax rates reduced from 18 to 11
1996	Credit activities exempted from turnover tax.State Budget Law defines tax and expenditure responsibilities of different levels of government. New Law on Foreign Investment reduces import duty exemptions for FDI projects, and clarifies some investment policies.	Regulations elaborate regime under Civil Code for protection of industrial property rights. Inward foreign exchange remittance tax lifted. Number of items managed by import quota reduced to six.Mining Law approved.
1997	Reforms provide scope for direct private sector rice exports. Restrictions on domestic rice trade are lifted. Commercial Code approved. Law on State Bank of Viet Nam specifies roles and functions of SBVN. Law on Credit Institutions establishes basis for supervision and regulation of banking system.Value Added Tax (VAT) Law	Number of goods subject to import controls to achieve national balances increased. Temporary prohibitions on imports of wide range of consumer goods imposed then lifted.Approval of certain foreign investment projects decentralised to selected provincial people's committees and industrial zones. Law on Cooperatives confirms continued government incentives for cooperatives.The

	introduces VAT to replace turnover tax in 1999. Corporate Income Tax introduces company tax to replace profit tax also in 1999. London Club agreement to reschedule Viet Nam's international commercial debt.	Fourth Plenum (Eighth Party Congress) calls for greater effort to develop agriculture and rural areas; and to reform and develop state enterprises, cooperatives, and individual and private enterprises.
1998	Forward and swap foreign exchange transactions permitted.Domestic investment legislation amended to improve incentives and simplify access for domestic investors. Foreign invested enterprises permitted to export goods not specified in investment licenses. Maximum tariff rate reduced to 60 per cent. Shift to tariffs from quota or licensing to manage imports of most consumer goods.Decrees 29 & 71 issued aimed at implementing democracy at commune level.	Private sector enterprises allocated quota to import fertiliser and export rice. Domestic enterprises allowed to export production directly without an export/import license. Business registration procedures greatly simplified.Intensified process of consultations with private sector to identify remaining regulatory constraints and to develop the Enterprise Law. National Assembly approves anti-corruption ordinance. The Sixth Plenum (Eighth Party Congress) renews support for economic reform.
1999	Enterprise Law approved. Business licenses requirements streamlined. Value added tax (VAT) implemented. Government issues plan to restructure and enforce minimal capital requirements in joint-stock banks.	Initial agreement on US–Viet Nam bilateral trade agreement. Viet Nam and China agreement on land boundaries followed by increased high level contact and economic cooperation. Party and National Assembly discipline senior government officials for corruption.
2000	Enactment of the Enterprise Law. Insurance Law approved in May 2000. A formal stock market commences operation in Ho Chi Minh City. Government announces decision to reduce public service workforce by 15 per cent. Party and government identify information technology as a key element of the development strategy and introduce reforms to increase competition and lower costs.	FDI law amended to streamline procedures, clarify land-use right provisions, provide greater flexibility in corporate structure, and liberalise foreign exchange controls. Tenth Party Plenum concludes that there is 'no other choice but to continue with regional and global integration'. Signing of bilateral trade agreement is followed by first visit by a US president to Viet Nam since reunification.
2001	Ninth Party Congress concludes with resolution confirming a leading role for the state, but also recognising a long-term role for private domestic and foreign investors in economic development. A New Socioeconomic Development Strategy for 2001–10 and 5 year plan to 2005 are endorsed. Amendments to Land Law clarify	Resolution of Third Party Plenum specifies timetable to accelerate state enterprise restructuring, and decree issued to facilitate corporatisation of state enterprises under the Enterprise Law. Bilateral trade agreement with United States ratified by United States Congress on 17 October and by Viet Nam National Assembly on 28 November. Becomes effective on 10

	stipulations on land prices and land-use planning, authorised levels on land allocation, compensation for land clearance, and transferring land-use rights. Decree 44/2001/ND-CP (2/8/01) allows enterprises, individuals, cooperatives and foreign investors to export and import all permissible goods. Government announces comprehensive master plan for public administration reform.	December. National Assembly amends Constitution to recognise role of private sector and to better protect private property rights. National Assembly given more formal power to oversee government actions, including power to pass no-confidence motions on senior government officials. National Assembly also approved 10 and 5 year development strategies.
2002	Fifth Party Plenum takes decisions supporting an enhanced role for the private sector and on improving the capacity and performance of grassroots organisations ('grassroots democracy'). The Plenum also decides that Party members are allowed to own private business.	New National Assembly elected with 115 of the 498 members elected to serve on a full-time basis. Labour Code amended in April 2002 to provide more labour market flexibility (especially in terms of wages and recruitment) and allow foreign investors to recruit staff directly.

Sources: Government of Vietnam, Communist Party of Vietnam, World Bank and Asian Development Bank reports on the reform processes.

---

throughout the 1980s by a *de facto* decollectivisation of agriculture and the growth of extensive parallel markets.

During the first half of the 1980s, Vietnamese policymaking was subject to contradictory influences, as the commitment to central planning was tempered by pragmatic responses to difficulties in implementing central controls. During that period, there was considerable uncertainty over the government's long-term aims and policy. The Five Year Plan (1986–90) continued to emphasise the leading role of the state sectors,[12] the need to broaden the collective economy and to restrict the negative aspects of the private economic sectors, but it was overtaken by the launch of the *Doi Moi* policy following the Sixth Party Congress in November 1986.

Reform came in response to the serious economic problems faced at various times in the 1980s. Great economic difficulties had been experienced in 1979–80, following the cessation of Western and Chinese aid, and as early as 1981 agricultural policy was modified, when the end-product contract system[13] was generalised and the role of the informal private sector in such areas as retail trade, handicrafts and artisanship was officially recognised.

One interesting characteristic of the Vietnamese system was its pragmatic flexibility—when it was evident that the system was not working, there was a willingness to experiment with changes. Such a response is not a necessary reaction; there are plenty of examples of regimes that respond to difficulties by resisting change and withdrawing into a defensive posture. Such flexibility and pragmatism, combined with resolve, in the Vietnamese communist system was not new, as it had been characteristic of the politics and military tactics of the more than three decades of struggle that had led to the creation of modern Vietnam.

This account emphasises that change came as a response to experience with success and failure of policies. However, there was also a willingness to learn from international experience. While it is difficult to gauge the influence of external examples, despite the limitations on travel and exposure to foreign influences in the pre-reform period, Vietnamese leaders have always been keen to study relevant international experience. Despite stringent efforts to insulate the society from hostile political influences in the post-unification period, the Vietnamese regime was not as controlled, closed or xenophobic a society as North Korea or Albania. Indeed, the theme of modernisation, which has always been a core objective for the Communist Party, incorporated concepts of learning and borrowing from relevant international experience.

There was an implicit recognition that, in many important areas, market economic systems had brought more tangible material and social benefits to many of Vietnam's neighbours than had been achieved by the existing policy regime. Viet Nam was also a member of the CMEA and was exposed to the ferment of debates and policy changes in the other CMEA countries during the 1980s. Also, while in that period relations with China were not close, the relevance of Chinese reforms would have been clear to informed Vietnamese leaders, many of whom had received training in China.

By 1986, at its Sixth Congress, the Party was ready to make a political commitment to economic renovation (*Doi Moi*), although it remained unclear how far economic reforms would be implemented. For some years the uncertainty of the political commitment manifested itself in cautious and somewhat tortuous language—in the early years the term 'market mechanism' was not in use, the economy being described instead as a 'multi-sector commodity-producing economy'. The period 1986–89 was crucial because this was the period when the process of change was initiated through a number of significant but still cautious reform steps. From 1989 onwards the pace of reform accelerated.

The somewhat cautious and pragmatic approach to reform, while frequently generating frustrations among external proponents of reform, had two great advantages.

First, in terms of the contemporary vocabulary of policy analysis, the reform process had very strong national ownership—it emerged from the national political process and at all times reflected decisions taken by the Vietnamese.[14]

Second, there was time for 'learning by doing' in the development of new institutions. The incremental process meant that at each step the effectiveness of new institutions and policies were tested and adjusted to Vietnamese conditions.[15] This process was particularly evident in the agrarian sector, which was subject to continuing crisis in the years prior to the adoption of *Doi Moi*.

NOTES

[1] Truong Chinh was a leading Party theorist, who was held responsible for the excesses of the 1954–57 land reforms, but remained influential and emerged as a key proponent of reform.

[2] Council of Ministers Decision 146, 26 November 1986, 'Development of the Family Economy'.

[3] Council of Ministers Decisions 169, 170 and 171, 14 November 1986, 'Renovation of the Management of State Farms', 'Policy Directions Towards the Private Economy and Private Business Enterprises in Agriculture, Forestry and Fisheries', and 'Reorganisation and Renovation of Management in Agricultural Cooperatives', respectively.

[4] The extent to which administrative constraints were relaxed varied considerably throughout the country depending on the actions of local level administrative authorities.

[5] Decision 217-HDBT, 14 November 1987, 'Renovating the Planning, Economic Accounting and Socialist Business of State Enterprises'. Subsequently, Statute 50-HDBT 'Regulations for State-Owned Industrial Enterprises', of March 1988 provided more details on the rights and responsibilities of state enterprises.

[6] Central Committee Resolution 10 'Renovation of Management of the Agriculture Sector', April 1988.

[7] For a nuanced interpretation see Fforde, who argues 'that implementation of Decree 10 was limited in scope' (1990:12), that '[t]he fact that Decree No. 10 was so rapidly implemented itself shows the power exercised over local cadres by the level superior to them' (1990:13), and that '[t]he reasons for the limited implementation of Decree No. 10—its lack of effectiveness outside the rather restricted micro area of cooperative management—are at root to do with the slow response of state organizations'.

[8] Council of Ministers Decree 27, 28 and 29-HDBT, 9 March 1988, on 'Rules and Policies on the Private Economic Sector in Industrial Production, Service Industries, Construction and Transport', on 'Rules and Policies on the Collective Economy in Industrial Production, Service Industries, Construction and Transport', and 'Rules and Policies on the Family Economy in Production and Service Activities', respectively.

[9] Politburo Resolution 16/NQTW, 15 July 1988, on the 'Renovation of Management Policies and Mechanisms towards Non-state Economic Sectors'.

[10] A subsequent World Bank Report (World Bank 1993b:27) recognised that the 'movement towards strengthening property rights accelerated in 1988, when a Land Law was enacted. While state ownership of land was maintained under this law, private land use rights granted by the state were also recognized'.

[11] Pragmatic accommodations were made. On visiting a very well run seafood canning plant, owned by the Ho Chi Minh City Peoples' Committee in 1989, one author complimented the general manager on the evident efficiency of the operation and enquired where he had learnt the business. Somewhat shyly he replied that before unification he had owned the factory.

[12] As, indeed, has the vocabulary of subsequent planning documents.

[13] The 'output contract system' was introduced into the agricultural cooperatives as early as 1979–80. This reform awarded the individual farmer more rights within the cooperative and the cooperative more rights *vis-à-vis* the state. Compulsory deliveries were replaced by a 'contract' under which families were allocated plots of land and were obliged to supply a certain amount of rice to the cooperative, and any surplus was available for disposal in any way the farmers wished, thus providing an incentive to increase production at the margin and to respond to markets.

[14] Fforde and de Vylder (1996:315) argue that '[t]he fact that until recently Viet Nam remained ineligible for IFI lending and conditionality has perhaps also contributed to making the reforms process more authentically Vietnamese'.

[15] A paradox of the international debates on reform is that those who have advocated 'big bang' movement to market institutions by application of a set of market economy blueprints derived from economic doctrine are, presumably unwittingly, engaging in a form of social engineering comparable to a neo-Stalinist model. The Vietnamese incremental approach on the other hand might be seen as closer to Karl Popper's liberal views on the most appropriate paths to social change. Stiglitz notes that '[t]he irony of it all is that the modern critique of utopian social engineering was based particularly on the Bolshevik approach to the transition from capitalism to communism, and the shock therapy approach tried to use the same principles for the reverse transition' (1999b:22).

7

STRATEGIC BUILDING BLOCKS OF
DOI MOI

AGRARIAN REFORM

Agrarian collectivisation was intended to be an important part of the socialist strategy. Great efforts were made to develop agriculture using cooperatives as the basic unit for organising production, as well as for the distribution of inputs and marketing of outputs. This was particularly true in the north, where the cooperatives were developed both as productive units and as providers of social services (such as crèches and kindergartens). Following unification, efforts were made to extend this system throughout the country. Agrarian reforms introduced during the 1980s represented a decisive shift towards the family farm as the basic productive unit. This was the most crucial initial building block of the reform process because it impacted on the majority of the population and the core of the economy.

There was some regional diversity in the agrarian reform process, as the history of agricultural organisation differed considerably between the north and centre on the one hand, and the southern provinces. Prior to the 1981 reforms, cooperatives in the north were organised based on farmers working in brigades for work points. Even then, however, there was considerable 'own account' (illegal) activity.

The experience of the south and in particular the Mekong was somewhat different. There were two successive waves of collectivisation in the Mekong. The first was stopped in 1979–80 in response to economic crisis, and although the second (started in the early 1980s) was declared successfully completed in 1985, cooperatives never played as decisive a role in the southern rural economy as they had done in the north.

Even in northern and central Viet Nam, farm households were important elements of the production system, although subject to policies aimed at establishing collective control through producer cooperatives. Reforms in 1981 and 1988 increased the autonomy of the farming household, with the 1988 reform decisively shifting most economic power from the producer cooperatives to households and essentially returning agricultural production to a family basis.

Under the 1988 reforms, cooperatives were still meant to provide a focus for various rural activities sponsored by the state, but probably in the majority of communes the cooperatives were reduced to only a minor role, their functions reduced to acting as local tax collectors, as the holder of residual property rights, and as an element of the formal state structure. A small group of cooperatives managed to shift successfully to a profitable service function. Some cooperatives retained some support from farmers, but were greatly diminished in importance.

Further measures introduced in 1989 reduced the direct involvement of the state in input allocation. The procurement of agricultural output at prices below those on the free market formally ended and the share of output procured by the state declined considerably. From 1989, there was a substantial surplus available for free market sales.

The reforms had a considerable impact on rural institutions. Farming families increased their control over land and other assets. The weakening of the state trading system at the local level permitted private traders to develop local markets, while many state trading enterprises became more responsive to market opportunities. Large-scale wholesaling often based upon access to foreign exchange and other key inputs (such as transport facilities) generally remained under the control of state agencies but these competed with each other.

The picture regarding land-use rights became clearer over many years. The formal legal position lagged behind events. While the formal legal framework remained ambiguous for some years, there was in practice a decisive shift in favour of family farms. Residual collective property rights remained socially important in northern and central regions, where it was common for families to hold their land on long-term contracts from the cooperative. In areas where the cooperatives were weak, enforcement of land-use rights probably reverted to the village or commune level. In the south, the situation was even more fluid, and land essentially returned to informal private ownership.

Other farm assets were privatised extensively. Livestock, machinery, brick kilns and other important sources of cooperative revenues were sold to farmers.

Liberalising agricultural and small scale trade and craft activities fundamentally changed the character of the Vietnamese economy, adding to the resilience of the economy during the subsequent decade of economic difficulties.

THE TRANSITION TO A MARKET SYSTEM—PRICE REFORM

For many years, the economy experienced repressed inflation, a typical characteristic of centrally planned economies. Open inflation surfaced during the late 1970s. For a decade, high open inflation was combined with the persistent symptoms of repressed inflation, such as rationing and shortages of inputs and consumer goods at official prices. As a result of the pressures on the planning system, there was a partial breakdown in the allocation of subsidised inputs and of state procurement of consumer goods to fuel the rationing system. Enterprises, agricultural cooperatives and individuals were thus forced to try to obtain the goods from non-official sources. State companies began to initiate direct relationships among themselves in order to obtain commodities, inputs and spare parts unobtainable through official allocations—an informal reform process in which the rules of the planning game were spontaneously modified.

Political leaders responded to spontaneous change by making a series of concessions while trying to regain control of the process. As early as 1981, industrial sector state enterprises were given the right to do business with each other and to sell their production freely after they had fulfilled their obligations to the state. Companies became increasingly interested in transactions on the parallel market where prices (and costs) were several times higher than official prices.

The 1979–81 reforms within agriculture and industry, simultaneous liberalisation of retail trade, a cautious price reform and limited decentralisation of foreign trade represented important movements towards a market system. Early attempts to reduce the extreme differences between free market prices and official prices were made in 1987 following the official announcement of *Doi Moi*.[1] Prior to the 1989 price reforms, however, the economy remained segmented between production within and outside the central plan. In the period 1989–92, 'step-by-step'[2] movement to reform institutions continued, cautiously in some areas (for example, in enterprise reform) but decisively action in other areas (for example, de-control of prices).

As a result of the increased economic autonomy granted to households and small businesses during the second half of the 1980s, the state sector was left in a sort of halfway house. Although state enterprises were still, in principle, subject to the planning mechanism, the central authorities lacked the instruments to enforce plan discipline. A good deal of autonomy was granted, and central plan targets and instructions were not rigorously enforced, but state enterprises were not yet subject to market discipline and their input/ output prices were not always market determined.

Even though a growing amount of economic activity fell outside direct state control by the mid 1980s, a number of key issues regarding the legal status of private economic activity remained unresolved (for example, access to land), many important policy issues related to the management of the emerging economic system had still be to addressed (for example, price controls, exchange rate management), and the political legitimacy of the emerging system needed clarification.

In 1987, the rationing system was abolished for many commodities, and official prices of non-essential goods were raised to a level close to free market prices. Administered prices of most consumer goods, and of a large number of agricultural and industrial inputs, were increased sharply in 1987 and 1988. However, differences between official and free market prices continued to be large in the markets for key agricultural products, such as rice, and for foreign exchange (and, as a consequence, in the markets for all imported goods).

By 1990, commodity prices were largely market determined and direct subsidies had been all but eliminated. These reforms were critical. Two central issues in the shift to a market system of economic coordination are the manner and timing of the shift from administrative to market prices, and the strategy for introducing a new set of 'rules of the game' whereby actors in the economy, particularly state enterprises, are constrained to respond to market prices by the discipline of a hard budget constraint. The economy was opened to the influence of international markets, although this partly involved official acceptance of a reality in which international trade was already much freer in practice than principle.

While price reform was highly successful, it was neither an instantaneous nor a smooth process. The authorities faced two dilemmas. The first related to the impact of price reform on those segments of the economy ill-adapted to respond to the new system. The potential political and social costs of collapse of large-scale enterprises were obvious and it did not make sense to force the premature collapse of enterprises which might, if allowed time to adjust, have a chance of viability. Another set of problems related to the impact of reform on consumers, in terms of both the risk of increasing open inflation as price controls were removed and the impact of large changes in relative prices.

The strong open inflation of the late 1980s facilitated the shift from official to market prices, as official prices became increasingly irrelevant even before they were formally abolished. There was increased competition as voluntary transactions between enterprises replaced central planning and state orders. A fundamental change took place in the entire economic environment, with profound effects on the behaviour of economic agents. The former sellers' market was replaced with the shift towards market-clearing prices.

First steps were made to put a more appropriate machinery of fiscal and monetary policy in place, while existing instruments were used to reverse dramatically the continuing very high inflation in early 1989. Price reform was accelerated. With the exception of a few social benefit items (such as electricity, house rent, medicines), consumer goods sold through state outlets were now sold at prices very close to the free market level and were frequently adjusted to keep pace with free market prices. The state budget was almost entirely relieved of the burden of directly funding price subsidies. A drastic devaluation brought the official rate of exchange close to the free market rate, resulting in positive real interest rates. With the 1989 price reform and increased autonomy for state enterprises, the attempt at to operate a centrally planned 'command economy', for all practical purposes, came to an end.

The speed and depth of the transformation of the price system were decisive for subsequent economic performance, both in terms of the move towards market determined prices and the shift in enterprise behaviour in responding to market opportunities and constraints. Viet Nam quickly moved to a price system as 'free' as those of many long-established and successful market economies. However, issues of enterprise ownership, management and control were confronted more cautiously.

EARLY REFORMS IN FOREIGN TRADE AND PAYMENTS

The decline and eventual collapse of economic aid from, and trade with, the CMEA compounded the macroeconomic problems faced in the late 1980s. In response, the government sought to diversify its external economic relations with an 'open door policy' that focused in particular on export development.

The transformation of the foreign trade regime was a potent force for change in the economic structures of the Vietnamese economy. Opening up to imports from world markets, encouraging national enterprises to take full advantage of export opportunities and exposing the local economy to the opportunities and challenges of technology available internationally have had profound effects on the commodity composition of production and on the choice of technology.

Planned economies which had been integrated into the CMEA could develop a structure of production with little reference to relative prices prevailing in world markets as prices were largely insulated from international influences. Exposure to world markets and to the price system prevailing in those markets could be expected to have powerful effects, both on activities which were no longer sustainable when faced with international competition and on those activities which benefited from the stimulus of international export opportunities.

In this as in other areas, the impact of Vietnamese reforms was conditioned by the fact that in reality, the system was at the end of the 1980s spontaneously adjusting ahead of the change in the policy regime. The central authorities practised what could almost be described as involuntary liberalisation. The flows of imports, both smuggled and countenanced by policy adjustments, provided the material basis for the rapid development of commodity markets and the ready availability of incentive goods, which was a striking feature of Viet Nam's economy towards the end of the 1980s.[3]

The high level of informal activity which characterised the foreign trade sector involved, among others, various actors within the state sector. Thus a good deal of the foreign trade which took place outside effective central state control involved state enterprises. Unrecorded trade is believed to have been of a similar size as official trade in some years.

In a sector in which the central government had little success in imposing its authority, it was perhaps not surprising that the direction of policy was unclear. The government made feeble attempts to implement a system of quotas and licenses. In 1989, it was officially recognised that informal trade had led to a great increase in goods supply on domestic markets, but some officials also argued that unregulated trade had resulted in the circulation of counterfeit goods, tax evasion and severe competition with domestic production. The government, however, concluded that mainly administrative measures, rather than trade restrictions, could reduce the deemed harmful effects of foreign competition. Certainly, the ready supply of low-priced imported goods throughout the country made a strategic contribution to expansion of the market and to decentralised growth in economic activity.

A critical determinant of performances of reforming economies is the degree of adaptability and resilience of the underlying real economy in the face of new trading opportunities and challenges. In this respect, Viet Nam's performance was in striking positive contrast to that of other CMEA members. The swift re-orientation and expansion of Vietnamese exports enabled the Vietnamese to withstand the shock of the sudden collapse of Soviet support, the continuing effects of the US-led trade boycott, and the absence of any compensating increase in non-Soviet assistance. This was partly the result of Vietnamese oil exports coming on stream, but was also the result of a rapid increase in non-oil exports to convertible currency markets.[4]

Opening up had particularly dynamic effects because of the Southeast Asian regional context. Neighbouring countries were experiencing very high rates of growth in international trade and were undergoing structural transitions, with rising labour costs providing incentives for them to move the more labour intensive export processing offshore. The potential for expanding trade and investment was enormous.

In the liberalised trading environment, state trading agencies remained powerful. They had access to financial resources and their 'owners' (either a line Ministry or a local authority) could retain control of foreign currency, depending on their negotiating position *vis-à-vis* central government. They were controlled by agencies at important levels of the state administrative system (line Ministries and local authorities) which also controlled other economic units as well as regulation and supervision of commercial activity. They were therefore a key part of a system of interlocking structures, which, combined with their access to cheap credit through the state banking system, gave them opportunities to reap economic rents in various ways.

In the subsequent process of reform during the 1990s, a private trading system grew up alongside the state trading system, often acting in cooperation with the state trading companies (for example, in gaining access to export commodities such as rice when the state enterprises continued to enjoy privileged access through quota systems and licensing arrangements).

Despite significant liberalisation, the Ministry of Trade retained considerable power to control business entry to foreign trade activities. The Ministry of Trade issued import and export licenses permitting businesses to engage in foreign trade.[5] Obtaining such a license could be a time consuming and expensive process.[6] Specified criteria to be registered to engage in foreign trade included minimum capital requirements, past foreign trade experience, and qualifications of enterprise personnel. While private manufacturing enterprises were permitted to trade directly in products closely related to their business, private trading companies found it much more difficult to obtain foreign trade licenses.

In addition, the government continued to operate a system of quotas and other controls on the import and export of some important commodities, including rice, textiles, garments, minerals, petroleum products, fertilisers, motor vehicles, equipment and machinery, and any second hand goods. Not surprisingly, securing favourable administrative decisions involved a less than transparent process.

The system operated more flexibly than might be apparent. For example, although most rice and garment export quotas were allocated to state enterprises, in many instances most of the actual work was subcontracted to private enterprises and the state enterprise just collected the rent associated with the quota (see, for example, ADB and IFPRI 1996). Export growth was an important priority, and steady progress was made in reducing private sector disincentives to participate in export trade, resulting in significant reductions in the share of foreign trade handled by centrally managed enterprises.

In the early stages of the reform process, as the trading system and domestic price system were liberalised, the exchange rate took on greater importance.[7] The evolution of foreign exchange policy was both unorthodox and successful. In contrast to widespread efforts in many developing mixed economies to defend official exchange rates at unrealistic levels and maintain exchange controls in the 1970s, the speed and degree of the movement towards uniform exchange rates and convertibility was remarkable.

The modification of the exchange regime involved a period in which private and official foreign exchange markets operated alongside each other, with large gaps between the parallel and official rates. In 1989, a dual foreign exchange system, with an official and unofficial rate, replaced a complicated system of multiple exchange rates. The formal system was based upon obligatory delivery, in principle, of a variable proportion of hard currency earnings to central authorities, whilst the large informal system included direct quasi-legal transactions between businesses, most of which were part of the state sector as well as an active small scale foreign exchange market, in particular served by the gold merchants. US dollars were held alongside gold as a monetary 'store of value'.

For a time in the late 1980s Vietnamese citizens had been free to hold dollars. After a period of relative laxity, in 1991 the central authorities attempted to enforce central control over foreign exchange markets, but without much success. Even after the holding of dollars and dollar transactions were made illegal, such activities continued quite openly. Moreover, many domestic transactions (notably real estate) were denominated in gold, which could be brought and sold freely in a well-developed free market.

In principle, the Dong remained unconvertible and enterprises that earned foreign currency were supposed to deposit it with the officially approved banks, retaining a right to use part. The system of control, however, was weak. The official foreign payments system was subject to a degree of risk, as banks were not trusted to honour obligations in hard currency. This encouraged those in receipt of hard currency to retain control over it, inhibiting development of an effective official exchange market.

Foreign exchange regulations were persistently and widely violated,[8] with currency not being deposited in banks, interest-bearing accounts being kept overseas and foreign exchange being used at the discretion of the institutions which earned it. The dollar circulated freely in the main urban centres and was used as an alternative, if not precisely legal, medium of exchange.[9]

It was typical for state enterprises to retain foreign exchange for lending, to finance joint ventures and even deposit abroad. Numerous attempts to tighten control over foreign exchange had little effect. Efforts to reduce the use of foreign currency within Viet Nam and to pressure Vietnamese to deposit foreign currency holdings in bank accounts were frustrated by the lack of trust in the banking system and the continuing gap between the state rate and the free market exchange rate.

Many of the dealers in foreign currency were state units, and their owners (Ministries and local authorities) were responsible for violations. Rates on the free market were reported in the official media.

By 1989 the margin between the official and free market rates was not high by the standards of many developing countries, although it continued to subsidise those who were able to gain access to foreign exchange at the official rate. During 1989, the margin averaged 12.2 per cent; in 1990 it was 9.4 per cent.

The Vietnamese experience illustrated how difficult it is to transform fiscal and monetary institutions at a stroke and that, irrespective of whether the rhetoric of 'big bang' stabilisation or gradualism is adopted, in practice a degree of financial instability and inflation is likely to be experienced during the transition. This suggests the need for second-best macroeconomic strategies, to live with financial instability and inflation and limit the damage done to the growth of market institutions. One second-best solution, implicitly accepted in Viet Nam, was a dual currency system. The free *de facto* circulation of dollars and gold not only facilitated foreign trade during the reform period but also provided a stable basis for transactions during periods of inflation, and by so doing increased the efficiency of domestic economic transactions.[10] Tolerance of a remarkably free foreign exchange market provided an unorthodox but effective mechanism for the facilitation of the growth of market transactions in a period (up to the end of 1991) in which it was not possible to stabilise the domestic currency supply and price level. Together with the movement of official exchange rates close to parallel market parity, the remarkable permissiveness in allowing the circulation of dollars provided a good monetary basis for the development of market transactions, sustaining growth in the real economy despite high levels of monetary instability.

NOTES

1   Free market prices tended to be several times higher than official prices.

2   A term much favoured by Vietnamese authorities in describing the *Doi Moi* process.

3   Already, in the early part of 1989, the availability of imported manufactures in Vietnamese markets was striking, both as a result of the initiative of state enterprises in speculating in imports outside their normal business and as a result of smuggling, particularly from China and Thailand. Large stocks of electrical and electronic equipment were to be seen not only in the big cities but in provincial centres. Clear evidence of the relatively free availability of goods at that time was provided by the sight of Soviet advisors returning to Moscow on Aeroflot flights loaded with consumer durables. The uncontrolled movements of goods could have slightly bizarre results, as in the case of one provincial trading enterprise in the

Mekong that had on display a collection of fine French cognac as a result of a whim of the management, or the quite unwitting sale of t-shirts displaying Rambo, smuggled from Thailand. The Vietnamese seemed to be quite astute in acquiring tradable commodities from CMEA trading partners. As a result, one author's home in Dar es Salaam is furnished with two charming Czech chandeliers.

4   The management of a state footwear firm, interviewed in Hai Phong in 1989, volunteered the information that the firm had substantially shifted its market from Eastern to Western Europe, despite its formal obligation to supply CMEA trading partners. The incentive for this shift was that the convertible currency generated by this trade was retained by the firm to fund its activities (including purchases from other state enterprises) rather than being surrendered to the State Bank as required by regulations.

5   Article 4 of Decree 89-CP (15/12/95), 'Revoking the Procedures for Granting Export or Import Permits for each Consignment', Government Gazette (15/3/96). Decree 33-CP (19/4/94), 'State Management of Export-Import Activities'.

6   Up until Decree 89-CP (15/12/95) was issued, traders also had to seek licenses for each individual shipment.

7   If the prevailing exchange rate does not realistically reflect the relationship between the domestic price and border prices, then rents will be available to be reaped. Governments can adopt a range of exchange rate regimes between strict controls and full convertibility, such as multiple exchange rate systems and selective export earning retention, in the attempt to influence the pattern of trade.

8   The realities of foreign exchange practice were brought home to both authors on separate occasions when visiting the State Bank with a senior international official and a number of government officials in early 1989. While waiting for our appointed interview, the international official decided to use the time to change dollars for dong at the official exchange rate. At that point the Vietnamese official reacted almost with alarm, urgently explaining that the official rate was much lower than the rate offered (illegally) by gold merchants—an early encounter with the pragmatism of Vietnamese officials.

9   Despite repeated statements of intent and reassertion of regulations, the dollar has remained as a currency in wide circulation, freely used for transactions.

10 The 'dollarisation' of the economy implied by the tolerance under this system was quite different from the dollarisation of the Argentine economy that ended in crisis in 2002, in which the peso was held at a fixed exchange rate with respect to the dollar. The cost to Viet Nam was the state loss of seigniorage on the money supply circulating in the form of dollars, but that was a reasonable price to pay for the flexibility achieved during the transition.

8

ONGOING REFORMS: BUILDING THE INSTITUTIONS FOR MACROECONOMIC MANAGEMENT

THE ONGOING REFORM AGENDA

When the Seventh Congress met in 1991, significant reforms had already been implemented. Farmers had been given medium-term land-use rights, prices and the exchange rate were largely market determined, and laws on foreign investment, private enterprises, and companies had been enacted. Economic growth had accelerated to 6 per cent, following a recovery in agriculture and strong service sector growth as the number of individual and household businesses increased. Growth in industrial output also accelerated, but mainly as a result of previous large investments financed by the USSR in the oil and electricity sector. Exports had increased to four times the level recorded in 1986, reaching just over US$2 billion. Viet Nam had made the first important steps to a market economy with a degree of macroeconomic 'shock therapy' without suffering a period of macroeconomic decline.

The imposition of very tight monetary policies in 1988–89 was initially remarkably successful.[1] In early 1989, prices were substantially decontrolled. The official exchange rate was adjusted to a level close to the free market rate. Considerable freedom was allowed in exchanging the dong for foreign currencies, and in practice widespread circulation of the dollar in local markets was accepted. Interest rates on deposits were increased to positive real levels, and credit supply was controlled.

Despite these initial achievements, the economy still faced difficult structural problems. Three commodities (oil, rice and seafood products) dominated exports, and there were doubts about whether the acceleration in export growth could be sustained. There was resurgence in inflation, which reached an annual rate of 67 per cent at the end of 1991, even though it had been brought down to single digit levels in 1989. The fiscal situation was still fragile, with the ratio of government revenue to GDP only 13.5 per cent. Total investment, at 15 per cent of GDP, was less than half that of most East Asian economies. Foreign investment approvals were increasing, but disbursements remained low. And there were domestic and international concerns about whether initial economic improvements could be sustained.

The government continued to intervene in micro aspects of investment and personnel decisions, and sought to limit outside influences on society. The 1980 Constitution provided little protection for the private sector and foreign investors. While the number of Vietnamese permitted to travel and/or study in market economies was increasing, travel continued to be heavily restricted, and few business people and policymakers had been exposed to the development experiences of market economies. The number of foreigners working in Viet Nam had increased, but official permission was still needed for internal travel. Foreign businesses and international agencies were not allowed to recruit local staff directly. Office facilities, hotels and housing of an international standard were not available, and the limited facilities that were available were very expensive. Personal contact between Vietnamese and foreigners continued to be actively discouraged by some state agencies.

Therefore, after achieving progress with stabilisation and liberalisation over 1989–91, renewed efforts were required to build on the initial growth in trade and foreign investment and to adjust the role of government still further. And as the economy was liberalised, the reform agenda shifted to the complex tasks of building institutions which could provide an effective environment for the market economy, consolidate the gains already made and sustain the acceleration in growth.

At the Seventh Congress in July 1991, the Party re-affirmed its commitment to the *Doi Moi* process and identified macroeconomic stabilisation as a key priority for socioeconomic development for 1992–95. This commitment was made in the face of a difficult external economic situation arising from the loss of assistance from the CMEA and the continuation of the embargo. In response to a sharp resurgence in inflation in the second half of 1990, and declining exports and budget revenue in 1991, the Party Central Committee placed the achievement of macroeconomic stability and the reduction of inflation as top medium-term goals.

The state enterprise sector was to be consolidated to concentrate on key sectors and the environment for private business was to be improved. Alongside its commitment to strengthening the market economy, the Party also committed itself to maintaining progress in the social sectors. Decisions were also taken to restructure and streamline the government administration and to initiate steps to revise the Constitution to accommodate these changes. Thus 1991 saw a renewed political commitment to continue with the next stage of the reform process.

The next round of reforms also focused on such institutional measures as the creation of a relevant system of business law, the redefinition of land-use rights, to the creation of a new fabric of financial institutions and reform of public administration.

THE PURSUIT OF FISCAL AND MONETARY STABILITY

An important aspect of a government's role in the market economy is its management of fiscal and monetary policy and its impact on macroeconomic stability. In the prelude to reform, the country had verged on hyperinflation, fed by weak public finances.

Under central planning, government is in principle able to transfer resources from the enterprise and household sectors through direct control over resource allocation, incomes and prices. However, the degree to which that was possible in Viet Nam was limited by the ineffectiveness of the planning system. The reform process had further weakened control, fuelling macroeconomic instability, resulting in the very high inflation from the mid 1980s.

Moreover, reforms in the price system and enterprise reform initially weakened the old fiscal base. With the shift from a centrally planned, state-owned economy it becomes both less feasible and less desirable to fund the state budget from transfers of surpluses from state enterprises. It is less feasible because prices and outputs can no longer be so readily manipulated to generate the required surplus. It is less desirable because the essence of a decentralised market system is that enterprises should control after-tax profits as a key incentive to performance and as a device to channel investment funds into profitable lines of activity. The share of revenue from state enterprises in total government revenue fell from almost 60 per cent in 1990 to around 37 per cent in 1996.

In the reform process, many of the direct instruments of economic control had to be replaced by indirect instruments, including those of fiscal and monetary policy, which form the box of tools for macroeconomic policy implementation in mixed economies. Despite starting from an initial position of pervasive controls over actors in the economy, it was difficult to put into place the instruments of fiscal and monetary policy which are a routine feature of most mixed economies.

One source of difficulty was the interdependence between macroeconomic reform and changes in the system at the enterprise level. Effective macroeconomic policy should provide an appropriate environment for decentralised decision making at the enterprise level, but successful reform of the state enterprise sector is, in turn, a necessary ingredient for successful stabilisation.

An objective of reform is to develop an enterprise sector which is not dependent on state subsidy and is faced with a 'hard budget' constraint. In the Vietnamese case, although the reform of the enterprise sector has been slow and incomplete, the government was willing to squeeze the state enterprise sector and accept significant redundancies. However, efforts to tighten access to subsidies from the state budget were offset to some degree by the weak credit system. As the government tightened access to budgetary resources, laxity in the provision of credit to state enterprises 'softened' budget constraints.[2]

As noted above, Viet Nam—like most reforming economies—suffered a bout of severe inflation during the early stages of the reform process. The monetarist view that inflation is associated with excessive growth in the money supply can be taken as a useful starting point for a discussion of fiscal and monetary stability, but it is also necessary to explore why money supply gets out of control. This can happen because governments lose control over their own budget and have to 'print money' to accommodate their borrowing requirement. Even if government can balance the state budget, the borrowing requirements of state enterprises might also need to be accommodated by expansions in money supply. This has emerged as a critical factor in most transitional economies.

In all these cases, the reasons for instability can be seen as either resulting from the inability of government to take the necessary action to control the source of the imbalance (for example, the lack of policy instruments needed to balance the state budget) or the unwillingness of the authorities to take action because of the undesirable consequences (for example, bankruptcy of state enterprises, or increases in unemployment). Achieving stability is both a matter of political will and of the availability of appropriate policy instruments to translate intentions into practice, as was illustrated by the Vietnamese experience in attempting to achieve stability.

In 1988–89, the Vietnamese authorities demonstrated the political will to implement a rigorous IMF-style policy package (without IMF financial assistance to sweeten the bitter medicine), including positive real interest rates, drastic exchange rate adjustment and efforts to balance the state budget. An attempt was made to check inflation through a draconian stabilisation program. This program had some success but then foundered because of the inability of the government to control money supply growth. This inability was a consequence of weaknesses in the government's fiscal base and the need to avert a downturn in the real economy in the face of the collapse of trade and aid with former CMEA countries. A more effective institutional framework was needed to implement stable fiscal and monetary policies in a market economy. This task was still only partially completed at the end of 2002, despite sustained efforts over more than a decade.

At first sight, it should be relatively easy to move from the tight state disciplines of central planning to the less onerous burdens of tax payment. However, an effective tax system needs to be built on a foundation of reliable accounting, experienced tax administration and a reasonable degree of voluntary compliance, none of which existed at the outset of the reform process.

Viet Nam took steps to create a new tax collection system and to strengthen central fiscal institutions after 1989, for example through the creation of the National Treasury system and the National Tax Collection Office and efforts to broaden the tax base. As part of the overall fiscal reform, towards the end of 1990, Viet Nam introduced new profit and turnover taxes, based on a relatively simple system, which did not formally discriminate on the basis of ownership, and steps were taken to introduce an orthodox system of personal income tax.

However, a lack of transparency remained in the system. With persistent problems in collection, receipts were slow to build up. Thus, at the early stages of fiscal reforms, revenues from foreign trade taxes in the 1991 budget were estimated at 900 billion dong (around US$100 million), compared with a formal hard currency foreign trade turnover of over US$4 billion.

Strengthening the capacity of the finance ministry has been a gradual process. Key ongoing issues include the relationship between central and local government, the extent to which central policymaking is sufficiently informed by analysis of the economic impact of policy, and corruption in tax administration. The fashioning of an efficient and equitable tax system is not merely a matter of an appropriate tax code. The Vietnamese authorities designed a tax system that in many ways was admirably neutral in its treatment of public and non-state sectors. To increase fiscal effectiveness, however, tax assessment needed to be made more predictable. Adequate wages needed to be paid to tax officials and effective discipline imposed. *Ad hoc* tax breaks for the state sector and 'special taxes' imposed by local authorities continued. Despite a fiscal system that is on paper highly centralised, there was (and is) in practice a considerable degree of provincial autonomy in revenue and spending matters.

Viet Nam also faced difficult challenges in seeking to control public expenditure. Prior to the resumption of financial assistance from the multilateral financial institutions in 1993, state resources to meet the considerable needs for investment and recurrent expenditure in infrastructure, rural development and the social sectors, were woefully inadequate, especially given the cessation of Soviet aid.

While the fiscal and monetary systems remained quite crude, they were used quite effectively by government to maintain a reasonable degree of macroeconomic stability through the 1990s. For example, the government responded to the acceleration in inflation towards the end of 1994 and in early 1995 by slowing capital expenditure and tightening the availability of credit. As a result, inflation declined during the second half of 1995. Another indicator of success in macroeconomic balance was the reasonable degree of stability in the exchange rate for Vietnamese dong.

Starting from a very fragile base, there was some success in improving fiscal performance.[3] By 1996 total government budget revenue was estimated to have risen to 23–24 per cent of GDP. Further improvement in fiscal performance was set as an important objective. The target was to maintain revenue collection at 24 per cent of GDP, and to reduce the fiscal deficit and ensure that it remained under 5 per cent of GDP, as part of a strategy to contain the rate of inflation to an annual rate of 10 per cent.

Restructuring of tax rates and tax administration, reducing and/or abolishing subsidies and better control over expenditure all contributed to the improved fiscal performance, which in turn contributed to the sustained reductions in the level of inflation.

By the mid 1990s, following successful implementation of stabilisation and initial market-orientated reform measures, the government formulated development objectives for a longer-term period. In formulating the 1996–2000 Five-Year Plan, the government issued a series of decisions relating to sectoral and regional development objectives for the period up to the Year 2010, and then to 2020.

The overall national development objective was defined in terms of the need to undertake industrialisation and modernisation in order to

build an industrialised country with modern technology and infrastructure, a rational economic structure, advanced productive relationships consistent with developing productive potential, high material and intellectual wellbeing, firm national security and defence, a prosperous people, and an equitable and civilised society (Communist Party of Vietnam 1996a:37).

Slow progress with enterprise and administrative reforms, low efficiency and competitiveness in domestic production, adverse climatic conditions and the impact of the regional economic and financial crisis led to rethinking of priorities and the revision of development plans. The Fourth Party Plenum (December 1997) emphasised that the immediate priorities were ensuring financial sector and macroeconomic stability and coping with the unfavourable impact of the regional economic crisis. The Sixth Plenum (October 1998) reaffirmed the need to sustain reforms focusing on industrialisation and modernisation, give priority to agricultural and rural industries and to other areas in which Viet Nam had a comparative advantage, and to increase economic competitiveness generally. The East Asian economic and financial crisis of 1997–98 also brought into greater focus the need to address continuing weaknesses in public finance and the financial system.

The increasing sophistication of the government in managing macroeconomic policy was demonstrated in 1998–99, when economic growth slackened as a consequence of the East Asian crisis, but the government swiftly adjusted its spending program and thereby avoided serious external and domestic instability.

MONEY AND BANKING REFORM

Efficient financial discipline is dependent on the existence of a financial system capable of applying good judgement to the provision of credit. Unfortunately, an effective two tier banking system cannot be created overnight.[4]

Viet Nam started the reform process with a banking system designed along Soviet lines. Under central planning systems, the main function of the banking system was to facilitate transactions and act as a component of the state accounting system; the banking system was not typically used as an active instrument of economic policy as macroeconomic aggregates were controlled directly through the planning system. In principle, any potential inflationary pressures resulting from excess monetary balances could be repressed by planning constraints on their use. Moreover, the allocative functions of the credit system were minimised—resources were allocated directly through the plan and the function of credit was merely to accommodate the physical allocations made by the planning system. Credit was allocated administratively and the interest rate was viewed neither as an allocative device nor as an incentive to savings. Given the limited functions allotted to monetary institutions, a banking system based on one tier of banking institutions combining the functions of central and commercial banks, was sufficient.

As the economy moved towards a more market-oriented system, it became apparent that existing financial institutions were woefully inadequate. There was no institutional distinction reflecting the differing functions of a central bank, responsible for managing monetary aggregates and overseeing key national policy instruments such as the exchange rate and interest rates, from the functions of commercial banks, operating to make allocative decisions through the provision of credit to enterprises and providing a range options for households and enterprises to hold liquid assets. Needless to say, there was a virtual absence of any other forms of formal financial intermediation or of equity markets.

The first step in financial sector reform therefore was the development of a two-tier banking system with a clear differentiation between the central (state) bank and commercial banks. The importance given by advocates of reform to the development of effective commercial banking particularly relates to the need for a proper financial context for enterprise reform. As enterprises are given greater autonomy, their access to automatic state subsidies is reduced and they are exposed to the rigours of the market, a process that lays the foundations for enhanced macroeconomic stability. The 'hard budget constraint' will be easily thwarted if enterprises have the option of unrestrained access to bank credits, while the absence of adequate credit facilities can constrain legitimate business. An effective banking system is therefore needed both to confront enterprises with the realities of market operation subject to budget constraints and to provide them with access to financial markets capable of operating according to market orientated principles.

The creation of a two-tier banking system is one step in the process of creating a mature, decentralised system of financial intermediation in which decentralised financial institutions operate autonomously and commercially, subject only to general banking regulations and directives which set limits within which they conduct day-to-day business and the learnt principles of prudent banking practice which provide a guide to business survival.

However, there are dangers in the transition. Newly created commercial banks may be subject to pressures to provide credit imprudently and may also be attracted to the potential returns from reckless lending. It may be difficult for a neophyte central bank to strike the right balance between encouraging autonomy and maintaining prudent supervision of the new commercial banks. Failure to control the process can have inflationary consequences and undermine the effort to expose enterprises to a market environment. An imprudent banking system can contribute to economic crisis—the East Asian crisis was partly fuelled by a lengthy period of imprudent bank lending (mainly by private banks).

It is not easy to create a commercial banking system with a sound portfolio of assets and reasonable profitability at a stroke, and certainly not in the context of the pressures rising from more general reform measures. Banking depends on trust and a culture of prudent banking behaviour, which needs to be acquired and demonstrated over the longer term. While established international banks can provide immediate access to effective banking, and arguably earlier and greater involvement of international banks would have been beneficial, Viet Nam, no more than other countries in the region, could not have been expected to abandon its commercial banking system to foreign domination. The practical and political constraints on the smooth development of a more commercial banking system are demonstrated by Vietnamese experience.

Formally, the basic structure of a market-based financial system emerged quite quickly. Following reforms in the banking system, the four state-owned commercial banks were, in principle, required to operate on a profit-making basis. In the early 1990s, a number of joint stock banks were also set up, some of which were in turn owned mainly by other state enterprises. These were small and operated within the framework of official interest rate policy. There were also a number of credit cooperatives and housing banks. A number of branches of foreign banks also opened.

In the early reform years, however, the Vietnamese banking system remained limited in its technical capacity to handle many basic banking functions, such as fund transfer, clearing and so on. These inadequacies resulted from technical weaknesses (absence of modern equipment, and so forth) and limitations in personnel and basic management skills, aggravated by low wages. The weakness of the banks can be seen as part of a more general phenomenon.

Even though a number of the key institutions appropriate to a market economy were put in place, making them work effectively proved difficult in the face of entrenched interests, established habits of work and a continued lack of clarity regarding the status of the state sector, especially the rights of banks to foreclose. As a result, financial discipline was lacking and the commercial banking system remains in poor shape at the end of 2002, with both the state and the banks suffering from a large overhang of questionable assets and unhealthy balance sheets. Financial intermediation remains ineffective. While an infant stock market now exists, the shares traded are too few and volumes too small for it yet to be a significant factor.

For some years, state banks in principle received subventions from the state budget intended to cover the large negative spread between deposit rates and lending rates, but in practice they were often not paid. Most state banks continued to lend mainly to the state sector, despite government statements asserting the need to treat all sectors equally. However, private sector businesses have been gaining increasing access to credit (Table 8.1).

After 1989, it was necessary to take action to prevent the collapse of a large number of state enterprises that had suddenly been deprived of access to subsidised inputs from the Soviet aid program. The financial performance of banks depended on the gross margin between loan rates and deposit rates, as well as on the performance of the loans themselves. On both counts, banks in Viet Nam faced difficulties and there have been sharp fluctuations in real interest rates.[5]

Although the state banks lacked the formal professional skills to carry out proper audits of their customers, they were in many instances well aware of the

Table 8.1   **Allocation of bank lending to enterprises in Viet Nam, 1991–2001 (end of year)**

	1991	1992	1993	1994	1995	1996	1997	1998	1999	2000	2001
Lending to state enterprises											
Share of total credit	90.0	81.7	66.9	63.0	57.0	52.8	50.0	52.4	48.3	44.9	41.9
Share of dong loans	88.5	75.9	55.7	51.5	44.8	39.6	41.8	48.3	..	..	..
Share of foreign currency loans	96.5	97.9	90.7	81.3	76.3	75.8	68.3	61.8	..	..	..
Lending to private enterprises											
Share of total credit	10.0	18.3	33.1	37.0	43.0	47.2	50.0	47.6	51.8	55.1	58.1
Share of dong loans	11.5	24.1	44.3	48.5	55.2	60.4	58.2	51.7	..	..	..
Share of foreign currency loans	3.5	2.1	9.3	18.7	23.7	24.2	31.7	38.2	..	..	..

Source: Derived from data in International Monetary Fund, 2001. *Vietnam: Statistical Appendix and Background Notes*, International Monetary Fund, Washington, DC; and International Monetary Fund, 2001. *Vietnam: Statistical Appendix and Background Notes*, International Monetary Fund, Washington, DC (and earlier issues).

risks involved. Banks would seek to recoup some of the losses from subsidised loans to non-viable enterprises by charging potentially profitable enterprises rates closer to commercial rates. While such cross-subsidisation improved the balance sheets of the banks, it reduced the efficiency of their role in resource allocation.

At the start of the 1990s central banking was in its infancy in Viet Nam. In principle, as early as May 1990 the State Bank of Viet Nam was endowed with the normal powers and obligations of a central bank in a market economy. But, given its earlier role, which combined the functions of a central and commercial bank, the State Bank of Viet Nam had a branch network at province level, with a high degree of formal branch autonomy, which created the potential for political pressures for targeted credit to be brought to bear at the provincial level. The State Bank also continued to have a close relationship with the state commercial banks, which placed in question for some time the degree to which the central banking and commercial banking roles had been separated. There has, however, been a gradual process of training and institutional development, which has increased the competence of the Vietnamese banks, while the entry of foreign banks into the Vietnamese economy has increased the sophistication of banking services available in Hanoi and Ho Chi Minh City.

By 1998, significant improvements had been put in place in the banking system in providing access to capital for the private sector. Clarification that state enterprises are limited liability enterprises and the issuance of regulations restricting government guarantees to state enterprises helped in providing more equitable access to bank credit. Amendments to the implementing regulations[6] for the Land Law to allow companies, cooperatives and private enterprises to mortgage land-use rights was also important, although land-use rights can only be mortgaged to Vietnamese banks,[7] and banks have concerns about the difficulties in foreclosing on mortgages to recover bad debts.[8] The private sector frequently cites the insecurity of title to land-use rights as a constraint to private investment. Despite the remaining impediments to private sector financing, there has been a marked increase in the share of total bank lending directed to the private sector in recent years. In 1997, however, the state enterprise share of total bank credit remained at almost twice the contribution of state enterprises to GDP, and state enterprises continued to have access to non-bank state funds.

Over the 1990s, the professional competence of the State Bank of Viet Nam has steadily improved and it has increasingly been able to establish itself in an important advisory role to government on macroeconomic policy and as a key player in ongoing discussions and negotiations regarding the need to undertake further bank reform and restructuring and refinancing of the commercial banking system, which is now at the top of the policy agenda.

Banking reform is one area where the critics of the slow pace of Vietnamese reform may appear to have some justification. Nevertheless, it should also be noted that while caution resulted in the slow growth of a modern banking system it also avoided the serious risks demonstrated in the performance of other economies in the 1990s. Accounts of developments in Russia indicate how the rapid development of an uncontrolled banking system can be the source of corruption, crime and severe disorder. Also, a rapid development of new private banks could have left the economy highly vulnerable to the finance and banking crisis that accompanied the regional downturn in 1997.

NOTES

1 The 1989 stabilisation engendered a good deal of international comment and analysis. See Dollar (2001), Fforde and de Vylder's ADB study (1996); and Wood (1989) for specific analyses of the stabilisation measures. See also van Brabant (1990) and Drabek (1990).

2   However, the concept of the 'hard budget' constraint is more ambiguous than rhetoric might suggest. In market economies, it is typical for firms to have access to credit and for creditors (including banks) to tide over firms with temporary losses and cash flow problems. A system which worked without credit would be woefully inefficient. Most enterprises require access to a credit market, and for the economic system to be efficient that market should provide access to funds on the base of the application of reasonable financial criteria. A 'soft budget' constraint implies that state enterprises (or, for that matter, private firms) have access to funds in excess of amounts justified by the application of sound financial judgements, which *ex ante* necessarily involves a strong element of judgment, exercised for example by competing commercial banks and other financial intermediaries.

3   Little information is available on the state budget during the early period of reform. The estimates here are drawn from IMF sources.

4   Various periods of difficulty faced by financial institutions in many fully developed market economies (for example, not only in Southeast Asia but even in Japan and the United States) suggest some of the complexities of creating an efficient credit market.

5   For example, there was a return to negative real rates in 1990 after the positive yield offered through much of 1989. The interest rates actually charged to state enterprises could be adjusted according to their viability

6   Article 13 of Decree 85-CP (17/12/96), 'Guiding Implementation of the Ordinance on the Rights and Obligations of Domestic Organisations with Land Assigned or Leased Land by the State', Government Gazette (28/2/97).

7   Buildings can be mortgaged to both domestic and foreign banks.

8   A mortgage sale generally requires the consent of the government and mortgagor (Circular 217-NHNN (17/8/96) and the sale must be conducted by an authorised body (Article 273(2) of the Civil Code).

9

INSTITUTIONAL CHANGE AND BUSINESS DEVELOPMENT

A pivotal ongoing component of the *Doi Moi* process has been the response of key economic actors to market opportunities. Early reforms facilitated increased contributions from households and businesses to economic activity, generating higher income and employment and reduced poverty during a period of profound restructuring of the economy. A strong supply response during the early stages of reform—especially the sharp jump in output resulting from increased household investment in agriculture and retail trade—was vital to macroeconomic stabilisation.

An important part of the ongoing *Doi Moi* process is the creation of new market institutions, including a legal framework for business that defines the accepted forms of business organisation and governs a wide range of business activities. So far, however, the process of creating many of the components of a formal legal and administrative environment for the market economy has been quite slow. In this, as in other areas, the economy has performed well despite the perceived weaknesses in the formal institutional framework. Changes in the behaviour of key economic actors have tended to move ahead of the adjustments to the formal institutional framework. The description of the process of change therefore emphasises the inter-play between formal and informal institutional development.

ACTORS IN VIETNAMESE BUSINESS ACTIVITY

As Viet Nam shifted towards a market economic system, economic performance increasingly depended on the decentralised decisions of economic actors responding to an economic environment influenced by public policy and newly emerging market institutions.

Key actors in the business sector during the reform process were farmers and other household business, cooperatives, state enterprises, domestic private enterprises and business involving foreign investment (in Vietnamese terminology 'foreign-invested businesses'). State enterprises have been important actors in larger scale and more formal economic activity, especially in industry, but the state share of total employment was much smaller than in most centrally planned economies at the beginning of transition and has fallen further during the transition period. Households have been important in rural and informal urban economic business activity and have provided employment for most of the population. Cooperatives played a role in agriculture, light industry, retail trade and other services. Formal private enterprises and foreign investors only became significant economic actors as the transition progressed.

INSTITUTIONS AND LAW IN BUSINESS AND ECONOMIC DEVELOPMENT

North argues that institutions[1] 'form the incentive structure of society, and the economic and political institutions, in consequence, are the underlying determinants of economic performance' (1994:360). In particular, institutions set the 'rules of the game' that accommodate and condition the participation of diverse actors in the economy. Effective institutions provide investors with confidence that contracts and property rights will be enforced. Such confidence is critical to ensuring increased investment. The most obvious institutions affecting business are the formal policies, laws, regulations and administrative arrangements that attempt to control and influence the behaviour of economic actors.

Creating an appropriate legal framework will eventually be part of a successful reform process. In examining the Vietnamese experience, however, it is striking that improvements in enterprise performance have usually preceded changes in the legal framework. It should be recognised when evaluating the urgency and timing of legal reform and the importance of formal legal arrangements during transition that informal institutions may evolve effectively ahead of the endorsement of the arrangements through legislation, while legislation may not be very effective if it is not in accord with established views and practices.

The Vietnamese experience is consistent with the views of those who emphasise that 'law develops over time and in interaction with changes in the socioeconomic environment' influencing the nature and content of laws and legal institutions.[2] In other words, market institutions, including formal legislation, evolve in response to social demand and need. Demand arises because legal institutions are needed to reduce the transaction costs of conducting business as economies develop. Legislation often formalises and reinforces informal arrangements that have emerged in response to need.[3]

While the importance of legal institutions in economic development is widely accepted, many attempts to accelerate economic development by transplanting laws have not produced the expected results (Berkowitz et al. 2000). John Gillespie has argued that the uneven reception of imported law in Viet Nam is consistent with experiences elsewhere in East Asia (Gillespie 2001a).

In the history of developed countries, most market institutions, including formal legislation, evolved in response to social demand. As an economy becomes larger, more open and complex, the demand for formal institutions to reduce risk and the transaction costs of conducting business increases. As the role of large private businesses increases, both national and foreign, the need for a more effective legal system—and for administrative practices (including tax administration) that are rule based rather than discretionary—also increases.

While formal business laws in market economies have tended to converge, attitudes to law and the role of key institutions still differ widely. This affects the way laws are implemented, and thus impacts on business decisions and economic behaviour. While formal institutions may remain in place, even if there is no demand,[4] informal institutions will only be sustained if supported by society. The sudden introduction of formal institutions can also undermine the effectiveness of informal arrangements.[5]

Informal understandings and interpretation are particularly important in developing and transition economies, where formal rules may not yet have adjusted to new economic needs and where formal institutions for enforcing formal rules remain weak and unpredictable, resulting in erratic enforcement. Even in relation to government regulations, informal understanding and interpretation of the intentions of government can be as important an influence on business behaviour as the formal 'rules of the game'.

Viet Nam's experience is consistent with a view that the formal legal institutions do not uniquely determine enterprise behaviour.[6] Even in rule-based societies, most contract and property disputes are settled informally (Pistor 1999), and politics can affect the way rules are interpreted.[7] Informal institutions (social practice and behaviour, and pressures to conform) provide alternative mechanisms for protection of property and rights. Informal institutions play an important role in all economies, including the most developed economies, and the relative roles differ from country to country and within countries (Berkowitz et al. 2000). Informal institutions linked to reputations have played an important role in more developed East Asian market economies (Pistor and Wellons 1999),[8] where recognition that a reputation is important to securing future business transaction provided strong incentives for performance. Pistor argues that

> [t]he concept of law as infrastructure fails to realise that formal law is but one set of institutions that govern behaviour. Where formal and informal institutions evolve over time, they tend to complement each other. In the context of a political or economic regime change, however, formal and pre-existing informal institutions compete. Formal law may be rejected or ignored and substituted with informal institutions that operate independently of and frequently in contradiction to the formal legal system (Pistor 1999:2).

While arguing that 'there is empirical evidence showing that the rule of law does contribute to a nation's wealth and its rate of economic growth', Richard Posner (a Chief Judge of the US Court of Appeals) argues that 'even very wide deviations from this capitalist rule-of-law ideal may not seriously compromise economic efficiency' (Posner 1998:2–3).

Even in economies with highly elaborate systems of commercial law, segments of the economy may operate on the basis of informal agreements, where there is a long-established trust between the contracting parties. The limitation is that under informal arrangements transaction costs are lower for those who are members of such informal networks than for outsiders, for whom a legally enforceable contractual system may be seen as a necessity.

In the case of Vietnam, the tendency of informal change to precede legislation and for business and government to engage in *de facto* arrangements to accommodate new norms of business behaviour may well have a differential impact on businesses, between those better able to understand and handle such an environment, with its uncertainties and need to cement informal relationships through discrete (and illegal) financial transfers, and those more at home in a more transparent legal environment.[9]

Viet Nam can draw on differing legal traditions in framing its new laws. Some observers argue that legal heritage impacts on institutional and economic development. Islam and Montenegro cite studies that argue that 'countries with French legal heritage have consistently poorer institutional quality than those with other legal traditions. It is argued that French civil law countries have been characterised by more interventionist and formal government apparatus' (2002:3). While French law had a major impact in the colonial era of Viet Nam, there was a long hiatus when the legal system was influenced more by Soviet thinking. Since the beginning of *Doi Moi*, Viet Nam has sought to learn from the business regulatory environments in neighbouring countries and OECD members, and from the experiences of other transition economies.

The view adopted in this study is that, although a well designed, clearly defined, generally accepted and enforceable system of laws is an optimal goal for the reduction of uncertainty and transaction costs, solutions exist that fall short of being optimal but are nonetheless workable. Differences in performance between systems may therefore depend more on the characteristics of the second-best solutions that emerge, which may involve informal arrangements and behaviour which by-pass inappropriate rules and regulations to establish workable ways of maintaining orderly business arrangements even in the absence of the certainties implied by the term 'rule of law'.

OVERVIEW OF INSTITUTIONAL REFORM PROCESSES IN VIET NAM

During the reform process in Viet Nam changes in formal rules have often responded to a spontaneous process of institutional development, accommodating changes in informal practices. This has critical implications for interpretations of the Vietnamese experience. On the one hand, the development and behaviour of businesses, both private and publicly owned, often moved ahead of reforms in policy, and informal stratagems were often effective in by-passing unhelpful formal constraints (McMillan and Woodruff 1999a, 1999b). Even within the state sector, corporate behaviour was varied and not easily characterised by reference to formal arrangements.

But first, it will be useful to highlight the most important formal legal changes. The 1992 Constitution was a milestone in laying the foundations for a private sector to compete with the state sector (Government of Vietnam 1992:18–19). The Constitution provided guarantees against nationalisation

(Article 23), stated that foreign investment and trade were to be encouraged (Articles 24 and 25), and specified that state enterprises should be run autonomously and be accountable for their performance (Article 19). Moreover, the Constitution stated that

> [t]he aim of the state's economic policy is to make the people rich and the country strong, to satisfy to an ever greater extent the people's material and spiritual needs by releasing all productive potential, developing all latent possibilities of all components of the economy—the state sector, the collective sector, the private capitalist sector, and the state capitalist sector in various forms—pushing on with the construction of material and technical bases, broadening economic, scientific, technical cooperation and expanding intercourse with world markets (Article 16).

It also noted that

> [i]n the private individual and private capitalist sectors, people can adopt their own way of organising production and trading; they can set up enterprises of unrestricted scope in fields of activity which are beneficial to the country and the people (Article 21).

There are areas where legal development has been important. The most important formal laws governing business introduced under *Doi Moi* are presented in Table 9.1. Legal developments have been very important in attracting foreign investment and have provided a strong signal to domestic investors that the government is serious in pursuing its stated intention to move towards a market-based allocation of resources, and a rules-based system of state management. The business community was receptive to some key pieces of legislation, most notably in the response to the Enterprise Law, which exceeded most expectations in terms of new business registrations.

STATE ENTERPRISE REFORM AND BUSINESS DEVELOPMENT: AN INTERNATIONAL PERSPECTIVE

Up until a couple of decades ago, the mainstream development profession tended to identify a potentially important role for state enterprises as development (even entrepreneurial) institutions. Megginson and Netter recently argued that '25 years ago proponents of state ownership could have just as easily surveyed the postwar rise of state owned enterprises and concluded that their model of economic organisation was winning the intellectual battle with free-market capitalism' (Megginson and Netter 2001:321). Multilateral financial institutions actively encouraged the development of state-owned development banks, financed state-owned industries, and supported the development of state-owned utilities. This support was not based on a

Table 9.1 **Formal laws governing business entities**

Law	Dates law approved and amended or repealed	Categories of business entities or arrangements addressed
Companies	Enacted December 1990 Amended June 1994 Replaced January 2000	Joint-stock companies Private limited liability companies
Private Enterprises	Enacted December 1990 Amended June 1994 Replaced January 2000	Private unlimited liability enterprises
Enterprise Law	Approved April 1999 Enacted January 2000	All private enterprises Allows state enterprises to be incorporated
State Enterprises	Approved April 1995	Entities with state invested capital (state corporations, public service enterprises, and business enterprises)
Cooperatives	Approved March 1996	Cooperatives
Financial Institutions	Approved November 1997	Banks and other financial institutions
Insurance services	Approved May 2000	Entities providing insurance
Bankruptcy Law	Approved December 1993	All business entities
Commercial Code	Approved May 1997	All business entities
Environmental Protection	December 1993	All business entities
Land Law	Approved December 1987 Amended November 1993 Amended December 2001	Applies differently to different entities
Labour Code	Approved June 1994	Applies (but not equally) to all entities
Mining	March 1996	All relevant business entities
Promotion of Domestic Investment	June 1994 Amended April 1998	All domestically owned business entities
Foreign Investment	Approved December 1987 Amended June 1990 Amended December 1992 Amended April 1997 Amended May 2000	Joint-venture entities Foreign-owned entities Business cooperation contracts Build-operate-transfer projects

Source: Central Institute for Economic Management/United Nations Development Programme (UNDP), 2001. Improving the Regulatory Environment for Business, Project Document VIE/ 01/025, United Nations Development Programme, Hanoi (unpublished).

particularly pro-state ideological view, but reflected a widely held pragmatic view that this would accelerate development investment levels above those that were likely to be achieved by relying solely on the private sector.[10]

The balance of conventional wisdom changed in the 1980s partly because of sharp ideological shifts, particularly in the United States and the United Kingdom, and partly because of pressures to improve fiscal balances and to increase economic efficiency. There was increasing support for the view that state ownership was only justified where there was a clear case of market failure that could not be addressed by less drastic interventions. Megginson and Netter argued that 'privatisation now appears to be accepted as a legitimate—often a core—tool of statecraft of more than 100 countries' (2001:321).

The influences at work that redefined views about the proper relationship between the state and the market included

- the obvious failures in the former CMEA economies
- a record of inefficiency and mismanagement of state enterprises in many developing countries
- a growing perception that government involvement in business distracted the attention of governments from their core responsibility
- ideological shifts in many OECD economies
- technological developments that allowed competition in markets that were traditionally seen as natural monopolies (for example, telecommunications).

The most persuasive case against state enterprises is that they are unlikely to face pressures to perform because, unlike private business, they are not faced with a 'hard budget constraint' (Kornai 1992). The market forces private businesses to perform by the ultimate sanction of failure if they are persistently unable to cover costs. In contrast, access to state subsidies, either directly from the state budget, or indirectly from state banks, means that state enterprises are not subject to the discipline of market forces.

The sceptical view on state enterprises argued that not only are they insulated from market pressures to perform efficiently, but they may also be subject to pressures to pursue goals other than efficient business operations. They may be instructed to pursue multiple (sometimes conflicting) objectives. In particular, state business enterprises can be subject to pressure from politicians, governments and interest groups to pursue unprofitable activities. While the case for subsidy is typically argued by reference to some legitimate social objective, the reality is that state enterprises can be used to further sectional interests, or to provide 'rents' to interested parties, often in a non-transparent fashion. In effect, state enterprises are often neither accountable to the market, nor to an efficient system of public supervision.[11]

Fashions change. With the increasing emphasis among development agencies in targeting poverty reduction directly, and growing recognition of the need for state intervention to support more equitable economic development, there appears to be a shift back towards a more sympathetic middle-ground vision of the important complementary role the state plays in a market economy. Rodrik suggests that there has been a major change in thinking from the 'Washington consensus' of the 1980s, where the priority was on 'rolling back the state, not making it more effective' (2000:1–2), and argues that the poor response to price reform and privatisation in Russia, and dissatisfaction with the impact of market reforms in much of Latin America, has contributed to this re-think. He argues that there is an emerging consensus on the need to improve the efficiency of the state as an essential complement to the market economy.

Others, arguing for a cautious path to reform, point to the social upheaval and lawlessness following rapid privatisation in Eastern Europe. Stiglitz argues 'that the destruction of social and organisational capital in the process of transition…may have played an important role in the failures in Russia and some of the other countries of the former Soviet Union' (1999b:7).

A recent World Bank study on ten years of transition experience in the former USSR and Eastern Europe also recognised the need for caution, concluding that policymakers 'face a difficult choice between (i) privatisation to ineffective owners in a context of weak corporate governance, with the risk of expropriation of assets and income of minority shareholders, and (ii) continued state ownership in the face of inadequate political commitment to transparent privatisation outcomes and limited institutional capacity to prevent asset stripping by incumbent enterprise managers' (World Bank 2002:xxviii).

The same report emphasises the importance of the business environment as much as the form of ownership, noting that

[c]reating an environment that disciplines old enterprises into releasing assets and labour and encourages new enterprises to absorb those resources and undertake new investments without tilting the playing field in favour of any particular enterprises, is central to economic growth (World Bank 2002:xix).

OVERVIEW OF STATE ENTERPRISE REFORM IN VIET NAM

Whatever the international debate, there are certainly examples in Viet Nam that lend strong support to the case for state enterprise reform, and for state enterprise divestiture. Overall, state enterprises have absorbed a large share of capital, but generated less output and less employment per unit of investment than other sectors. Despite strong output growth, state enterprise employment fell during the late 1980s and early 1990s, and only recorded very modest growth subsequently. Moreover, there are regular reports in the domestic press of cases of inefficiency, mismanagement, and corruption associated with state enterprises.

This, however, is not the whole story. Experience with individual state enterprises is variable. Some state firms adjusted remarkably quickly to the requirements of the market economy, in contrast to others that continue to operate inefficiently, surviving through state protection and (often hidden) subsidies, and others that largely ceased operations. With state enterprises dominating exports and industrial output, Viet Nam's impressive economic performance during the early transition period would not have been possible without strong performance by a significant segment of the state enterprise sector. State enterprises made an important contribution to recent economic growth and remain an important source of government revenue.

A crucial aspect of growth performance in Vietnam in the 1990s was that, although the state enterprises expanded rapidly, they did not 'crowd out' the growth of the non-state sector in most sub-sectors. The share of state enterprises in official national output estimates actually increased in the period up to 1997, even though this was a period of such dynamic growth in private activities that visitors returning to Viet Nam in the late 1990s after a decade away could readily assume that there had been a decisive shift in the balance of the economy towards the non-state sector. In the late 1980s, the visitor would have stayed in a state-run hotel, eaten at state-run restaurants, been entertained at a state-run night club, hired a car from a state-run company, and bought basic consumer requirements from a state store or cooperative. By 1997, a typical visitor would have obtained such services from domestic private and foreign-invested enterprises (the latter enterprise often a joint-venture in which the state retained a minority interest).

STATE AND NON-STATE BUSINESS DEVELOPMENT IN VIET NAM SINCE *DOI MOI*

Data inconsistencies and inadequacies make it impossible to present a precise statistical picture of the changes in the economy from official sources, but there have been a number of clear trends. During the early stages of *Doi Moi*, there was an acceleration in growth of output from farm households and household business (mostly trade and simple processing), and this growth has been sustained over much of the *Doi Moi* period.

The state sector recorded modest growth in the first years of *Doi Moi*, but output (and state employment) declined sharply in 1989 and 1990. There was a rapid build-up of foreign investment, and a recovery in growth in state enterprise output, in the early 1990s. With the fast growth in larger-scale production, domestic private businesses' (including households) share of total output declined during the early 1990s, but continued to be the major source of employment growth. The role of cooperatives in agriculture, retail and other service industries dropped sharply during the early stages of reform as many cooperative activities and resources were transferred to the private sector.

A cyclical turning point was reached in 1997. Even before the onset of the Asian financial crisis, approvals of foreign direct investment (FDI) were declining, and FDI inflows dropped sharply following the onset of the East Asian financial crisis, although output resulting from FDI continued to increase at faster rate than other sectors. As the formal barriers to domestic private sector activity were lifted in the late 1990s, there was a sharp jump in the number of formal domestic private enterprises, and initial estimates indicate that the domestic private sector recorded higher growth than the state sector in 2001. Official data on state and non-state sector growth rates are presented later in Figure 12.1.

Interpreting the data is tricky, given the incentives and opportunities to under-report private sector output, but according to official series state sector output growth equalled or exceeded private sector growth in most years in the decade to 1997, except for 1989 and 1990 when state output suffered from the collapse of economic cooperation arrangements with the former USSR. The surprising conclusion from these data is that the state's share of official GDP increased over much of the reform period,[12] despite reductions in barriers

Figure 9.1   GDP growth, 1986–2000

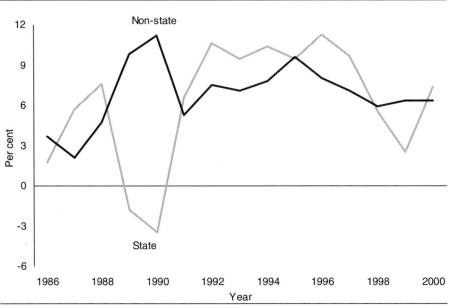

Figure 9.2   Share of GDP by sector, 1986–2000

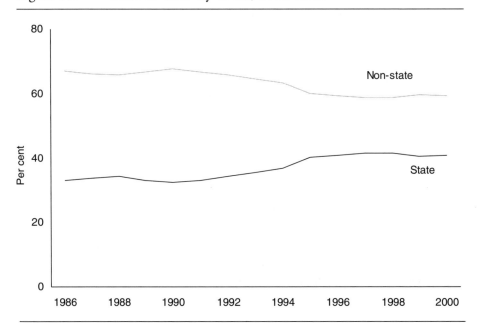

to private sector investment, and increased competition, including strong competition resulting from a much more open external trade regime.

Changes in the balance of ownership have not been uniform across sector and industries. At the sectoral level, state and cooperative involvement in the agricultural sector and most retail businesses is now negligible. Cooperatives no longer play a pervasive role in the economy, but play more limited roles in marketing activities in some areas such as handicrafts. The state sector share of retail activity has declined. Although the state share of industrial output has declined in recent years, it remains higher than it was at the beginning of *Doi Moi*. The household and cooperative share of industrial output has declined over the transition period. The formal domestic private sector is just beginning to emerge, but plays a significant role in some industry and service groups, as discussed later in this chapter.

The strong growth in state enterprise output distinguishes Viet Nam's reform experience from the experiences of most transition economies, and the experiences of most East and Southeast Asian economies. Moreover, growth was initially accompanied by declining state enterprise employment, and later by only modest growth in state employment, indicating significant improvements in output per worker in state enterprises.[13] Official figures indicate that output per state enterprise worker increased 3 times from 1995 to 1995, and by about another 25 per cent from 1995 to 2000. In interpreting these data, it should be noted that a substantial part of the early productivity increases resulted from formally laying off workers who were already not working. There may also have been an increase in sub-contracting work to the emerging private sector. Nevertheless, it is also clear that there have been significant improvements in state enterprise productivity since the *Doi Moi* process started.

STATE AND NON-STATE INDUSTRIAL OUTPUT, 1995–2000

In the second half of the 1990s, the relative output performance of the ownership groups grew more in line with expectations regarding the results of reform (Table 9.2). The state share of industrial output declined from just over 50 per cent to 42 per cent (in constant 1994 prices), the share of the domestic private sector declined from almost 25 per cent to just over 22 per cent, and the share of foreign invested enterprises increased from 25 per cent to 35 per cent. State

Table 9.2   Share of industry group output by ownership, 1995 and 2000

Industry group	1995				2000			
	Total	State	Domestic non-state	Foreign investor	Total	State	Domestic non-state	Foreign investor
TOTAL	100.00	50.29	24.62	25.09	100.00	42.03	22.43	35.54
1. Mining	13.47	2.34	0.65	10.48	13.56	1.78	0.55	11.23
Coal	1.62	1.60	0.02	-	1.15	1.12	0.02	0.01
Oil and gas	10.49	0.03	-	10.46	11.22	0.02	-	11.20
Metal ores	0.23	0.18	0.04	-	0.11	0.09	0.02	-
Stone and others	1.12	0.52	0.58	0.02	1.08	0.55	0.51	0.02
2. Manufacturing	80.54	41.98	23.97	14.59	80.47	34.31	21.87	24.29
Food and beverages	26.13	12.46	8.68	4.99	20.18	9.32	6.63	4.23
Tobacco products	3.85	3.83	0.01	0.01	2.87	2.85	0.01	0.01
Textile products	5.97	3.39	1.54	1.04	4.81	2.59	1.25	0.97
Garments	2.85	0.99	1.34	0.52	3.06	1.03	1.36	0.67
Leather tanning and processing	3.45	1.32	0.90	1.23	4.57	1.38	1.24	1.95
Wood and wood products	3.22	0.69	2.24	0.29	1.89	0.40	1.33	0.15
Paper and paper products	1.88	1.14	0.45	0.29	2.10	1.08	0.77	0.24
Publish, print, copy recorded materials	1.46	1.35	0.08	0.04	1.12	1.00	0.10	0.02
Coke and refined petroleum products	0.33	-	0.04	0.29	0.05	-	0.05	-
Chemicals	4.92	3.73	0.47	0.72	6.09	3.79	0.68	1.61
Rubber and plastics	2.20	0.97	0.92	0.30	3.50	1.13	1.59	0.77
Non-ferrous metals	8.90	5.96	2.50	0.44	8.89	5.22	1.99	1.68
Metal production	3.32	2.01	0.32	0.98	2.95	1.25	0.36	1.34
Metals products	2.26	0.40	1.59	0.26	3.15	0.46	1.77	0.92
Machinery and equipment	1.30	0.89	0.26	0.14	1.23	0.71	0.22	0.29
Computer and office equipment	0.03	0.03	-	-	2.62	-	0.03	2.59
Electrical machinery and apparatus	1.05	0.77	0.14	0.15	1.88	0.89	0.33	0.66

Radio, TV and communications equipment	2.00	0.96	0.12	0.92	2.36	0.36	0.03	1.97
Medical and precision instruments	0.20	0.04	0.11	0.04	0.23	0.04	0.02	0.16
Assembly and repair of motor vehicles	1.41	0.20	0.21	1.00	1.09	0.15	0.15	0.79
Produce/repair other transport equipment	1.83	0.66	0.35	0.82	3.63	0.50	0.42	2.70
Furniture	1.91	0.18	1.58	0.14	2.13	0.14	1.46	0.53
Recycling	0.09	-	0.09	0.00	0.07	0.00	0.07	-
3. Electricity, gas and water supply	5.99	5.97	0.01	0.01	5.97	5.95	0.01	0.02
Production, distribution of electricity and gas	5.27	5.25	0.01	0.01	5.44	5.43	-	0.01
Supply, purification and distribution of water	0.73	0.72	-	-	0.53	0.51	0.01	0.01

Source: Derived from GSO, 1997 and 2001, Statistical Yearbooks.

and private sector industrial output both recorded solid growth over this period (58 per cent and 72 per cent respectively), but output from foreign invested projects grew much more rapidly, increasing by 168 per cent.

Mining accounted for about 13.5 per cent of the value of total industrial output. Foreign investors dominated mining. Foreign capital in oil and gas alone accounted for 11.2 per cent of industrial output in 2000. Coal (mostly state) and precious stones are the only other significant mining activities, each accounting for about 1 per cent of total industrial output.

Manufacturing accounted for about 80.5 per cent of industry in both 1995 and 2000, but there was a drop in the share of state manufacturing, from 42 per cent to 34 per cent. The share of domestic private manufacturing declined from about 24 per cent to 22 per cent, while the share of foreign invested manufacturing increased from nearly 15 per cent to just over 24 per cent. There were marked declines in the share of food processing, tobacco, textiles and wood products, and increases in garments, leather goods, rubber, plastics, electrical machinery, computer and office equipment, and transport equipment. State enterprises continued to account for virtually all of the nearly 6 per cent of industrial valued added from electricity, gas and water supply.

IMPLICATIONS FOR PRIVATE BUSINESS DEVELOPMENT AND STATE ENTERPRISE REFORM

Viet Nam has surprised many observers (the authors included) by rapidly increasing productivity, accelerating economic output, and rapidly expanding its exports to market economies, despite the dominant role of state enterprise in industry and external trade. Most donors had been advising the government that an increased private sector role was essential for sustaining economic growth and reducing poverty.[14] The strong state enterprise performance therefore needs to be analysed.

The strong state enterprise performance was undoubtedly due in part to preferential treatment and access to resources, the low starting base, restrictions on competition (especially in the earlier periods of reform), and the weak governance and accountability mechanisms which have meant that many state enterprises managers face strong personal incentives to expand output and turnover. Under-reporting of private sector activity also affects the picture of relative sectoral growth.

Some of the larger scale industries dominated by state firms increased their share in total production (for example, power, building materials, and telecommunications) as a secular phenomenon at this stage of Vietnamese development. The rapid build-up in official development assistance and FDI has also boosted state enterprises in the power, water supply, construction, and construction material sectors. In addition, during the early 1990s, the output of state-owned heavy industry expanded as a result of earlier investments (most notably Soviet investments in oil and power development).

In the lighter industrial and processing sectors, state enterprises continued to benefit from protection provided by the state (for example, in garments and in key agricultural commodities, through preferential access to export quotas). Some state firms achieved genuine competitive successes in export markets, including in joint ventures with private foreign investors.

By contrast, agriculture, the sector with the highest proportion of private (household) activity, grew more slowly than the overall average. Although buoyant growth was achieved in historical and international comparative terms, the expected secular trend is for the proportion of agriculture in total output to decline as the economy grows.

Despite the above points, the relatively effective performance of state enterprises in Viet Nam needs further explanation, particularly in light of conventional wisdom regarding the ineffectiveness of state enterprises and the failure of state enterprises with similar preferential treatment in other developing countries. This raises a number of important questions.

- What special factors, if any, contributed to strong state enterprise performance in Viet Nam?
- Can this strong performance be sustained in the future?
- Why has the private sector taken so long to develop, especially in the industrial sector?
- Are there lessons to be learned that can be replicated elsewhere?

Much of the material in the following chapters in this section is an attempt to answer these questions.

NOTES

1   Institutions as defined by North 'Institutions are the humanly defined constraints that structure human interaction. They are made up of formal constraints (e.g. rules, laws, constitutions) and informal constraints (e.g. norms of behaviour, conventions, self-imposed codes of conduct) and their enforcement characteristics' (1994:360).

2   Pistor and Wellons (1999) identify this approach with the work of the eighteenth century economist Adam Smith and the nineteenth century German sociologist Max Weber.

3   For example, in the development of land law in many countries, legislation has included formalising and accommodating customary tenure arrangements that have developed historically.

4   Pistor notes that informal institutional arrangements in East Asia, which had been seen as a source of stability, became 'increasingly regarded as an impediment for future economic development. While many formal rules had long been on the books, a demand for them was created only with the economic regime change, which in some cases (Korea, Taiwan) was accompanied by a political regime change' (Pistor 1999:6).

5   Messick argues that attempts to impose formal institutions can even be counterproductive noting that 'a variety of studies, in settings as diverse as medieval Europe and contemporary Asia, show that informal mechanisms based on incentives provided by repeat dealings can ensure the performance of contracts that no court has the power to enforce. One early, and surprising, finding of this research is that in some instances the sudden introduction of a formal mechanism to resolve legal disputes can disrupt informal mechanisms without providing offsetting gains' (Messick 1999:118).

6   Pistor argues that Asian experiences show that economic development is possible even when rational legal systems play a subordinate role: 'For much of the period of high speed economic growth in East Asia since the late 1950s, the law that had much earlier been transplanted from the West played only a marginal role...It was supplemented by negotiated bargains between governments and business elites, as well as by rulings and decrees issued by the executive which had extensive discretionary powers. Large parts of the society remained outside the realm of formal law. Private transactions were governed by customary rules and disputes settled out of court' (Pistor 1999:5).

7   Upham (2001:19) notes that while both George W. Bush and Al Gore promised in the 2000 US elections to maintain the rule of law 'they also each promised to appoint judges who would support certain positions on abortion, affirmative action, and other highly politicized issues'.

8   See also Van Arkadie (1990) for a more general discussion of the interplay between formal and informal institutions.

[9] One may speculate that the disproportionate weight of foreign investors from the region may not only reflect geographical proximity but also the greater ease with which firms from the region adapted to the Vietnamese environment.

[10] There were counter views—for example the case against state enterprises was put vigorously by Peter Bauer (for example, see Bauer and Yamey 1957:155–61), but in the 1960s and 1970s such views were in the minority and tended to be viewed as away from the mainstream.

[11] The fact that this line of argument is so universally popular among the staff of multilateral funding institutions may be that the description fits so well the lack of accountability and 'hard budget constraints' in their own organisations (which are enterprises owned by many states, and which are themselves asked to achieve multiple objectives).

[12] The jump in the state share in 1995 is partly due to a shift in constant prices from 1989 prices to 1994 prices, but even allowing for this the trend remains the same.

[13] As with all data on Viet Nam, this table should be seen as indicative. Estimates of state enterprise employee numbers were reported separately prior to 1995. From 1995, state enterprises employees are estimated as total state employees, minus state employees working in science and technology, state management and national defence and public security, education and training, health and social relief, culture and sport, activities of the Party and mass organisations, and community and personal services. Moreover, different official statistics give quite different estimates of output levels and growth prior to 1995.

[14] World Bank (1995a:xii) warned that '[o]verwhelming international evidence indicates that there are limits to what reform without divestiture of non-strategic enterprises can accomplish and sustain. Divestiture of non-strategic state enterprises will be critical to encourage entry by private business in productive sectors'

10

STATE ENTERPRISES

STEP-BY-STEP STATE ENTERPRISE REFORM

In contrast to the rapid progress in divesting land-use rights for agriculture, forestry and aquaculture, the approach to state enterprise reform has been cautious. Before 1998, the only substantial divestiture of whole enterprises was the relatively rapid liquidation and/or mergers of (mostly small) non-viable enterprises from 1991 to 1994. The equitisation[1] program adopted by the Seventh Party Congress in 1991 made particularly slow progress, with only 14 small and medium sized enterprises equitised by September 1997 (Communist Party of Vietnam 1991a).

More rapid progress was made in sharpening the incentives facing state enterprises by hardening the budget constraint and introducing competition (both domestic and through foreign trade). This had a positive impact on enterprise productivity, with substantial reduction in state enterprise employment during the late 1980s and early 1990s.

While reforms in the ownership of state enterprises moved at a slow pace, the negative consequences have not been as apparent as many external commentators had predicted. Characteristics of the sector that may have mitigated expected negative consequences include the following factors

- state enterprises accounted for a relatively small share of national employment and a smaller share of national income than in most other transition economies

- there were relatively few large-scale, capital intensive state enterprises. Most enterprises were decentralised geographically with considerable management discretion enjoyed by the diverse 'owning' agencies within the national and lower level branches of government
- sound macroeconomic management limited government budget resources to subsidise state enterprises, thus hardening budget constraints
- Viet Nam did not experience the institutional collapse that occurred in Eastern Europe. Despite limited formal legal infrastructure, property rights and basic rules governing commercial relationships continued to be enforced
- foreign direct investment was encouraged to introduce new capital, technology and marketing skills to state enterprises
- early reforms were introduced to increase competitiveness and improve incentive structures, including trade liberalisation, property right reforms (for example, long-term land-use rights), and the relaxation and subsequent abolition of official price controls (Mallon 1998b:14–15).

STATE ENTERPRISE REFORM FROM *DOI MOI* UP UNTIL THE EIGHTH PARTY CONGRESS[2]

The need to improve the efficiency of, and incentives for, state enterprises was a recurring subject of development policy debate well before *Doi Moi* was announced. Lengthy sections of resolutions from past Party Congresses had been devoted to options for improving state enterprise efficiency. This reflected the strong commitment for the state, and state enterprises, to play a leading role in the nation's development.

The strong commitment to a leading role for the state was maintained in policy statements throughout the early *Doi Moi* period, but in recent years there has been somewhat less emphasis on the contribution of state enterprises, and a gradually increasing emphasis on a role for private domestic investors in the nation's long-term development. Elements of the state enterprise reform program during the early *Doi Moi* period included

- commercialisation to increase efficiency
- re-registration, restructuring and liquidation
- pilot equitisation
- establishing the basis for leasing and divestiture
- developing a legal framework (including the Law on State Enterprises)
- development of enterprise groupings (state corporations).

Commercialisation of state enterprises

Promulgation of Decree 217 in late 1987 marked the first post *Doi Moi* step towards a broad-based state enterprise reform program aimed at placing state enterprises on a commercial footing, with increased autonomy and financial responsibility.[3] This decree put into effect a Party Resolution[4] to give greater autonomy to state enterprises and to introduce a 'socialist cost-accounting regime'. Subsequent implementing regulations further clarified relationships between government agencies and state enterprises under the new system.[5] While 'the people' retained ownership of state enterprises, enterprise assets were 'placed under the direct management and utilisation of the collective of workers and the director for the development of production and business'.[6] Employees were to remain 'masters of the enterprise'—approval of a general meeting of employees would still be required for decisions on major issues such as development strategies, annual business plans (which must also be approved by government agencies), profit distribution and employee welfare policies.

Important changes introduced under Decree 217 included

- the introduction of a profit based accounting system. Profits were to be assessed based on actual costs and revenues (not on plan directives)
- replacement of physical output targets with profit targets for most enterprises. Physical output targets were to be limited to the production of goods of 'strategic importance'
- increased autonomy for enterprise managers in production, personnel and financial decision making
- abolition of budgetary support as well as the state supply of inputs, and restrictions on selling in the open market
- limitation of subsidies to on-lending through state-owned commercial banks. Bank credit was to be provided to state enterprises on a commercial basis
- allowing enterprises, except those with high levels of public investment, to retain depreciation charges.

A crucial change was the introduction of economic contracts as the basis for transactions between business entities. Economic arbitration offices were established to assist in enforcing contracts.[7] State enterprises had to purchase inputs directly from suppliers, rather than being supplied by the state. Except for a few products that had to be sold at government mandated prices,[8] state enterprises could sell on the open market.

Initially, only large-scale state enterprises were permitted to undertake direct external trade and were legally able to retain only a portion of foreign exchange earnings,[9] but subsequent reforms, aimed at boosting exports, relaxed restrictions on state enterprise capacity to engage in external trade.[10] Follow-up regulations helped define an economic role for state enterprises independent of the broader functions of government,[11] to clarify corporate governance provisions[12] and to permit state enterprises to enter joint ventures and forms of economic cooperation with other entities, including private enterprises and foreign investors.[13]

Increased autonomy, harder budget constraints, and improved profit incentives contributed to significant restructuring of state enterprises. Pressures to restructure intensified with the cessation of economic aid from, and trade with, the former socialist bloc countries in Eastern Europe over 1990–91. While Decree 217-HDBT was a turning point, serious problems persisted. In May 1990, the government initiated a review of the early experience with state enterprise reform to assess the need for further reform.[14] With harder budget constraints and increased competition—between state enterprises, with the emerging private sector, and from imports—the numbers of loss-making enterprises also increased. There were growing concerns about the lack of accountability for the use of state assets and the rapid increase in numbers of state enterprises, particularly at the local level. There was also concern that decision making was constrained by ambiguity and inconsistency in regulations, and overlapping responsibilities between management and government agencies. Following this review, the Seventh Party Congress in 1991 noted that

> …the weakest aspect of the state-run sector as a whole remains its inefficiency in business operations. A fairly large number of state-run industrial enterprises, especially those under district management, are beset with difficulties. Many state-run trading enterprises have made losses: quite a few have been misused by private businessman for illegal activities (Communist Party of Vietnam 1991a:77).

The Seventh Party Congress renewed the commitment to greater state enterprise autonomy, and an expanded private sector role, stating that

> all enterprises, regardless of the system of ownership, should operate in accordance with a system of autonomy in business, co-operation and competition, and are equal before the law…The private capitalist sector is to develop without limits in terms of scale and location in sectors and professions that are not prohibited by law (Communist Party of Vietnam 1991a:154).

While the Party still maintained that state enterprises were to continue to play a leading role in the economy, there were also calls for consolidation of the state enterprise sector, including the liquidation of non-viable enterprises and the equitisation of non-strategic state enterprises. Subsequently, the government introduced a second round of reforms.

Re-registration, reorganisation and liquidation of state enterprises

The decentralisation of authority to establish state enterprises under Decree 217-HDBT was followed by a proliferation of new state enterprise registrations, particularly at the local level. Local authorities had strong incentives to establish new state enterprises because they were able to exercise greater discretion in using state enterprise resources than they could with other state resources. However, increasing reports of financial failure and irregularities prompted government action to strengthen central control over state enterprises.

A second round of reforms started in 1991 which focused on reorganising and consolidating the state enterprise sector. The government issued a decree in November 1991 requiring all state enterprises to re-register or close.[15] The decree specified criteria for establishing state enterprises, with commercial viability the main criterion for non-strategic enterprises.[16] Minimum legal capital requirements were specified for different categories of state enterprises. Authority for approving the establishment of state enterprises was limited to the Prime Minister, Minister, or Chairman of the Provincial or Municipal People's Committee depending on the scale and/or nature of the enterprise. State agencies, and/or organisations with state management functions, were not allowed to operate as state enterprises.

When that Decree was issued, there were an estimated 12,297 state enterprises (Nguyen Ngoc Tuan et al. 1995:2). By 1 April 1994, 6,264 state enterprises had been re-registered. The reduction in state enterprise numbers was achieved through liquidation (about 2,000) and mergers (about 3,000). Increases in average capital of state enterprises reflected the ongoing revaluation of state enterprise assets and mergers, and the impact of growth in investment in the state enterprise sector from domestic sources and joint ventures with foreign investors.

Most liquidated and merged enterprises were small locally managed state enterprises with less than 100 employees and 500 million dong in capital (about US$45,000 at that time). The assets of liquidated enterprises were generally sold to bidders from either the state or private sector. Total assets of liquidated enterprises accounted for less than 4 per cent of total state enterprise assets and about 5 per cent of state enterprise turnover (Tran Ngoc Trang 1994). Money raised from the liquidation of state enterprises was first used to pay outstanding debts and surplus funds were transferred to the state budget.

In March 1994, instructions were issued for a second phase of re-registration.[17] All re-registered state enterprises would continue to be monitored to ensure compliance with their certificate of registration. The new decision also required all umbrella entities, such as unions of enterprises and state corporations, to be registered as commercially viable business entities or be dissolved. The process of mergers and liquidation under the second phase of the re-registration process led to further, more modest declines in the number of state enterprises, to an estimated 5,500 at the end of 1997.

Equitisation and divestiture

The Seventh Party Congress called for pilot activities to dissolve or change the ownership of enterprises that did not need to be retained under state ownership (Communist Party of Vietnam 1991a:14). A Party resolution[18] agreed that the conversion 'of a number of eligible state enterprises into joint-stock companies...[which]...should be undertaken on a pilot basis and under close guidance, and experience should be drawn with utter care before divestiture is conducted on an appropriate scale'.[19] The National Assembly approved a pilot equitisation program in late December 1991, and the government issued a decision to proceed with this pilot program in mid 1992. It aimed to increase efficiency through improved management and incentives; mobilise increased capital for investment, and allow enterprise employees to become owners of the enterprise.

Equitisation was in effect a form of partial privatisation—state enterprises were to be transformed into joint-stock companies and a proportion of state shares in the enterprise were to be sold.[20] Implementing guidelines specified that pilot enterprises should be small or medium size and potentially profitable, but not 'strategic enterprises'. Shares in equitised enterprises were to be registered, transferable and inheritable and be available to both employees and persons outside the enterprise. No single individual was allowed to own more than 5 per cent of all shares, and no institution could own more than 10 per cent. Enterprise employees were to be given preferential access to enterprise shares and provided with suitable redundancy and/or retirement packages as appropriate.

The Ministry of Finance was authorised to coordinate and work with the Central Institute for Economic Management, the Ministry of Labour, War Invalids and Social Affairs, the State Bank and other government agencies to implement the pilot program. A Central Steering Committee for Enterprise Reform (CSCER) was established in September 1992 to oversee government initiatives in reforming state enterprises.[21] Line ministries and the chairpersons of provincial and municipal People's Committees were assigned to establish divestiture steering committees to develop divestiture plans for submission to the CSCER and the Ministry of Finance for approval. Complex implementing arrangements provided opportunities for interested parties to slow progress.

Initially, seven enterprises volunteered for the pilot program, but these later withdrew. Subsequently, 21 new enterprises were selected, and the government later ordered the selection of another 200 enterprises. Most enterprises subsequently withdrew. Despite follow-up instructions[22] calling for acceleration, implementation remained slow. Only 17 enterprises had been equitised by the end of 1997, despite a 1996 government directive instructing that 150 enterprises were to be equitised by the end of 1997.[23]

In the lead up to the Eighth Party Congress, a review by the Central Institute for Economic Management concluded that equitised enterprises increased turnover and profit with no compulsory redundancies, and increased wages paid to workers (Le Dang Doanh 1995). Why then was it so difficult to gain the support needed to facilitate more rapid equitisation? Reasons given at that time included

- concerns by managers that they would lose the preferential treatment given to state enterprises (access to land, quotas, subsidised credit, and less strict financial reporting requirements)[24]
- the lack of clear and transparent guidelines on equitisation procedures, especially those for valuation, formal classification of what enterprises could be equitised, and what to do with the social welfare services, funds and facilities provided by state enterprises prior to equitisation
- the fact that many state enterprises are too small for a joint-stock company structure to be economic
- the lack of liquidity in share trading because of restrictions under equitisation and the lack of formal share-trading institutions
- the limited institutional capacity to implement equitisation

- complex institutional arrangements that provided opportunities to slow progress
- political concerns about the impact of equitisation on the leading role of the state in the economy and, consequently, on state control over the economy.

Following the Eighth Party Congress in mid 1996, the government issued a series of new regulations to address these concerns. These will be discussed later.

Legal framework for state enterprise activities

The general legal framework governing business enterprises has evolved slowly and has gradually reduced differences in treatment between enterprises. The National Assembly approved the Law on Foreign Investment in 1987 and Laws on Private Enterprise and on Companies in 1990. As discussed earlier, the 1992 Constitution was also an important milestone in defining the rights of the non-state sector to operate alongside the state sector (Government of Vietnam 1992).

The 1993 Law on Bankruptcy and the 1995 State Enterprise Law were meant to facilitate improved governance and the closure of non-viable state enterprises. The Law on State Enterprises made progress in

- clarifying responsibilities and accountability and establishing state enterprises as limited liability entities[25]
- distinguishing between state public service enterprises[26] and business enterprises
- clarifying rights to establish and dissolve state enterprises,[27] and the role of the government in exercising ownership rights in enterprises, including defining those rights that can be delegated to central ministries and/or provincial/municipal people's committees
- defining the rights and responsibilities of state enterprises, including rights with regard to equitisation, divestiture and selling assets
- defining the rights and responsibilities of the chief executive, senior management, and the board of management
- specifying the rights and role of state management agencies and worker groups in day-to-day management decision making.

The law also addressed the rights and obligations relating to the management of investments by the state (or state enterprises) in other enterprises.[28]

State business enterprises were subject to similar corporate governance structures as private enterprises, and profit maximisation was to be their main objective. State business enterprises had the right to 'transfer, lease, rent and mortgage properties under their management, except important equipment and factories that are prescribed by the state...[and]...land and natural resources'.[29] Autonomy in day-to-day management decisions, in mobilising capital and in allocating profits, was guaranteed within state guidelines. State enterprises were guaranteed the right to decide the level of salary and bonuses of employees within the framework of norms established by the state. State enterprises were required to comply with accounting and auditing standards established by the state and 'to make public its yearly financial report and other information, with a view to allowing a correct objective assessment of the enterprise's operation'.[30]

The government retained the power to exercise ownership rights in state enterprises, including making decisions on the main components of the business development plan for the enterprise, promulgation of model statutes governing the organisational and operational arrangements, making decisions on capital structure, allocation of profits, sale or lease of major assets, and organisational arrangements to protect the rights of the state as owner of the capital of the enterprise, making decisions on management structures, appointment of senior management positions, making decisions on salary norms and allowances paid to employees, board members, and the chief executive of the enterprise.

A Board of Management was to be established for each state corporation and large state enterprises to 'manage the activities of the enterprise, and be responsible to the government, or a state management body delegated by the government, for the development of the enterprise in accordance with the objectives assigned by the state'.[31] Board members were appointed for a term of five years, contracts were renewable, and provision was included for performance contracts.[32] The workers' collectives were to be consulted on key management issues, including the collective labour accord, the use of enterprise funds directly related to the interests of labourers, business plans and assessment of business performance, measures to improve working conditions, training opportunities, and the wellbeing of workers. They also were given the right to propose candidates for the Board of Management.[33]

However, key provisions of these two laws were never enforced. Few bankruptcy cases have been brought to the economic courts[34] and the law is widely seen as providing very little protection for creditors. Few state enterprises have published financial reports as provided for in Articles 12 of the Law on State Enterprises. There have been great delays in issuing implementing regulations and in effectively implementing key provisions. There has been little enforcement of provision of financial and performance reporting, despite the establishment of the General Department for the Management of State Capital and Assets in Enterprise in the Ministry of Finance with specific responsibilities for ensuring the financial accountability of state enterprises. The government continues to face serious difficulties in enforcing its ownership rights to sell or equitise state enterprises. The classification of state enterprises as public service or business enterprises (as required under the state enterprise law) was delayed by the absence of criteria and clear allocation of responsibilities for the process.

The main reasons for poor enforcement were that there was limited national understanding of the purposes of the laws and limited, if any, national demand for the laws. The two laws were approved because disbursements under a World Bank-funded structural adjustment loan were conditional on them being approved. There was little consultation with the business and financial sector in drafting the laws. This experience demonstrates the limited role of legislation as an instrument of change, where the laws are neither supported by a consensus of the concerned parties nor respond to a demand arising from within the society.

State corporations

The need to streamline state enterprise administration and to separate state ownership from state regulatory and public service functions has been a central proposition in the enterprise reform debate since the reform program started. The administrative grouping of enterprises under umbrella organisations was seen by the authorities as facilitating this separation.

Many state enterprises had for many years been grouped under unions of enterprises based on decisions issued by the government in 1978. New regulations governing unions of enterprises were issued in March 1989 which defined two alternative models for unions of enterprises:[35] as a legal entity formed as a voluntary association of members,[36] or as a stronger entity responsible for all enterprises covering specific public services such as power, postal services, rail transport, and air transport. In the second model, membership was to be compulsory, member enterprises would not have a fully independent legal status, and the assets of member enterprises would belong to the union of enterprise. The proposals were resisted by both unions and member enterprises, and the institutional *status quo* prevailed.

While the Political Report of the Seventh Party Congress in 1991 called for enterprises to be grouped into large state corporations (Communist Party of Vietnam 1991b), Decree 388 (requiring re-registration of all enterprises) was vague on procedures for re-registration of existing Unions of Enterprises and state companies and corporations. The government issued two decisions in March 1994 specifying procedures for the re-registration of corporations and enterprise unions, which provided for the registration of two categories of state corporations, commonly referred to as Decision 90 and Decision 91 State Corporations.[37] All state corporations, companies and enterprise unions were required to re-register as state corporations or state enterprises or be disbanded. Enterprise unions and other entities that only provided administrative services were required to be disbanded.

The stated objective of this decision was to consolidate enterprises in order to rationalise state enterprise supervision, and to facilitate the abolition of line ministry and local authority control over state enterprises. Arguments in support of state corporations focused on the economies of scale from larger state business entities, the increased scale needed for domestic enterprises with external competitors in domestic and international markets, the need to free state administrative resources to focus more on managing a reduced number of businesses better, and the idea that large state businesses were essential for the state to play a leading role in the industrialisation and modernisation of the economy.

Decision 90 State Corporations were required to have at least five member entities and total legal capital of VND 100 billion. Ministers and heads of the People's Committee at the provincial or municipal level could approve the establishment of Decision 90 State Corporations. Decision 91 State Corporations could only be established with at least seven member entities, a total legal capital of VND 1,000 billion, and the approval of the Prime Minister. State corporations were not subject to the Company Law. They did not own their member entities, and were not holding companies like the South Korean *chaebols*. Many of their powers were more administrative in nature, similar to the enterprise groups (*jituan*) in China.

There is little evidence that the state corporations model has been successful in meeting stated policy objectives. Corporations have not resolved conflicts over the exercise of ownership rights. The state still directly exercises control over final decisions on major policies, investment plans and on the appointment and dismissal of senior management. Government officials from line ministries continue to intervene in the management decisions of corporations.

Member enterprises complain about direct involvement of state corporation officials in the day-to-day management of enterprises and argue that the state corporations merely add another layer of bureaucracy without producing any value added from their members' contributions. Profitable member enterprises complain that they have to cross-subsidise inefficient enterprises, endangering their own viability in the process. Profitable state corporations are sometimes pressured to provide social services that would normally be a government responsibility. A lack of consolidated financial statements makes it difficult to assess the financial impact of state corporations, and suggests that there has been little improvement in terms of accountability and transparency. Amongst the first 18 Decision 91 Corporations established (see the following table), a number were well under the specified minimum capital requirements.

There has been considerable debate about the desirability of the state corporation model. Many external commentators have been especially critical of this approach, arguing that Viet Nam should learn from the problems with the South Korean *chaebols*. Frequently raised concerns included

- the potential for state corporations to strengthen state monopoly positions and reduce the competition that had stimulated enterprise performance[38]
- state corporations with monopoly powers could evolve as a pressure group opposed to further reform and opening up of the economy
- potential inefficiencies resulting from profitable enterprises cross-subsidising loss-making enterprises within the corporations.

The actual extent to which Decrees 90 and 91 contributed to increased monopoly powers has not been thoroughly studied. In some sectors, member enterprises have to compete with other members of the same corporation, other enterprises (both private and state), and imports. In the case of Vinafood 1 and 2, key policies that protected these entities from competition have been lifted since they were established as state corporations (Table 10.1).[39] However, where there are natural monopolies, the domestic market is concentrated and/or trade barriers remain significant, there is potential for corporations to coordinate the operations of their member enterprises to exploit possible monopoly positions. Certainly some state corporations have continued to use monopoly pricing (for example, in telecommunications and aviation), and the government has only permitted the introduction of very limited competition in these sectors. Partly in response to these concerns, the government has formally included the study of options for regulatory and institutional reforms to prevent abuses of monopoly power in its reform agenda.

The Law on State Enterprises clarified the legal status of state corporations as legal entities with the same rights and obligations as state enterprises. The law states that state enterprises generally have the right to decide whether to join as members of state corporations, but provision is included for compulsory membership when this is of special importance.[40] The law requires that state corporations to establish a Board of Management and Control Commission to supervise the executive and to make major policy and investment decisions,

Table 10.1   **Decision 91 State Corporations**

State corporation	Member enterprises (excluding j-v)	No. of joint-venture enterprises[1]	Legal capital (billion dong)[1]
Electricity Corporation of Viet Nam	34	-	19,332
Coal Corporation of Viet Nam	47	4	824
Viet Nam Petroleum Corporation (PETROVIETNAM)	17	4	761
Cement Corporation of Viet Nam	14	4	2,235
Viet Nam National Shipping Lines (Vinalines)	24	12	2,145
Viet Nam Airline Corporation	20	6	1,043
Viet Nam Post and Telecommunication Corporation	88	6	4,740
Viet Nam Rubber Corporation	32	2	2,700
Viet Nam Steel Corporation	17	4	1,336
Viet Nam Coffee Corporation	68	-	276
Viet Nam Tobacco Corporation	12	-	550
Viet Nam Paper Corporation	18	-	1,028
Viet Nam Textile and Garment Corporation	53	2	1,186
Northern Food Corporation—VINAFOOD 1	30	2	194
Southern Food Corporation—VINAFOOD 2	33	3	568
Viet Nam Chemical Corporation	50	14	..
Viet Nam National Gem and Gold Corporation	12	-	12
Viet Nam Ship Building Corporation	22	2	204

Note: [1] At the time the decision to establish the Corporation was issued.
Source: *Government Gazette*, various issues.

and to appoint an executive team led by a chief executive to take responsibility for the day-to-day operations of the Corporation.[41] Recent regulations on equitisation require state corporations to administer the equitisation of selected member enterprises.

STATE ENTERPRISE REFORMS FOLLOWING THE EIGHTH PARTY CONGRESS

The Political Report to the Eighth Party Congress in mid 1996 criticised the slow pace of state enterprise reform, noting in particular the slow pace of reforms aimed at improving enterprise efficiency and accountability and also the lack of progress in the pilot equitisation program. At the same time, the report stressed that calls for mass privatisation were inappropriate.

The Eighth Congress stated that 'the state economy plays the leading role and, together with the cooperative sector, will become the foundation of the economy' but that it was also important to 'create favourable economic and legal conditions for private entrepreneurs to feel assured in investing in long-term business' (Communist Party of Vietnam 1996a:50). The Congress noted an urgent need to improve the efficiency and transparency of state business. It also highlighted the need for a greater focus on improving financial management of all state enterprises, and to rely on profitability indicators to evaluate the performance of state business enterprises while also using social indicators to evaluate the efficiency of state public service enterprises.

Continuing slow progress with enterprise and administrative reform,[42] concerns about the low efficiency and competitiveness in domestic production and the impact of the Asian economic crisis led to a notice from the Politburo in April 1997 calling for an acceleration of the equitisation process.[43] The Fourth Party Plenum (December 1997) emphasised the need for financial sector and macroeconomic stability if Viet Nam was to cope with the unfavourable impact of the regional economic crisis and for a renewed focus on state enterprise reform.

The resolution of the Fourth Party Plenum charged that some officials are 'inefficient, bureaucratic, corrupted, overbearing, oppress the people, hinder economic development and cause indignation amongst the people' (Communist Party of Vietnam 1996b). This resolution highlighted the need for accelerated enterprise reform as the third of six priority program areas. Priorities for enterprise reform included: accelerating the equitisation program; developing the legal basis for small state enterprises (less than VND 1 billion in capital) to be restructured (merged, divested, leased, or contracted out under performance contracts), incorporating state business enterprises as limited liability or joint-stock companies under the Company Law; promulgating regulations to deal with supervision of enterprises with monopoly powers; and introducing regulations imposing compulsory auditing and publication of annual reports. The resolution also sought action

- to encourage farmers to buy shares in equitised agriculture processing and trading enterprises
- to allow foreigners to be buy shares in equitised enterprises
- to formulate policies and legislation to control monopolies
- to improve the state corporation model to strengthen vertical and horizontal cooperation
- to reorganise inefficient corporations.

Further calls to accelerate broader economic reforms were made less than a year later at the Sixth Party Plenum (October 1998). Subsequently, implementation of state enterprise reform activities has accelerated, but the government continues not to meet its own targets for equitising enterprises. These continuing delays, despite the increasingly strong Party and government commitment to substantially reducing the numbers of state enterprises, suggests that resistance to change is still strong at intermediate levels and within state enterprises.

'Compulsory' equitisation

Decree 28, issued in May 1996, abolished the enterprise management's right to veto equitisation decisions and provided clearer guidelines on responsibilities for action. At the same time, a Central Steering Committee on Equitisation was established, chaired by the Minister of Finance, to oversee the equitisation process.[44] Decree 28 was amended in March 1997[45] and replaced by Decree 44 in June 1998.[46] Both decrees sought to mobilise increased capital and new technology to develop state enterprises and to encourage employee owners of enterprises to play the role of real owners, to increase incentives, and incomes.[47] The options to be followed in equitisation were clarified, specifying the responsibilities of government agencies and enterprise management in implementing equitisation, defining worker entitlements, and establishing a central committee for reform of enterprise management.[48] Importantly, Decree 44-CP included an appendix that listed the categories of state enterprises which could not yet be equitised, and those enterprises in which the state had to retain controlling or special shares.

Subsequent implementing regulations listed the steps that had to be followed in the equitisation process. Decisions on the equitisation of enterprises with a total of VND 10 billion (about US$900,000 at that time) were delegated to relevant ministers, or provincial chairpersons.[49] Bonus and welfare funds were to be distributed to current employees to purchase shares. Decree 44 included provisions for equitisation through the issuance of new share capital,[50] selling part of existing state equity in a state enterprise, separating and selling part of an existing state enterprise, and selling all state equity in an enterprise.[51] State corporations were required to prepare lists of member enterprises to be equitised.[52] Participation by foreign investors was also permitted on a pilot basis, subject to the approval of the Prime Minister.[53]

The above changes addressed many of the constraints to accelerating equitisation.[54] Whereas only 17 state enterprises were equitised from 1992 until the end of 1997, some 102 enterprises were equitised in 1998, 249 in 1999, 212 in 2000, and 197 in 2001.

Despite this progress, the government recognises that further changes are required to meet ambitious targets to reduce state enterprise numbers substantially by 2005. Part of the problem is that many state enterprises are not suited to the equitisation process either because they are not viable in their current form or because they are too small to operate under a joint-stock management structure. Consequently, the government has also stepped up its efforts to improve the regulatory framework for divestiture, leasing and contracting out of state enterprises.

A second concern relates to the undervaluation of equitised enterprises and a lack of transparency in the sale of shares in equitised entities. Undervaluation results particularly because land-use rights do not have to be factored into enterprise valuations, although they are typically the most valuable asset. While this undervaluation is not a great problem from an economic efficiency perspective, lack of transparency in share sales and the broad public perception that access to shares is usually limited to (the often already privileged) state enterprise management and employees, state officials connected with the enterprises, and business partners of the enterprise are cause for public concern. This will become a growing concern as larger and more profitable state enterprises are equitised.

Divestiture, leasing and contracting-out of state enterprises

The government issued regulations setting out procedures for divestiture and dissolution of state-owned enterprises in mid 1996, and amended these in April 1997.[55] Implementing instructions were issued in mid 1997.[56] In September 1997, the government issued Decree 103 on the Regulation on Contracting Out, Leasing and Divestiture of State Enterprises.[57] Prior to this decree, there had been informal experiments with leasing and contracting out services and assets as a means for improving state enterprise efficiency. Indeed, some state enterprises earned a substantial proportion of their income from contracting out assets (including rights to use land and export quotas). However, there had been no transparent system for pricing and allocating these 'leasing' arrangements and it is difficult to assess the extent of such arrangements, but they were reported to be significant in areas such as retail services. Decree 103 aims to provide a more transparent process to facilitate the divestiture, leasing or contracting out of state enterprises with legal capital of less than VND 1billion (about US$70,000), or up to VND 5 billion for loss-making enterprises.

The stated objectives of this decree were to increase the efficiency and competitiveness of the state run sector; to 'promote the labourer's right to mastery', and create employment and higher income opportunities for workers, reduce state costs and responsibilities for business management. The scope of the decree was limited to the restructuring of whole enterprises, and specifically did not apply to the sale or leasing of parts of enterprises.[58] Substantial preferences (reductions in the sale price of up to 70 per cent) were given to labour collectives to buy these enterprises. Larger preferences were given to collectives guaranteeing to retain the most workers. Other individuals or entities could purchase enterprises at up to a 50 per cent discount if they retained all workers for at least one year. Further reduction in sale price of 20 per cent could be obtained for immediate cash payments for enterprises.[59] There are also provisions for state enterprises to be assigned free of charge to labour collectives, provided the collective commits to increasing investment, maintaining employment, and not dissolving or selling the enterprises for at least three years.

A critical concern with Decree 103 was the lack of transparency in valuation procedures. Combined with the substantial discounts offered, there would appear to be considerable scope for privileged persons to acquire state assets at very low prices. Public concerns about the lack of transparency and restricted access to these potentially profitable opportunities—and questions as to why employees fortunate to have had the benefits of state employment should be entitled to special privileges—have slowed implementation of this decree. Nevertheless, 37 state enterprises were sold, and 4 contracted out during the period 1999 to 2001. Another 60 enterprises (43 in 2001) have been assigned to labour collectives.

Corporatisation: transformation of state enterprises to limited liability companies

The Enterprise Law included provision for state enterprises to be corporatised as state-owned limited liability enterprises. A decree outlining the procedures for corporatisation was issued in September 2001.[60] Detailed implementing regulations were issued in January 2002 authorising ministers and the heads of provincial people's committees to approve the corporatisation of individual state enterprises.[61] Under these regulations the Prime Minister's approval is required for the corporatisation of any members of Decision 91 State Corporations.

These actions were in response to instructions given in the resolutions of the Third Party Plenum, and the five-year plan endorsed by the National Assembly, to accelerate actions to transfer all state business enterprises into state limited liability enterprises. The aim is to transfer all state business enterprises into limited liability enterprises by the end of 2005. Given the past pace of state enterprise reform, this appears to be an ambitious target.

The government has also ordered that new regulations be drafted to specify the relationship between subsidiaries of state corporations, and to increase the accountability of subsidiary enterprises. Options being considered include the transformation of state corporations into holding companies.

FUTURE DIRECTION OF STATE ENTERPRISE REFORM: RECENT RESOLUTIONS ON STATE ENTERPRISE REFORM

The Third Party Plenum resolution

The Third Party Plenum[62] called for further acceleration of reforms to increase state enterprise efficiency. Efficiency was to be assessed 'based on a comprehensive view in economic, political and social aspects; in which the return on capital shall be one of the major criteria to assess the efficiency of operating business enterprises with the results in implementing social policies as the major criterion to assess the efficiency of public utility enterprises'. The resolution notes that it is not essential for state enterprises 'to hold a large share in all branches and sectors and products of the economy'. Acceleration of the equitisation process was seen a key to achieving 'radical change for improving the efficiency of state enterprises'. The Resolution of the Third Party Plenum instructed that during 2001–05, the government should

- basically complete the restructuring of existing state enterprises: equitising state enterprises where the state does not need to retain 100 per cent ownership; liquidating inefficient state enterprises; transferring, selling and leasing small state enterprises which cannot be equitised and the state does not need to keep control
- corporatise as limited liability enterprises all state enterprise's where the state was to retain 100 per cent of equity. Amend the existing mechanism and policies to establish a consistent legal framework that ensure autonomy and accountability in state enterprise business operations
- reform and clean up state enterprise finances; resolve unrecoverable debt and labour redundancies and devise measures to prevent their recurrence
- reform and enhance the business efficiency of state corporations to establish several strong economic groups
- invest to develop and set up new state enterprises where needed in key sectors, branches and important localities
- reform and modernise the technology and managerial capability inmost state enterprises.

The resolution clarified that the state is to retain 100 per cent ownership in state business enterprises involved in producing explosive materials, toxic chemicals, radioactive materials, and cigarettes, and managing the national power transmission grid and international and national communication networks. The state will retain a controlling share in larger enterprises that 'contribute significantly to the state budget and/or spearhead the application of hi-tech, and breakthrough technologies and also contribute considerably to macro-economic balances', and in state enterprises that 'provide necessities for…rural populations and ethnic minorities in the mountainous and remote areas'. Enterprises belonging to Party organisations shall be subject to the same restructuring as other state enterprises, while enterprises belonging to political and social organisations will be required to register under the Enterprise Law.

The state will retain 100 per cent ownership of public service enterprises in areas such as 'printing money, flight controls, maritime control, radio frequency management and distribution; production and repair of weapons and military hardware and equipment for national defence and security; enterprises entrusted with special national defence tasks and enterprises operating in strategic locations and combining the economic operations and national defence tasks in accordance with the government decisions'. The state will retain a controlling share of public service enterprises responsible for 'technical inspection of large transport vehicles, publication of academic books, political papers and books, current event and documentary films; management and maintenance of the national railways and airports, management of watershed irrigation system, plantation and protection of watershed forests; water drainage in large cities; lighting system of cities; management and maintenance of land roads, bus and coach stations, important waterways; production and supplies of other products and services as provided for by the government'. The resolution also noted that households and non-state enterprises will be encouraged to provide public goods and services.

The resolution called for a Competition Law to be issued 'to protect and encourage enterprises from all economic sectors to compete and cooperate on equal footing within the common framework of the law'.[63] It called for steps to be taken to monitor and assess the efficiency of state enterprises regularly and to strengthen accounting, auditing, reporting and publication of information on the financial performance of state enterprises. A state Finance Investment Company is to be established to manage state shares in business enterprises on a pilot basis. Mechanisms were to be developed for tendering out the provision of public goods and services.

The government plans to 'rearrange and strengthen those corporations that are vital to the national economy while merging or dissolving other state corporations'.[64] State corporations are to be retained and strengthened in petroleum exploitation, processing, and wholesaling; the supply and distribution of electricity; the exploitation, processing and supply of coal and other important minerals; metallurgy; heavy manufacturing; cement production; post, telecommunications and electronics; airlines; maritime; railway; chemicals and chemical fertilisers; key consumer good and food industries; pharmaceuticals; construction; wholesale grain trading; banking; and insurance. State corporations are to be transformed as holding companies, on a pilot basis, with member entities corporatised as limited liability enterprises, with a minimum capital of VND 500 billion.[65]

A number of specialised economic groups are to be established based around state corporations, but with private sector participation. The government argues that economic groups are seen as important in allowing Vietnamese enterprises to compete internationally in sectors such as petroleum, telecommunications, electricity and construction. At the core of these groups will be conglomerates operating at home and abroad with a minimum capital of VND 10 trillion (US$667 million).

Government state enterprise reform agenda

The government expressed concern that 'only 40 per cent of the SOEs operate at a profit, 29 per cent have prolonged losses and 31 per cent break even' and considered state enterprise restructuring as 'key to enhancing the competitiveness of the economy and ensuring successful integration'.[66] In its report to donors in December 2001, the government noted a recent acceleration in state enterprise reform

> ...government decrees and other legal documents have been issued to provide guidelines for equitising state enterprises, for the divestiture, leasing and contracting out of state enterprises, and for the transfer of state enterprises into single-member limited companies, creating the basic legal framework to facilitate the operation of state enterprises within a socialist-oriented market mechanism. Initial progress has been made in adjusting the number, structure, and size of state enterprises. The number of state enterprises has been reduced from more than 12,000 to just over 5,000, and it is planned to further reduce the numbers by one-half, maintaining only those operating in key economic areas, especially in public services (Government of Vietnam 2001).

The stated objectives of accelerated equitisation are to create enterprises with a variety of owners, including a large number of workers; utilise the capital and assets of the state in an efficient manner to mobilise domestic capital for business development and create a dynamic and efficient management mechanism for state enterprises; enhance ownership of the workers, shareholders and promote supervision of enterprises by society; and ensure harmonised benefits between the state, the enterprises and labourers. The government also intends to include the value of land-use rights in enterprise valuations, and to identify options to ensure that valuations better reflect market value. Options to be piloted include public tendering for shares, and the sale of shares through intermediary financial institutions. Revenue from the selling of shares are to be used to implement redundancy policies, and for re-investment by the state in business development. While equitisation remains the preferred policy, efforts will also be made to accelerate the transfer, divestiture, merging, and/or liquidation of state enterprises that are not suited to the equitisation process. Increased efforts are to be made to build public understanding of, and support for, these policies.

IMPLICATIONS FOR DEVELOPMENT

Achievements and remaining constraints

State enterprise reform has been one of the most contentious areas of Viet Nam's economic reform process. The most substantial changes occurred during the late 1980s and early 1990s in response to the cessation of economic cooperation with the former Eastern European countries. During this period nearly one-third of the workforce was made redundant. Subsequently, the number of state enterprises, and the share of state enterprises in GDP, remained little changed over most of the 1990s.

With the benefit of hindsight it is possible to identify the impact of three tracks taken in reforming state enterprises in Viet Nam. The most significant influence was from the track exposing state enterprises to some of the rigours of the market, by forcing them to compete—on a gradually more level playing field—with each other, with imports, and with an emerging private sector. Direct subsidies were abolished, and many indirect subsidies reduced (but far from eliminated). The net result is that most state enterprises face a less elastic, if not hard, budget constraint, and operate in a substantially more competitive environment.

Another track involved a protracted effort to develop a new policy and regulatory framework to restructure and improve state enterprise efficiency. The net result of this track was a plethora of decrees, decisions, directives and circulars dealing with enterprise restructuring. The issuance of regulatory documents in Viet Nam is generally a time consuming, labour intensive process, involving many rounds of meetings and consultations. Sustaining this effort for such a protracted period suggests a strong commitment for change from at least some parts of the leadership. However, if there was such a strong commitment to reform, the obvious question is why many policy reforms were largely ignored by those responsible for their implementation. Why was Decree 388,[67] issued in late 1991, enforced quite effectively, but Decision 202,[68] issued a few month later, largely ignored despite repeated follow-up instructions urging action? Both regulations should have been implemented at a similar period of time, and both would have potentially important costs for some interests. Follow up regulations were issued in both cases in an attempt to facilitate implementation. These questions are raised, although the authors are unable to provide definitive answers. The processes of consultation and debate in drafting new policy documents and regulations have had a powerful educational impact, changing attitudes that eventually contributed to the acceleration of reforms. It is not possible, however, to determine whether faster reforms would have been possible if the government had taken a more authoritarian line in imposing implementation.

The third track was to allow pilot reforms and experimentation—to learn by doing. This had been the track adopted in many of the earlier reforms in agriculture, and with cooperatives, trading and other services. However, this approach was markedly less successful in the case of state enterprise reform. This was no doubt due to the fact that reforms in the area of state enterprises had much more clearly discernible costs to many of the officials responsible for implementing these measures.

The various tracks complemented each other, gradually building the support for state enterprise reform, needed to accelerate reform in the face of resistance from vested interests. State enterprise reform is a difficult process that requires substantial inputs of political capital. Leading proponents of reform in Viet Nam have noted the need to weigh up the potential gains of reform with the probability of success in deciding where to focus their efforts.

Viet Nam has achieved relatively strong economic growth and reductions in poverty via a combination of rather cautious changes in state ownership, increasing competition, and step-by-step removal of barriers to private sector development. But, there remain important questions about the appropriate pace of further reform and appropriate goals in striking a balance in the structure of ownership.

One interesting analytical issue relates to the relative importance of measures to change the structure of ownership as compared to measures to increase competitiveness and exposure to market forces. A possible interpretation of the Vietnamese experience is that promotion of competition is more important than promotion of changes in ownership.

Pace of state enterprise reform

Despite official commitments to accelerating state enterprise reform, resolutions of both the Eighth and Ninth Party Congresses maintained that the state was to continue playing a leading role in economic development. Of all recent Party policy resolutions, the continuing commitment to state-led economic development provoked the strongest criticism by multilateral financial institutions and OECD donors,[69] with many warning that state enterprises have been a (if not the) major impediment to achieving strong and sustainable economic growth and that economic growth and stability can not be sustained without accelerated state enterprise reform.[70] Those arguing for faster reform say that even greater progress could have been achieved with faster dismantling of state enterprises. They argue that this would have facilitated much greater private sector investment and employment creation.

An alternative view is that a stable set of state institutions, including state enterprises, along with market liberalisation have helped lay the foundations for a competitive private economy. A steady organic growth of private business has provided greater stability, more equitable distribution of the benefits of growth, and a more solid base for future development than may have been achieved by attempts to 'kick-start' a private sector through the rapid transfer of state assets despite the absence of an appropriate institutional environment, with the attendant risks of ineffective enterprise management, asset stripping and the hasty creation of private property rights of questionable legitimacy.

Even within the Party there are conflicting views. Some senior Communist Party and government leaders have persistently criticised lower administrative levels for failing to meet state enterprise reform targets. The lack of national consensus on the direction of state enterprise reform was clearly recognised in the resolution of the recent Third Plenum of the Ninth Party Congress

> ...a high degree of unanimity of perception is yet to be obtained regarding the role and position of the state economic sector and state enterprises ... many issues remain unclear, entailing conflicting opinions, yet practical experiences have not been reviewed for proper conclusions. There are many weaknesses and bottlenecks in the state administration of state enterprise...Mechanisms and policies are entangled with many inadequacies...failing to generate a strong motivation for managers and workers in enterprises to raise labour productivity and business performance; a segment of state enterprises' managers fail to meet professional and moral requirements. The Party's leadership and the government's guidance...are still incommensurate to this important and complex task.[71]

Implications for future reform

Despite the acceleration of state enterprise reforms in recent years, and regardless of the arguments about the pace of reform, there is clearly much unfinished business. Probably the most important incentive for the state to accelerate state enterprise reform is an increasingly public debate about equity, corruption and the misuse of state assets in the reform process. Most Vietnamese state enterprises are small. It will never be economic to implement effective governance of state investments in many of these small state enterprises. The more viable option—if the state is to achieve its objectives of increasing efficiency and reducing corruption—is for most of the small state enterprises to be sold. But the same public concerns about corruption and equity which lend support to the case of divestiture also require a greater transparency in the processes by which state assets are sold.

There is now a growing private sector with the capacity to buy the smaller state enterprises, but public bidding for the sale, or leasing out, of all of the smaller state enterprises will be essential in retaining public support for the process. Government policy seeks to ensure that workers have preferential access to state assets under public bidding processes, but there are questions as to why preference should be given to state enterprise workers, who are not among the more disadvantaged groups in society.

Although the case of divestiture of the smaller state enterprises is strong, the state retains an unequivocal commitment to retaining and strengthening state enterprises engaged in some core industries and services, and in the provision of public services. In this regard, Vietnamese policymakers cite the examples of other successful East Asian and European economies in which an active role of the state has been combined with effective use of market instruments. Given this approach, the challenge is to improve governance of these enterprises, and to improve performance incentives for enterprise manages, in order to sustain the growth in labour productivity achieved in recent years. It is not difficult to envisage a gradual relaxation of the state's position with regard to state ownership over time, as a large-scale domestic private sector emerges with the legitimacy, resources, and capacity to acquire and develop these businesses.

In discussions in the donor community in Hanoi, there was at times a certain reluctance to deviate from the 'Washington consensus' on the role of the state, because of a belief that this might lend support to groups opposed to further reform. But it is also important that experience and pragmatism, and not ideology, drive policy advice. Experiences of difficulties faced in other transition economies have demonstrated not only the failure of the central planning model, but also failures of poorly designed and managed reform efforts that neglect the important role that effective institutions (state and private) play in developing competitive market economies. There are limits to short-cutting development processes by simply copying models from long-established market economies.

In an analysis of the reform process, perhaps the key question of political economy is not whether it conforms to some abstract model of transition to a market economy, but rather what are the concrete patterns of interest engendered by the reform? In the Viet Nam case, an interesting aspect has been the degree to which those in the system have been able to benefit from the reform process and have therefore found it acceptable. Given that the Party highlighted conflicting internal views in the resolution of the Third Plenum, achieving consensus for more accelerated reforms in this area will require more time and debate in the Party and government.

NOTES

1. In Vietnamese, equitisation (*cæ phÇn hāa*) refers to the transformation of a company to a share-holding company. Under the old Company Law this implied a divestiture of shares because this law required a share-holding company to have at least seven shareholders. The new Enterprise Law allows for the state to be the single owner of limited liability companies, but requires at least three shareholders in joint-stock companies.

2. See Mallon (1996) for more detail.

3. Decision 217-HDBT (14/11/87), 'Renovating Planning, Economic Accounting and Socialist Business of State Enterprises'; and reinforced by Statute 50-HDBT, (3/88) 'Regulations for State-owned Industrial Enterprises'.

4. Resolution of the Third Plenum of the Sixth Party Congress (Communist Party of Vietnam 1987b).

5. Decree No. 50-HDBT, (22/3/88) provided details on implementing Decree 217-HDBT. Decree No. 98-HDBT (2/6/88) defined the rights and limits of worker unions in state enterprise decision making. Decision 93-HDBT (2/12/89) defined the powers of management in making management decisions. Decision 332-HDBT (23/10/91) provided details on the rights and responsibilities of enterprises regarding the management of state assets.

6. See Article 4 of 'Regulations for State-owned Industrial Enterprises' attached to Decree 50-HDBT (22/3/88).

7. The legal basis for these changes was reinforced by State Council Ordinances on: Principles of Accounting and Statistics (29/9/88); Economic Contracts (29/9/89); and Economic Arbitration (12/1/90).

8. By the early 1990s, controls were limited to public utilities and services, petrol, fertilisers, cement, steel, sugar and paper.

9. In practice, even before the controls were relaxed, many state enterprises showed little enthusiasm to transfer convertible currency to the State Bank.

10. Decision 218-CT (16/8/89), 'Foreign Earnings Management', and Decree 64-HDBT (10/6/89), 'Management of Import Export Business', and the devaluation and unification of the exchange rate.

11. Decree 50-HDBT (22/3/88), 'Regulations for State-owned Industrial Enterprises'.

12. Decree 144-HDBT (10/5/90), Decision 316-CT (1/9/90), Directive 408-CT (20/11/90), Directive 138-CT (25/4/91), Decision 332-HDBT (23/10/91),

13. Decree No. 28-HDBT (22/3/89), 'Regulation on Joint-Ventures', and Decree 38-HDBT (10/4/89), 'Economic Cooperation in Production, Distribution and Services'.

14. Decision 143-HDBT (10/5/90).

[15] Decree 388-HDBT (20/11/91), 'Establishing and Liquidating State Enterprises', Directive 393-CT (25/11/91) and Circular 34-CT (28/1/92). Later amended under Decree 156-HDBT (7/5/92) and Decision 196-CT (5/6/92).

[16] Strategic state enterprise was not defined, but was understood to include enterprises that contributed to national defence, public utilities and enterprises producing basic factors of production (for example, steel and cement), and key services such as banking.

[17] Decision 90-TTg (7/3/94), 'Work to Re-arrange State Enterprises'.

[18] Specifically, a resolution of the Second Plenum of the Seventh Party Congress.

[19] Resolution 2-NQ-HNTW (4/12/91).

[20] Decision 202-CT (8/6/92), 'Implementing Experiments to Convert State Enterprises to Share Holding Companies', and Decision 84-TTg (4/3/93), 'Accelerating the Pilot Scheme for Converting State Enterprises into Share Holding Companies'.

[21] Decision 84-TTg (1/3/92), 'Establishing a Central Steering Committee on Enterprise Reform'. This committee is now chaired by the Minister for Planning and Investment.

[22] Decision 84-TTg (4/3/93), 'Accelerating the Pilot Scheme for Converting State Enterprises into Share Holding Companies'.

[23] The target was specified in Article 3 of Decision 548-TTG (13/8/96), 'Establishment of the Equitisation Steering Committee under Decree 28-CP (7/5/96) of the Government'.

[24] One of the first equitised enterprises, the Refrigeration Electrical Engineering Company, faced initial difficulties in retaining export permits after equitisation.

[25] Law on State Enterprises, Article 1.

[26] A state public service enterprise was defined as 'a state enterprise that produces and provides public services pursuant to state policies, or directly involved in the discharge of defense or security tasks' (Law on State Enterprises, Article 3 (4)). More detailed definitions were subsequently provided in Decree 56-CP (2/10/96) 'On Public Utility State Enterprises'.

[27] The Prime Minister's approval was required for state corporations and large state enterprises to be established. Ministers and Heads of the People's Committees of the Provinces and Municipalities were allowed to approve the establishment of other state enterprises.

[28] Law on State Enterprises, Articles 49–54 (and Article 3 for definitions of state predominant and special shares).

[29] Law on State Enterprises, Articles 7–8. State enterprises also had the right to 'reject and denounce all requests for supply of resources not prescribed by law from any individual, agency or organisation, except voluntary contributions for humanitarian or public utility purposes'.

[30] Law on State Enterprises, Articles 10–12 (quote from Article 12(2)).

[31] Law on State Enterprises, Article 29.

[32] Law on State Enterprises, Articles 31(2), 34 and 35.

[33] Law on State Enterprises, Articles 41–42.

[34] By itself, this would not be bad. A good bankruptcy law could encourage problems to be resolved without having to resort to the courts. The problem, however, has been that bankruptcy actions have been slow, costly and often unsuccessful.

[35] Decree 27-HDBT (23/3/89), 'Replacement of the Charter for Unions of Enterprises'.

[36] Directors of member enterprises were to be represented on the Board of Directors of the Union of Enterprises. The head of the Union of Enterprises was to be elected by member enterprises, subject to the approval by the government.

[37] Decision 90/TTg (7/3/94), 'Work to Re-arrange State Enterprise', and Decision 91-TTg (7/3/94), 'Pilot Work to Establish Business Groups'.

[38] Article 2(2) of this decision does emphasise that, in establishing business groups, efforts should be made to 'limit both monopoly powers and disorderly competition'.

[39] Most importantly private enterprises were allowed to engage directly in external trade in agricultural commodities (including rice). Agriculture trade reforms were key conditions of an ADB-financed agriculture adjustment program.

[40] Law on State Enterprises, Article 7 (1.d).

[41] See Chapter V of the Law on State Enterprises. See also Decree 39-CP (27/6/95), 'Model Charter on the Structure and Operations of State Corporations'.

[42] Resolution 8/1998/NQ-CP (16/7/98) notes that 'impediments in the system of institutions and administrative procedures remain large. Some cadre, especially at the executing level, still cause hindrances and harassments to the production and business activities of the population and the enterprises. Implementation of the policies and regulations of the state, including correct ones which are promulgated in time, has not been serious…'

[43] CPVN Central Committee Notice 63-TB-TW (4/4/97). 'Opinion of the Politburo on Proceedings with Active and Stable Implementation of the Equitisation of state Enterprises'.

[44] Decision 548-TTG (13/8/96), 'Establishment of the Equitisation Steering Committee under Decree 28-CP (7/5/96). This committee was then abolished under Decree 44-CP in 1998.

[45] Decree 25-CP (26/3/97), 'Amending a Number of Articles of Decree 28 (7/5/96) on the Transformation of a Number of State Enterprises into Joint-Stock Companies', Directive 568-TTg (20/8/97), 'Accelerating the Equitisation Program'.

[46] Decree 44-CP (29/6/98). 'The Transformation of State Enterprises into Joint-Stock Companies'.

[47] Decree 44-CP (29/6/98). 'The Transformation of State Enterprises into Joint-Stock Companies', Article 2.

[48] Decision 111-CP (29/6/98). 'Establishing the Central Committee for Reform of Enterprise Management'. This decision repealed earlier decisions establishing the Central Steering Committee for Reform of Enterprises (Decision 83-TTg, 4/3/93) and the Central Steering Committee for Equitisation (Decision 548-TTg, 13 /8/96).

[49] Decree 44-CP (29/6/98), Article 17. The cut-off value in Decree 28-CP was VND 3 billion: this had been increased to VND 10 billion in Decree 25.

[50] This allowed an enterprise to be transformed into a joint-stock company, new shares to be issued, and these new shares to be sold to fund expansion, thus diluting state equity.

[51] Decree 44-CP (29/6/98). 'The Transformation of State Enterprises into Joint-Stock Companies', Article 7.

[52] Decree 44-CP (29/6/98). 'The Transformation of State Enterprises into Joint-Stock Companies', Article 15.

[53] Article 3 of Decree 28-CP (7/5/96), 'Transformation of a Number of State Enterprises into Joint-Stock Companies'. This is not allowed under the current Company Law, but exceptions are often made for 'pilot' reforms.

[54] Directive 20 CT-TTg (21/4/1998). 'Stepping up the Reorganisation and Renewal of State Enterprises', and Directive 659-TTg (20/8/97), 'Speeding up the Equitisation of State Enterprises'. Decision 1021-CP (1/12/97). 'Setting-up Working Teams for Restructuring State Enterprises in Hanoi and Ho Chi Minh City' was also aimed at accelerating equitisation.

[55] Decree 50-CP (28/8/96), 'The Establishment, Re-organisation, Dissolution and Bankruptcy of State Enterprises', and Decree 38-CP (28/4/97). 'Amending and Supplementing a Number of Articles of Decree 50-CP of 28/8/96'.

[56] Circular 8-BKH/DN (11/6/97), 'Guiding Implementation of Decrees 38-CP and 50-CP', and Circular 25-TC/TCDN (15/5/97), 'Guiding the Order, Procedures and Principles for Financial Settlement when State Enterprises are Dissolved'.

[57] Decree 103-CP (9/9/97), Regulation on Assigning, Selling, Business Contracting or Leasing State Enterprises.

[58] Decree 103-CP (9/9/97), Article 2.

[59] Decree 103-CP (9/9/97), Articles 51–52.

[60] Decree 63-CP (14/9/01), 'Transforming State Enterprises into Single Owner Limited Liability Enterprises'.

[61] Circular 01/2002/TT-BKH (28/1/02).

[62] Central Party Committee Resolution 05-NQ-TW (24/9/01), Resolution of the Third Plenum of the Ninth Central Party Committee 'On Continuing to Restructure, Reform, Develop and Improve the Efficiency of State Enterprises'.

[63] The Competition Law is scheduled for consideration by the National Assembly during 2003.

[64] Presentation by Deputy Prime Minister Nguyen Tan Dung to a two-day workshop on state enterprise in March 2002 (as reported in *Saigon Times Weekly*, 9 March 2002).

[65] Government reports indicate that about 60 per cent of state enterprises have capital of under only VND 5 billion (about US$330,000).

[66] Presentation by Deputy Prime Minister Nguyen Tan Dung to a two-day workshop on state enterprise in March 2002 (as reported in *Saigon Times Weekly*, 9 March 2002).

[67] Decree 388-HDBT (20/11/91), 'Establishing and Liquidating State Enterprises', reinforced in Directive 393-CT (25/11/91) and Circular 34-CT (28/1/92). Revised and strengthened in Decree 156-HDBT (7/5/92) and Decision 196-CT (5/6/92).

[68] Decision 202-CT (8/6/92), 'Implementing Experiments to Convert state Enterprises to Share Holding Companies', and followed by Decision 84-TTg (4/3/93), 'Accelerating the Pilot Scheme for Converting state Enterprises into Share Holding Companies'.

[69] This was a major topic of 'dialogue' between government and donors during the preparation of the last two five-year development plans, and at most CG meetings.

[70] The World Bank warned that '[o]verwhelming international evidence indicates that there are limits to what reform without divestiture of non-strategic enterprises can accomplish and sustain. Divestiture of non-strategic state enterprises will be critical to encourage entry by private business in productive sectors' (1995a:xii).

[71] Central Party Committee Resolution 05-NQ-TW (24/9/01), Resolution of the Third Plenum of the Ninth Central Party Committee 'On Continuing to Restructure, Reform, Develop and Improve the Efficiency of State Enterprises'.

11

HOUSEHOLD AND PRIVATE BUSINESS DEVELOPMENT

THE EMERGING NON-STATE SECTOR

Prior to *Doi Moi*, the domestic private sector largely comprised households engaged in farming, handicrafts and limited retail trade services. At the time of the Sixth Congress, the Party distinguished between a socialist sector (state enterprises, collectives and households) and non-socialist enterprises. The state allowed small-scale non-socialist enterprises to operate in a few industries and services, but restricted private commerce to trade in unprocessed agricultural products (Nguyen Van Dang 2001).

The role of household business in the economy expanded during the late 1980s and early 1990s, and households businesses are now an important contributor to output and employment, especially in the agricultural and service sectors. In contrast, the role of cooperatives has diminished sharply. The 1997–98 Viet Nam Living Standards Survey (VLSS) found that nearly 62 per cent of the population depended on farming (mostly household farms) and another 24 per cent depended on non farm self-employment. Only 25.7 per cent of the labour force was engaged in wage employment. Those engaged in non-farm self-employment generally enjoyed higher living standards than other groups.[1]

More recently, there has been a marked expansion in private firms in terms of numbers, employment and output, reflecting significant progress in deregulating domestic private sector involvement in industry and service activities, and especially in external trade, since 1999. The domestic private sector now accounts for most employment and recent employment growth; dominates agricultural output; and accounts for an increasing share of trade and other key services. Changes in the non-state share of industrial output have been more modest.

STRIKING THE APPROPRIATE BALANCE BETWEEN PRIVATE AND PUBLIC ECONOMIC ACTIVITY

Private sector growth has made a significant contribution to growth and reducing poverty. The key to reducing poverty in Viet Nam has been growth in employment and livelihood options for rural households and the self-employed in the urban informal sector. In Viet Nam, as elsewhere in the region, the number of jobs created for every unit of investment is much greater in the private sector than the state sector.

With capital as a critical constraint, the incentive for the private sector is to maximise output through the adoption of relatively labour-intensive processes. With preferential access to credit and natural resources, easier access to foreign investment, and weaker incentives to maximise profits, Vietnamese state enterprises have invested in more capital-intensive industries, so that typically state enterprises have created fewer jobs per unit of investment.

Thus the private sector has made a particularly strong contribution to employment growth. The private sector absorbed many of the workers laid off from the state sector, and much of the large annual increase in new entrants to the workforce. State enterprises' share of employment fell from 9.3 per cent of the total in 1988 to 5.1 per cent of the total in 1995. The proportion of public servants in the workforce fell from 4.8 to 3.6 per cent over the same period.

Private enterprises are also more flexible and innovative than state sector entities, a factor which is likely to be particularly important in the development of modern manufacturing and service sectors. The life cycle of most manufactured products is limited. Innovation and adaptability are essential to maintain growth momentum. And innovation will be of critical importance in continuing Viet Nam's successful integration into the international economy. Although Viet Nam has had remarkable success in promoting exports, for that process to be sustained, further increases efficiency will be required to effectively compete in an increasingly competitive international market. Innovation is even more crucial in the modern service sectors.

The growth of a lively and competitive private sector can also act as a stimulus to improved state enterprise performance. Efficiency gaps between state and private enterprises are generally reduced when state enterprises are forced to compete with each other and with suppliers from other sectors (including importers and other domestic producers). As argued above, one reason for Viet Nam's economic success in the 1990s was that, even before the growth of private sector, the state sector was not monolithic; parts of it operated on a decentralised and competitive basis. Measures that promote private sector development and increase the competition faced by state enterprises will contribute to further innovation and growth in efficiency in state enterprises.

Another important reason to promote private sector development is that the government simply does not have the administrative or financial resources to implement manifold commercial business activities while also implementing its ambitious social and physical infrastructure development programs.

The administrative difficulties (for both the government and businesses) of the government being involved in too wide a range of business decisions will become more onerous as the number of business entities needed for Viet Nam to grow and compete increases, particularly in small and medium-scale labour-intensive service and manufacturing activities.

Although the case for encouraging the private sector is strong, this does not imply that a completely *laissez faire* approach is appropriate as a strategy to ameliorate Viet Nam's development constraints. While a strong private sector helps generate growth and reduce poverty, it cannot guarantee an equitable distribution of increased output. Recent poverty studies suggest that, while past patterns of development have greatly reduced poverty, the better-off segments of the population have benefited more than the poorest.

The state needs to continue in a leading role to ensure the equitable distribution of the health and education services, supply the physical infrastructure needed to facilitate the geographical spread of development and service the fast growing urban centres, and should even selectively invest in directly productive activities, where foreign or domestic private investment are not sufficient.

EVOLUTION OF PRIVATE SECTOR POLICY

The movement towards acceptance of a fully active role for the private sector by the Vietnamese authorities has been gradual, and policies have often been ambiguous. There was much more rapid and less ambiguous acceptance of the role of the markets than of the private business. And, for some time, it appeared that foreign private business was more acceptable than national private firms. Household business activity was considered much more acceptable than private firms which employed large numbers of workers. While Viet Nam's Constitution guaranteed that 'enterprises belonging to all components of the economy...are equal before the law' (Government of Vietnam 1995:Article 22), enterprises have not enjoyed equal administrative and regulatory treatment.

Managers of all forms of enterprises were vulnerable to *ad hoc* interpretation of the changing legal and regulatory framework by officials in government and administrative agencies because of ambiguities in public policy. Difficulties also arose because of the rapid pace at which new laws were issued and because regulations were sometimes inconsistent and overlapping; and because the roles, responsibilities and accountability of different government agencies were not clear. There were also counterproductive attempts to regulate far too much.[2] Consequently, regulations often added unnecessary transaction costs in business and provided opportunities and incentives for corruption.

Early reforms fell short of providing an adequate policy and regulatory environment. This was not only a matter of the regulations as such but also of bureaucratic attitudes. Former Prime Minister Pham Van Dong noted in 1993 that drastically changing society's way of thinking was one of the most difficult aspects of the reform process. The stigma attached to traders under Confucianism, and to any business activity under Communism, 'is not easily undone overnight' (Tuong Lai 1999:5). While some adjustments were made in a surprisingly flexible manner, there were also inevitable tensions.[3]

Prior to the enactment of the Enterprise Law in 2000, legislation and regulations governing different business entities were promulgated on an *ad hoc* basis to meet the needs of an emerging market economy. Specific legislation was enacted for different categories of owners and for different forms of investment. Restrictions on capital structure were specified for different categories of business entities. Registration responsibilities were spread amongst different government agencies depending on the ownership and form of the business entity. All this tended to restrict entry and make it difficult to adapt to changing economic opportunities because it limited businesses' flexibility to increase capital and/or change the nature of their activities without going though a costly and time-consuming process of re-registration. Such rigidities hurt smaller enterprises the most because compliance costs were spread over a relatively small base, and this encouraged them to continue operating on an informal basis.

There are a numbers of areas in which private businesses have been constrained by the policy regime. One area in which private business was at a distinct disadvantage was in establishing joint ventures with foreign investors. Foreign investors had an incentive to select a state enterprise as a partner in order to get easier access to decisionmakers in order to facilitate administrative approvals. More direct discrimination included regulations that allowed state enterprises, but not private enterprises, to contribute land-use rights as equity in ventures with foreign investors.[4] Private enterprises also faced tighter restrictions on transferring land-use rights.

Land has been a constraint on private sector development and remains one of the more contentious ideological issues. The constitution clearly states that all land belongs to the people (that is, it cannot be owned by individuals). However, individuals and business entities can acquire long-term rights to use land. Rights to use land are usually by far the most valuable assets held by Vietnamese households and business entities.

The lack of freehold title to land need not be a constraint, provided that there are efficient markets for trading land-use rights.[5] This, however, has not been the case. Markets in land-use rights remain poorly developed and inefficient. It is difficult for private individuals or businesses to mortgage, and thus raise finance for investment, from their most valuable asset. Commercial banks are concerned about the difficulties in foreclosing on mortgages in a cost efficient manner to recover bad debts.[6] Actors in the private sector frequently cite the insecurity of title to land-use rights for commercial and industrial purposes as one of the most important constraints to private investment.

Vietnamese businesses and professionals also have been disadvantaged in terms of access to the latest business, market, trade, and professional literature and information. While controls on access to the internet have progressively been relaxed since late 1997, costs remain high because of monopoly pricing.

While the situation has gradually improved, the costs of international telecommunications, books, newspapers and magazines were higher than elsewhere in the region for the same reason.

During the decade prior to the passage of the Enterprise Law, reforms aimed at promoting private sector development were gradually instituted. A Party Plenum in 1989 called for a multi-sector economy with various forms of ownership and the Seventh Party Congress in 1991 stated that 'the private capitalist sector will be allowed to engage in those businesses prescribed by the law and beneficial to the national economy' (Nguyen Van Dang 2001). Changes to the Constitution (1992) and the Land Law (1993) provided signals to private enterprises that the state was moving towards protecting key property rights.

These policy and legal changes, and associated administrative reforms, helped promote social and political acceptance of the private sector, thus increasing private sector confidence that the reform process would be sustained. Changes in business policies were reinforced by a gradual opening up of economic and social life. People had greater freedom to make their own decisions. By the mid 1990s, permission was no longer required for internal travel[7] and the number of Vietnamese travelling to market economies on business and to study was growing. Personal contact between Vietnamese and foreigners was much more frequent and only likely to be restricted in exceptional circumstances. There was increased access to international perspectives and experiences through television, movies and other media.

A decisive shift in policy towards actively promoting the development of domestic private sector firms was quite late in coming. A pivotal change occurred with the extensive consultations and public discussion leading to simplification of business licensing and registration requirements during the late 1990s and the enactment of the new Enterprise Law from 2000. Subsequent resolutions from Party plena in 2001 and 2002, and constitutional change (December 2001), have reinforced the legitimacy of private sector firms. The Fifth Party Plenum in 2002, resolved to allow Party members to own private firms. A deputy head of the Party Central Economic Committee summarised the changes as follows

> [w]e used to advocate an economy of which a large proportion of output would come from the socialist sector, and wanted to eliminate gradually the non-socialist sector. Nowadays, we have shifted to a multi-sector economy. Many new economic sectors have taken shape, and they co-exist with such conventional ones as the people, collective and private-owned sectors. Each

sector has an important role in the economic structure and serves as a constituent of the socialist oriented market economy. These sectors are allowed to develop, cooperate or compete with one another healthily. An enterprise may contain different forms of ownership. The legal system has gradually shifted to one of general provisions governing all the sectors…

…Previously, we used to believe that central planning was characteristic of socialism and would not accept market relations. Nowadays, we consider the market both the basis and object of planning which is orientative and particularly important in macroeconomic terms. We recognize the market as instrumental in helping enterprises select their scope of production and business plans. Thereby, we have established the elements of the market: goods, services, technology, information services, consultancy, marketing, legal framework, finance, banking, auditing, insurance, capital and labour (Nguyen Van Dang 2001).

EMERGENCE OF DOMESTIC PRIVATE ENTERPRISES IN THE 1990s

Before *Doi Moi*, private business was mostly limited to household businesses, often with uncertain legal status, and operating mainly in the black economy. By the end of the 1980s, however, there were very many traders operating throughout the country, and much small-scale private activity in both urban and rural areas, albeit mostly still without official approval. The number of household businesses increased from about 0.84 million in 1990 to 2.2 million by 1996.

Following approval of the Company Law in 1990 the number of private companies increased steadily, with 190 joint-stock companies, 8,900 limited liability companies, and 21,000 private enterprises registered by 1996.

From the beginning of the *Doi Moi* period the private contribution to light industry, including handicrafts, household and small industries, grew at a lively rate. Most of the former industrial and service sector cooperatives engaged in light industry were disbanded, or reorganised as private enterprises. By 1995, there were over 400,000 production units operating outside the state sector, which generated around 30 per cent of total industrial sector output.

Private businesses have been even more important in the service sector, where they account for about half of total output. They dominate retail trade activity, with their share increasing from 41 per cent in 1986 to nearly 76 per cent in 1996. The state share of the service sector (including public administration, education and health) averaged around 45 per cent through the 1990s. Excluding public administration, education and health, the state accounted for about 22 per cent of value added in services in 1996.

A recently-published survey of developments in small and medium-sized private business between 1991 and 1997 concluded that

[g]enerally speaking, small-scale enterprises in Vietnam were considerably larger and more robust in the 1997 survey than they had been six years earlier. Income, capital and assets have all grown, among the urban as well as the rural enterprises. Furthermore, higher levels of value added per worker unveil growth not only in size, but also in efficiency. The increases in labour productivity are universal and in many instances remarkable. In Hanoi it increased by as much as 70 per cent. This growth has been linked to a general increase in the capital intensity of enterprises. Workers today have much more machinery and equipment at hand than six years ago (Ronnas and Ramamurthy 2001:327).

The lively growth of the national private sector, despite what seemed to be an unhelpful, if not hostile, regulatory environment, has been a particularly striking aspect of Vietnamese development. As noted earlier, casual observations suggest that the rate of private sector growth has probably been considerably greater than that reported in official statistics. In part, this is evidence of the extraordinary vitality of Vietnamese entrepreneurship. This has been demonstrated not only in Viet Nam, but also by overseas Vietnamese in contexts as diverse as North America and the former Soviet economies. It may be that if entrepreneurial 'animal spirits' are strong enough, they can overcome quite negative regulatory environments. A long-established pragmatic culture amongst segments of the administrative system, and amongst political leaders, probably also facilitated entrepreneurial activity.

Thus, somewhat paradoxically, while the regulatory and administrative system resulted in distortions of incentive structures and possibly a sub-optimal allocation of resources, it did not prevent the vigorous growth in non-state economic activity. While the high degree of discretion left to officials in implementing many policies and regulations left the system open to abuses and corruption, it also provided for a degree of flexibility whereby businesses became adept at manoeuvring around regulations and maintaining cooperative relations with local officials.

Observation suggests that, at the local level, many businesses establish close relationships with government and party officials.[8] Many businesses also have family members who are involved in the public sector. In addition to helping negotiate administrative and regulatory hurdles, this can be important in enforcing contracts and in enforcing property rights. However, it is also apparent that many business people tend to be quite discrete about the degree of their success, not wishing to attract too much official interest.

PRESSURES FOR PRIVATE SECTOR REFORM

The strong focus on employment growth

Grassroots pressure to improve economic opportunities and increase living standards has been important in driving the reform process. Continuing improvements in living conditions were important in sustaining the credibility of the government and the Party, and strong backing of Party and government leaders has helped in removing formal institutional barriers to business development. Agriculture and the household sector presently provide the majority of employment in Viet Nam, but this is generally low productivity, low income employment with minimal growth prospects. The private sector has been seen as crucial to increasing employment and incomes.

During the late 1990s, concerns about the potential impact of the Asian financial crisis and declining foreign direct investment reinforced growing domestic pressures to reduce barriers to private sector development. The Fourth Plenum (December 1997)[9] called for broader enterprise reform and the introduction of a more consistent regulatory framework for all types of business entities in order to achieve a more level playing field, and announced initiatives to

- amend the law on domestic investment to make it more readily applicable for different forms of enterprises[10]
- develop a new enterprise law to apply to a range of different business entities and with more transparent governance requirements
- streamline procedures for business registration, and for issuing residence permits and travel documents, to facilitate business development and employment generation[11]
- clarify regulations on the inspection and monitoring of enterprises by government agencies[12]
- distinguish clearly between civil and criminal breaches of the law and take strong action to punish criminal business activity
- develop a regulatory environment conducive to healthy competition and establish institutions to resolve commercial disputes in line with the principles of a market economy.

With growing economic turmoil in neighbouring Asian countries, pressure for action had intensified by the time the Fifth Plenum was held in July 1998. This plenum stressed the need for action to mobilise and utilise more effectively the large amounts of untapped capital still 'under the mattresses' in Viet Nam. There has been increased (or at least more public) policy debate about the positive employment, distributional and equity impacts of small private domestic investments compared with the more capital intensive investments typically made by state enterprises and foreign investors. There has also been more public discussion in the media about the adverse impacts of unnecessary and poorly drafted regulations in facilitating corruption, and stifling investment and employment growth.

Interactions between civil society and the bureaucracy

The growing public debate about administrative barriers to business development reflects grassroots discontent with cumbersome and costly administrative procedures and also the public dissemination of more sophisticated analysis of the equity implications of administrative and regulatory constraints to private sector development by research organisations such as the Central Institute for Economic Management (CIEM), and the Viet Nam Chamber of Commerce and Industry (VCCI).

Public dissemination of information about the employment and equity implications of administrative and regulatory constraints to private sector development have helped increase public awareness of the issues and helped to build support for reform. For example, CIEM produced and widely disseminated a report analysing the experiences with the old Company Law which concluded that cumbersome business procedures are circumvented in practice, encourage corruption, and add unproductive costs to doing business (CIEM 1998). The report drew public attention to the reality that the opportunities for corruption increase as civil servants are given greater discretion in making administrative decisions affecting the profitability of business activities. Given increasing public concern about corruption, the widespread distribution of these findings undoubtedly helped mobilise support for subsequent reform.

As businesses have developed, managers have had to deal with an increasing number of officials from outside established networks in order to secure licenses, pay taxes, secure financing, receive quality certification, and so forth. Business people became more aware of the administrative barriers to enterprise development. This, and the increasing number of entrepreneurs who do not have direct access to decisionmakers, has helped create demand for more transparent rules of the game. Business people began to see benefits in working with other business people, the Party, government officials, and the media, to push for change. Increased demand for change coincided with more systematic consultation between the state and the business sector to address business constraints.

The VCCI has been the dominant business association in recent efforts to improve the enabling environment for business. The VCCI differs from its counterparts in most market economies in terms of its close relations with the government. Most of its staff have worked with the government, and the government has financed much of VCCI's infrastructure. While external observers may argue that the VCCI is constrained in criticising the state, because of the close links with the Party and the government, at least some domestic business people argue that it is especially effective in presenting business complaints to the government because of its close links with the senior leadership of the government and the Party. It has played a visibly proactive role in pushing for the reforms embodied in the Enterprise Law and related business regulation reforms.

In addition, more independent business associations have begun to emerge which represent the interests of the new private sector (for example, the Young Entrepreneurs' Association) and representing industry interests in dialogue with the government and in public policy debate through the domestic media.

The resolution of the 2002 Fifth Party Plenum

There is now increasing senior level recognition of the contribution of the private sector to socioeconomic development, and increasing top down pressure for change. The Fifth Party Plenum (March 2002) stressed that the private sector is

> ...an integral part of the national economy. In the past years, the Party and state reform guidelines and policies have enabled the private economy to grow vigorously nationwide, spreading out to all branches and sectors which are not prohibited by laws and have mobilised more social resources in production and business thus generating more jobs and procuring further for the state budget and making an important contribution to GDP growth (Communist Party of Vietnam 2002:n.p.).[13]

The Plenum endorsed measures to create an attractive business climate and a fair and competitive playing field for all enterprises and set priorities for further reform to support private section development, including further improving the Enterprise Law and reducing remaining barriers to the entry of new businesses; changing the land law and mortgage procedures to make it easier for the private sector to use land-use rights as equity and/or collateral; facilitating lending to the private sector through the provision of guarantees and consulting services; changing the accounting system to encourage private enterprises to adopt professional accounting systems that distinguish more clearly between civil and criminal violations of commercial regulations; asking national leaders to promote the image of the private sector; and allowing business people to retain Party membership.

While these trends represent important progress, much remains to be done. For example, the Fifth Party Plenum endorsed the establishment of business associations, but details of their legal status are still to be resolved. Consultations on business issues are still done on an *ad hoc* basis. Thus, progress in reducing barriers in one area is often (at least partially) undermined by administrative inertia, or new decisions and circulars emanating from line ministries and/or provincial authorities. The Fifth Party Plenum also noted concerns about both the weaknesses of the private sector and problems in ensuring compliance with business regulations, stating that

> Vietnam's private economy is basically of small scale and capital and equipped with obsolete technologies, low levels of management and expertise as well as competitive edge. Many private economic businesses have not strictly observed work rules regarding working allowances and conditions for employees; quite a few units have evaded tax or violated laws.[14]

The following section describes the process of business regulation reform that was aimed at both promoting private sector development and developing a simplified and more enforceable regulatory environment for business.

THE ENTERPRISE LAW

The consultative processes adopted during the drafting of the new Enterprise Law[15] reflected a crucial turning point in government relations with the business sector. Consultations between government, the business community, the media, and members of the National Assembly were protracted and substantive, resulting in widespread support for, and awareness of, this legislative reform. Reform proposals also included explicit reference to regional experiences with private sector development. The substantive consultations appear to have helped build business confidence that the government and Party were serious in their commitment to private sector development.

The enactment of the Enterprise Law in 2000,[16] and related regulatory reforms, greatly improved the institutional environment for private business. Key implementing regulations (on registering business and cancelling licenses and permits contrary to the Enterprise Law) were issued in March 2000.[17] The net impact of these changes was to help

- reduce ambiguities and inconsistencies inherent in earlier legislation
- provide an umbrella framework for a range of business entities previously governed by different legislation (joint-stock companies, limited liability companies (including corporatised state enterprises), and private firms)
- clarify mechanisms to protect investors and enterprises against state interference in the operations of the enterprise
- simplify enterprise registration procedures
- introduce partnerships as a new form of business
- clarify the rights and interests of company members, and especially the interests of minority shareholders
- clarify mechanisms for decision making within the company structure.
- protect the interests of lenders by clarifying the conditions for withdrawing capital from company
- clarify procedures for profit distribution to protect the interests of shareholders
- define procedures for transferring ownership of non-cash assets
- clarify procedures for merging or breaking-up an entity, and for shifting from one form of entity to another.

In related reforms, the government revoked the need for about 150 business licenses and permits, and simplified many remaining business licensing procedures. While enforcement remains an issue—and many licenses are still required—regulatory reforms have greatly reduced establishment costs and the time required to register businesses. Simplified procedures have reduced opportunities and incentives for corruption, reduced uncertainty about the legality of business operations, and allowed investors to focus their efforts on business development. A very tangible impact of the changes has been the marked reductions in the time lapsing between submission of dossiers requesting business registration, and the eventual approval (from an average of about 90 days to 7 days), and reductions in the typical fees paid to consulting firms for registering a company from about VND 10,000,000 to VND 500,000.[18]

These administrative changes were of greatest benefit to smaller enterprises because the costs of complicated procedures are largely fixed: that is they were not related to the size of the enterprise. For small enterprises, these costs could account for a large percentage of their total costs structure. Larger enterprises could spread fixed costs over a larger cost and revenue base. Costs of complex and less transparent regulations were particularly high for those without personal access to decisionmakers in the bureaucracy (for example, firms in isolated and rural areas and firms headed by ethnic minorities, women and other groups that are underrepresented in government). Thus, simplification of procedures helped to reduce the bias against such groups establishing new businesses.

RELATED INITIATIVES GIVING GREATER RECOGNITION TO THE PRIVATE SECTOR

Many initiatives have been introduced since approval of the Enterprise Law which have the potential to improve further the regulatory environment for small enterprises. Since February 2000, private enterprises have been allowed to convert, transfer, lease, provide their assets as collateral and capital contribution to banks or to joint-ventures. The Ninth Party Congress (March 2001) endorsed a Socio-Economic Development Strategy for 2001–10 that included a commitment to move towards equal treatment for all enterprises. A Public Administration Reform Master Plan approved by the Prime Minister in September 2001 is a potentially important step towards addressing remaining administrative barriers to private enterprise development. The December 2001 meeting of the National Assembly amended the Constitution to provide clearer recognition of the long-term role for the private sector in the economy, and formally approved the Socio-Economic Development Strategy for 2001–10.

The strong official endorsement of the private sector appears to have had a significant impact in building investor confidence, and in increasing pressure on those mid-level officials who have been reluctant to implement streamlined business procedures.

IMPACTS OF THE ENTERPRISE LAW

The net result has been a rapid acceleration in the registration of new businesses, including businesses that previously operated in the 'grey' economy. During the first year of enactment, 14,444 enterprises were newly registered under the Enterprise Law—about 2.5 times the number of registrations in 1999 under earlier legislation. By the end of 2001, some 35,000 enterprises had been newly registered under the Enterprise Law. Some of these enterprises were already operating informally, but most were newly established. Some existing companies prefer to establish new companies as part of their expansion plans in order to benefit from tax incentives offered to new businesses.

Not only did the number of private businesses grow at a high rate, but their average size and diversity of business activity of sole proprietorship and limited liability companies also expanded. The rate of growth in output by the domestic private sector has exceeded that of both state enterprises and foreign invested enterprises since 2000. Despite this growth, nearly all Vietnamese private enterprises remain relatively small.

The most significant growth has been in the number of new joint-stock companies. The number of joint-stock companies registered in 2000 exceeded the number of joint-stock companies established in the previous nine years. The number of limited liability enterprises newly registered under the Enterprise Law almost equals the total number of such enterprises registered under the old Company Law. The rate of growth in the number of new sole proprietorship enterprises has also accelerated. In addition, some 4,000 existing enterprises increased their chartered capital and/or broadened the scope of registered business activities.

Not only did the number of private businesses grow at a high rate, but the average size and diversity of business activity of sole proprietorship and limited liability companies also expanded. With the rapid expansion in numbers of joint-stock companies, the average registered capital of joint-stock companies declined, from VND 11 billion in 1991–98 to VND 4.2 billion in 2000. Prior to the Enterprise Law there were only a few, relatively large share-holding companies (including equitised state enterprises).

In mid 2001, the Steering Group for Enterprise Law Implementation (SGELI) estimated that the total registered capital of private enterprises had reached VND 24,000 billion (US$1.65 billion), that newly registered companies have created 300,000 new jobs, and that newly registered sole proprietorship businesses have created another 200,000 jobs.

Prior to the enactment of the Enterprise Law most new enterprises were registered to engage in trading activities. Some 61 per cent of enterprises were primarily engaged in trading services, 26 per cent in manufacturing and processing, 3 per cent in construction, and the remainder in other services and

Table 11.1   **Number of newly registered enterprises, 1991–2001**

Type of enterprise	1991–98	1999	2000	2001[a]
Sole proprietorship	26,708	2,427	6,412	2,709
Limited liability company	12,163	3,147	7,304	3,976
Joint-stock company	316	208	726	543
Partnership	-	-	2	0
Total	39,187	5,782	14,444	7,228

Note: [a] First five months of the year.
Source: CIEM and Enterprise Department, Ministry of Planning and Investment.

Table 11.2   **Average registered capital of new enterprises, 1991–2001 (VND million)**

Type of enterprise	1991–98	1999	2000	2001[a]
Sole proprietorship	197	400	439	546
Limited liability company	1,006	1,360	1,091	1,276
Joint-stock company	11,832	5,316	4,223	4,923
Partnership	-	-	550	88
TOTAL	542	1,099	959	1,297

Note: [a] First five months of the year.
Source: CIEM and Enterprise Department, Ministry of Planning and Investment.

general business. Following enactment of the Enterprise Law, trading activities still account for the largest share of new business registrations, but the share of manufacturing and other services has increased. Some 42.7 per cent of the businesses registered during 2000 were engaged primarily in trading services, 31.4 per cent were in industry and construction, 3.9 per cent in agriculture and 21.9 per cent in other services and general business. The sector classification system for registered enterprises is still evolving, and thus these numbers should be seen as indicative. However, the figures suggest that private investors are now more prepared to make longer-term business investments.

There is also some indication of more equal regional distribution of newly established enterprises. During the period 1991–98, some 72 per cent of all enterprises were established in the southern provinces, mostly in and around Ho Chi Minh City. While the number of enterprises registered continued to increase throughout the country, the share of newly registered enterprises in the southern provinces fell to 56 per cent of total newly registered enterprises, while registrations in the northern provinces increased to 32 per cent, and registrations in the central provinces increased to 12 per cent of the total during the first five months of 2001. The acceleration in new registrations in the northern and central provinces is particularly pronounced for the larger limited liability and joint-stock companies (Table 11.3). However, most new business registrations continue to be concentrated in the major cities.

COOPERATIVE SECTOR

Official data suggest that cooperatives played an important role in all sectors prior to the start of *Doi Moi*, accounting for 35 per cent of gross social product in 1985. Cooperatives accounted for 43 per cent of valued added in agriculture, 24 per cent of industry and 18 per cent of general trade in 1987 (see General Statistical Office 1989, 1992). Subsequently, the share of cooperatives fell sharply, with the most rapid declines being in agriculture and trade. By the mid 1990s, cooperatives accounted for less than 1 per cent of GDP.

The role of cooperatives in agricultural production fell to virtually nothing after the 1988 agriculture reforms. The role of cooperatives in industrial output fell sharply after 1988 to about 1 per cent of industrial output by 1994. Most cooperative production capacity was transferred to the private sector. Price reforms, relaxation of restrictions on private sector development, state enterprise reforms, and the loss of East European markets all contributed to reduced incentives for cooperative forms of industrial production.

The 1996 Cooperative Law and the new cooperatives

In response to concerns about the declining role of cooperatives, the government drafted a Law on Cooperatives which was approved by the National Assembly in 1996.[19] The law included provisions for cooperatives to receive up to 50 per cent reductions on land-use rents and taxes for the first two years of operation and preferential access to credit. Family members of cooperative employees, many of whom will also be engaged in the private sector, are to benefit from 50 per cent reductions on tuition fees in government training institutions and from government financed training.[20] On the other hand, regulations on inheritance of investments in cooperatives are vague, being largely left to regulations in the Statute of Individual Enterprises. The policy objectives in providing such differential treatment to cooperatives are not specified in the regulations.

Table 11.3   **Newly established enterprises, by region, 1991–2001 (per cent)**

Type of enterprise	1991–98	1999	2000	2001[a]
Northern provinces	16.9	18.2	28.4	32.1
Private enterprise	6.4	4.4	7.7	7.4
Limited liability company	10.3	12.2	18.4	21.0
Joint-stock company	0.2	1.6	2.2	3.7
Central provinces	11.4	10.4	13.1	12.0
Private enterprise	8.8	6.5	8.3	6.3
Limited liability company	2.6	3.4	4.3	4.9
Joint-stock company	0.1	0.5	0.5	0.8
Southern provinces	71.7	71.4	58.5	55.9
Private enterprise	52.7	30.9	28.7	23.8
Limited liability company	18.4	39.1	27.5	29.1
Joint-stock company	0.5	1.5	2.3	3.1
Total	100.0	100.0	100.0	100.0

Note: [a] Year to June
Source: CIEM and Enterprise Department, Ministry of Planning and Investment.

Table 11.4   **Cooperatives re-registered under new cooperative law (June 2001)**

	Number prior to new law	Number transformed with business license	Number transformed but without business license	Number closed	No action
Cooperatives	9,810	4,250	1,203	1,088	3,269
Per cent of total	100	43.3	12.3	11.1	33.3

Source: CIEM 2001. Report to CIEM Workshop on Implementation of the Cooperative Law, www.ciem.org.vn.

Subsequently, the government issued a comprehensive set of implementing regulations.[21] The Ministry of Planning and Investment (MPI), the Ministry of Agriculture and Rural Development (MARD), and the Central Union of Cooperatives soon thereafter organised training courses throughout the country to encourage the transformation of old cooperatives, and/or re-registration of cooperatives, under the new Cooperative Law. Steering committees were established at the provincial and at district levels, to facilitate transformation at the commune level. The due date for transforming cooperatives under the new law was 31 December 1998, but many cooperatives had still not been transformed by mid 2001 (Table 11.4).

Newspaper reports indicate that there was more rapid progress in transforming cooperatives in the second half of 2001 and in the first quarter of 2002 (*Viet Nam News*, March 2002). The Fifth Party Plenum in March 2002, was critical of 'the errors of Party organisations and authorities from central down to grassroots levels' in failures to develop the collective economy, and stressed the need to 'accelerate, develop and improve the efficiency of the collective economy' (*Nhan Dan News*, 4 March 2002). The Plenum concluded that

> the collective economy and cooperatives are crucial for individual households and small and medium-sized enterprises to lean on each other to survive and grow in the fierce competition of the market economy. The collective economy and cooperatives also constitute a means, which combines with the state economy in addressing social issues, reducing hunger and poverty and raising community awareness…the collective economy should be developed in diverse forms with cooperatives as the mainstay to…guarantee that the collective economy and state economy become the bedrock of the socialist-oriented market economy.

It is not at all clear, however, how realistic these resolutions are (at least in terms of the economic contribution of cooperatives) as the share of cooperative output in GDP was less than 1 per cent in 2000, roughly the same share as in 1996 when the new law was approved. Recent studies indicate that there continues to be ambiguity about the role of cooperatives, the relative roles and responsibilities of cooperative management and members, and of the rights of local authorities to interfere in basic cooperative management decisions (CIEM 2001).

LESSONS AND ISSUES FROM RECENT PRIVATE SECTOR REFORM EXPERIENCES

Informal institutions have played a key role in that rapid expansion of household and micro business in Viet Nam during the *Doi Moi* period. However, as firms grow, and commercial transactions expand beyond village, provincial and national borders, so the demand for more formal institutions grows. But it takes time to develop new institutions and, in planning institutional development, it is important to recognise that new institutions need to reflect local realities and meet demands from the business community. Access to formal institutions, especially if they are 'over-designed', may be very expensive for many entrepreneurs. The challenge is to maximise the benefits from both existing (often informal), and new institutional arrangements. Institutional reform should generally focus on complementing, rather than displacing, existing market institutions.

The recent acceleration in growth of formal private enterprises reflects increasing private investor confidence that an institutional and policy environment is emerging that will protect their property rights. The turnaround in the state approach to private sector development is reflected in the Enterprise Law. While the thrust of earlier business legislation was that private enterprises might be permitted if they complied with government controls, the Enterprise Law codifies mechanisms to protect the rights of citizens to establish and operate private businesses. It also establishes the right of investors to be protected from undue official interference, provided businesses operate legally. Other factors that have contributed to increased confidence over the last 2–3 years include

- a clearer commitment from the country's leadership about the long-term role for the private sector in economic development
- the fundamental change in thinking at all levels of society reflected in the process of recent regulatory reform and drafting of the Enterprise Law
- commitments to the private sector that are increasingly reflected in state policies, legislation and other institutional reform affecting the private sector
- simplified procedures that have reduced opportunities and incentives for corruption, reduced uncertainty about the legality of business operations, and allowed investors to focus their efforts on business development.

REMAINING CHALLENGES

Although the government and Party have left some key questions unresolved about the appropriate balance in the roles of the state, markets and market institutions, ambiguities about the state commitment to private sector development have been reduced in recent years. Meanwhile, accelerated business development continues to contribute to employment growth, and thus to poverty reduction.

The challenge lies in sustaining this progress. This will require continued efforts to address remaining institutional inadequacies that result in high transaction costs and thus constrain business investment and employment growth. Continuing progress in improving consultations between the state and business people will be useful in identifying remaining inadequacies.

Successful institutional reform and development requires broad support. Institutional reform usually results in both winners and losers. Policymakers need to understand the distributional consequences of proposed reforms. In some cases, sustained efforts are required to build support for reforms. Formalising consultative processes and requiring regulatory impact assessments (that also incorporate consultative processes) could add to the quality of new policy and regulatory documents. There is also a need to develop the capacity of research agencies and associations in undertaking applied research, and in preparing policy submissions, on business development issues.

The domestic business media played an important role in securing support for the Enterprise Law, and for complementary regulatory reform. The media could play an increasingly important role in increasing awareness of private sector constraints and business issues, and in providing the greater transparency needed to succeed with anti-corruption efforts.

Learning by doing and by empirical observation have been important inputs into Viet Nam's reform program. Viet Nam has actively studied experiences in other countries in planning reforms, and experiences from more successful provinces have been extended elsewhere throughout the country. Competition between regions for investment can help in developing the most appropriate institutions as it 'highlights successful institutions and promotes demand for them' (World Bank 2001b:4). However, it is also important that such competition does not lead to new distortions in the form of protection and other subsidies for investors.

Regulatory reform has reduced the discretion of civil servants in making decisions affecting business investments. This has the potential to facilitate private sector development and reduce some opportunities for corruption. But there are contradictory tendencies. With a growing role for the private sector, and increased contracting out of the provision of public goods and services to the private sector, improved transparency and accountability in public procurement and policy process is also needed. Otherwise, efficiency gains could be dissipated through new types of corrupt relationships between the state and private sector.

NOTES

1. Vijverberg and Haughton (2002) found that participation in non-farm self-employment was 'associated with a higher standard of living…and…greater economic mobility'.

2. The proliferation of new decrees, laws and policy reforms may, at least, partly reflect the fact that donors often see such measures as important indicators of success for institutional building technical assistance projects and policy based lending.

3. Kornai (1992:579) argues that such tensions are inevitable in post-socialist societies.

4. Article 11(6) of Decree 85-CP (17/12/96), 'Guiding Implementation of the Ordinance on the Rights and Obligations of Domestic Organisations with Land Assigned or Leased Land by the state', Government Gazette (28/2/97, p.14).

5. The state retains ownership of land in Hong Kong, and parts of Australia, with land-use rights leased on a long-term basis.

6. A mortgage sale generally required the consent of the government and mortgagor (Circular 217-NHNN (17/8/96)) and the sale must be conducted by an authorised body (Article 273(2) of the Civil Code).

7. People still had to register when changing addresses, and some restrictions on moving addresses between provinces.

8. Officially, Party members were not allowed to engage in private business prior to the Fifth Party Plenum in 2002.

9. Fourth Plenum of the Eighth Party Congress (December 1997)

10. Amended in April 1998. The Law on the Promotion of Domestic Investment was intended to address concerns of domestic investors that foreign investors received preferential treatment, but cumbersome and ambiguous procedures meant that relatively few domestic businesses applied directly to benefit from the incentives provide under this law.

[11] Steps were taken soon after to simplify business registration and on the issuance of visas for domestic and foreign business people. Business registration reforms were included in Circular 5/1998/TTLT-KH&DT-TP (10/7/98). 'Procedures for Establishing and Registering Private Enterprises and Companies'.

[12] Actions on these issues were reflected in Decree 61/1998/ND-CP (15/8/98), 'Inspection and Control Work with Regard to Enterprises' and Directive 16/1998/CT-TTg (31/3/98), 'Settlement of Enterprise Petitions'.

[13] Resolution of the Fifth Plenum of the Communist Party of Vietnam Central Committee (Ninth Tenure) on Renovating Mechanisms and Policies to Encourage and Facilitate Private Economic Development. See also the Government Action Plan to Implement the Resolution of the Fifth Plenum (Decision 94/2002/QD-Tty, 17/7/02), Cong Bao, Hanoi.

[14] A decree addressing this issue was being discussed in early 2002.

[15] This section draws on research undertaken as part of the CIEM/UNDP project on 'Improving the Regulatory Environment for Business' which has supported business reforms since 1997.

[16] This law replaced the old Company Law and Private Enterprise Law.

[17] Decree 02/2000/ND-CP(2/3/00) on registering business under the business law, and Decree 03/2000/ND-CP (2/3/00) and Decision 19/2000/QD-TTg cancelling licenses and permits contrary to the Enterprise Law.

[18] Actual costs vary substantially. Estimates are as reported by the Steering Group for Enterprise Law Implementation, and have also been widely reported in the domestic press.

[19] National Assembly (3/4/96), 'Law on Co-operatives'.

[20] Decree 15-CP (21/2/97), 'Policies to Promote the Development of Cooperatives'.

[21] Decrees 02-CP (2/1/97), 15-CP (21/2/1997), 16-CP (21/2/97), and 41 to 46-CP (29/4/97).

12

THE PATTERN OF ECONOMIC GROWTH

PRELUDE TO GROWTH: ECONOMIC STAGNATION IN THE 1980s

The economic difficulties facing the country in the period leading up to the implementation of *Doi Moi* were described earlier. Following an initial economic recovery immediately after formal reunification in 1976, attempts to impose central economic controls and conflicts in Cambodia and in the border area with China contributed to economic stagnation and increasing macroeconomic imbalances during the late 1970s. Annual economic growth averaged only 0.4 per cent in the five years to 1980. With population increasing by about 2.3 per cent each year, this represented a decline in per capita income. Prices increased by an average of more than 20 per cent each year. Individuals attempted to meet basic needs by producing and trading outside official channels.

Despite some economic recovery and growth in national output in the first half of the 1980s, public sector and trade deficits continued to increase sharply. By the mid 1980s, inflation soared and output growth fell sharply. Agricultural growth slowed, and paddy production per capita fell by 1 per cent in 1986 and a further 8 per cent in 1987. Following the poor harvests of 1986 and 1987, large areas of the country experienced near-famine conditions.

The reliability of the economic growth data for the 1980s is particularly uncertain. Data was collected to estimate net material product under a centrally planned accounting system. The available series indicates low but positive growth for the years 1985–89. However, a decline in agricultural value added was recorded in 1987 and a decline in industrial output in 1989. At best, per capita economic growth was around 2 per cent per annum, and was probably lower.

The *Doi Moi* process outlined in the previous two sections of this study was initiated during a mounting economic crisis in the late 1980s. There was a gradual relaxation of the administrative controls on private sector activity and domestic trade. In early 1987, many of the checkpoints that had been established to limit domestic trade were reduced, and private markets for agricultural goods developed rapidly.[1] In mid 1987, substantial price reforms were introduced with the official price of most non-essential consumer goods raised to close to the market price and rationing cut back. At the same time, the dong was substantially devalued. However, government attempts to reduce imbalances through currency, price and wage reforms were poorly coordinated and initially ineffective. Large macroeconomic imbalances persisted, and economic prospects were uncertain.

THE TURNING POINT: 1989–92

The critical turning point in Vietnamese economic performance came in the period 1989–92, when growth in GDP rose from 4.7 per cent per annum (1989) to 8.1 per cent per annum (1992), and inflation had been reduced to less than 20 per cent (Figure 12.1). The economic history of the period 1989–92 is therefore of particular interest.

The striking improvement in economic performance happened in a period in which Viet Nam experienced a sharp decline in external assistance. External assistance from the Eastern Bloc declined sharply and then abruptly stopped in 1990–91 as a consequence of the dramatic political changes in the Soviet Union. Access to finance from the International Monetary Fund, World Bank and the Asian Development Bank continued to be blocked by the US government until 1993, and few OECD countries provided assistance at the time.

Recently, claims have been made that Viet Nam is an example of the success of foreign aid in promoting poverty-alleviating growth (Development Economics Vice Presidency 2002). Claims could possibly be made for the effectiveness of external assistance in later periods, but the crucial period for reform and the turning point for economic performance was characterised by a sharp reduction in the level of foreign aid. Indeed, a simplistic interpretation of Figure 12.1 might suggest that higher levels of investment were required to achieve constant and then declining levels of growth during the mid 1990s. This apparent decline in investment efficiency occurred as ODA and FDI inflows were increasing. Of course, the real story is much more complex.

Economic management in the years 1989–92 had to meet the difficult challenge of achieving a degree of monetary and price stability at the same time as encouraging expansion in the real economy during a period in which the economy faced a tight external constraint. Policymaking in that period involved a large degree of economic crisis management. The response on the part of the Vietnamese authorities was a pragmatic combination of implementation of market liberalisation (Chapter 7) and fairly orthodox macroeconomic stabilisation.

Figure 12.1   **Financing development and growth, 1986–2001**

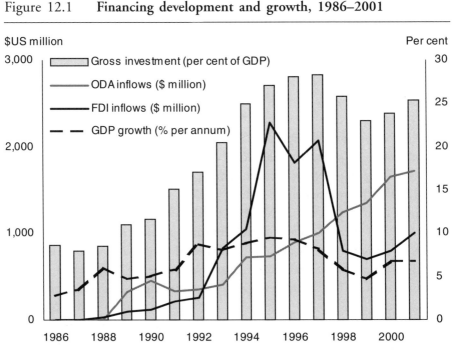

Source: Data from General Statistical Office (various years), *Statistical Yearbooks*, Statistical Publishing House, Hanoi; and International Monetary Fund (various years), *Recent Economic Developments*, International Monetary Fund, Washington, DC.

In 1989, the Vietnamese authorities implemented a rigorous IMF-style policy package (without IMF assistance to soften the social costs).[2] When the program was introduced, the economy was experiencing hyperinflation, with price increases of 774 per cent in 1986, 223 per cent in 1987 and 394 per cent in 1988. In the semi-reformed economy, there were enormous imbalances between the official economy and free market transactions.

The package of measures introduced in 1989 helped to reduce inflation to 35 per cent in 1989. The initial success was not sustained because of the inability of the government to control money supply growth given the weak fiscal base and the need to avert a collapse in the real economy.

In 1991, as the full effects of the decline in trade with the CMEA countries took hold, there was a significant decline in both exports and imports. The avoidance of a decline in real GDP at that time (GDP grew 5.8 per cent in 1991) was an indication of government policy success, although price stabilisation had not yet been achieved. Inflation again rose to 67 per cent in 1990 and 1991, before the government again tightened monetary policy and the real economy expanded, bringing inflation back down below 20 per cent. Since 1992, inflation has remained below 15 per cent.

The critical factor influencing economic performance was a vigorous response in real output to the early reform efforts. The cumulative effects of the land reforms, liberalisation of domestic trade, price reforms, including an increasingly realistic foreign exchange regime, and greater macroeconomic stability, stimulated a strong supply response. In 1992, both agricultural and industrial output expanded rapidly. As crude oil exports expanded, the decline in exports was reversed and imports could be increased. The economy turned the corner with little external assistance.

ACHIEVEMENT OF RAPID GROWTH: 1993–97

During the first half of the 1990s, the Vietnamese economy moved from economic crisis to buoyant growth. This was sustained until the East Asian economic crisis began to impact on Viet Nam in 1998. Real GDP growth rose to an annual rate of 8 per cent in 1992, and stayed at 8–9 per cent through 1997. Increasing supply and prudent government financial policies ensured inflation was kept under tight control from 1992.

An important qualitative aspect of the economic performance was that growth extended to all sectors, with relatively strong growth in agriculture making an important contribution to overall growth. While, in a statistical sense, the industrial sector led GDP growth, expanding at an average annual rate 13–14 per cent per annum in each year 1993–97, the growth rate in agriculture in the range 3.5–5 per cent per annum in each year over the same period was also impressive compared with long-term historical trends and international experience. Agriculture still had sufficient weight in the economy (in 1994, it still accounted for 27 per cent of GDP) that lively growth in agricultural output was an irreplaceable component of the high overall growth. The high rate of agricultural growth ensured national food security, which had been at question in the 1980s, but also contributed substantially to exports and ameliorated the widening gap between urban and rural incomes (Table 12.1).

In this period, the inflow of external finance became more important. Foreign direct investment rose to US$832 million in 1993, US$1,048 million in 1994 and US$2,074 million in 1997. During that period, Viet Nam participated in the boom in East Asian investment. Aid flows built up more slowly and during the 1993–1997 period remained of minor importance in overall development financing compared to the flows of private investment.

Table 12.1   **Annual growth rates, 1994–2000[a]**

Year	Inflation	GDP[b]	Industrial output	Exports	Non-oil exports
1995	12.7	9.5	14.5	28.2	30.9
1996	4.5	9.3	14.2	41.1	43.5
1997	3.6	8.2	13.8	24.6	28.9
1998	9.2	5.8	12.5	2.4	5.3
1999	0.1	4.8	11.6	23.2	16.2
2000	-0.6	6.8	17.5	25.2	15.9
2001 est.	0.8	6.8	14.2	3.8	12.5[c]

Notes: [a] The IMF report from which the data in this table are abstracted also presents IMF staff estimates that give a lower GDP growth rate for 1997–2000 apparently mainly because the IMF staff estimate growth rates for services significantly below official estimates. IMF staff estimates show the service sector growing less than 1 per cent 1998–99—considerably below the GDP growth rate and even below population growth. Official government estimates show services growing below the GDP growth rate and as such seem reasonable enough. On balance, the government estimates appear more plausible.
[b] Constant 1994 prices. [c] Growth during the first 10 months of 2001.
Source: Official government estimates as presented in International Monetary Fund, 2002. *Vietnam: selected issues and statistical appendix*, Country Report 02/5, International Monetary Fund, Washington, DC.

PROXIMATE SOURCE OF SUCCESS: EXPORT-LED GROWTH

The obvious and immediate engine of growth was the expansion in exports. Between 1989 and 1997 the dollar value of Vietnamese exports rose seven-fold. This high export growth rate had a pervasive influence. It generated fast income growth. In the agricultural sector, it sustained a growth rate in excess of the expansion of the domestic food market. Rapidly increasing export earnings, supplemented by capital inflows, generated the foreign exchange needed to fund imports, including capital goods. Entry into new branches of trade stimulated technical transfer and innovation. Buoyant foreign exchange earnings made it easier to liberalise the foreign exchange regime and protection levels.

Underpinning the early growth in exports were
- the initiation and subsequent growth of petroleum exports
- agricultural expansion, which both ensured food supply and made a significant contribution to export growth
- a rapid expansion of seafood and aquaculture exports during the 1980s and 1990s
- a diversification of agricultural exports to coffee, tea, cashews, pepper, cinnamon, rubber, fruit and vegetables, especially during the mid to late 1990s
- a rapid expansion of exports of garments and footwear throughout the 1990s so that by the middle of the decade they accounted for a large share of exports
- a steady expansion of handicraft exports (fine arts, pottery, glassware and embroidery) and wood products
- the emergence of electronic equipment as a fast growing export by the end of the decade (exports of electronic equipment declined in 2001 in line with the sharp rise in international demand for electronic products).

Geographic proximity to high income, and/or rapidly growing, Asian economies has also been important as these countries are the major markets for Vietnamese exports. Japan was the major market for Vietnamese exports in 2001, followed by China, Australia, Singapore and the United States.

An important characteristic of the export performance has been its diversity. The initiation of the export of crude oil at the beginning of the decade was important, as it helped fill the foreign exchange gap resulting from the end of aid from, and the decline in trade with, the CMEA. Crude oil exports expanded

Figure 12.2   **Export growth in selected Asian economies, 1986–2000**

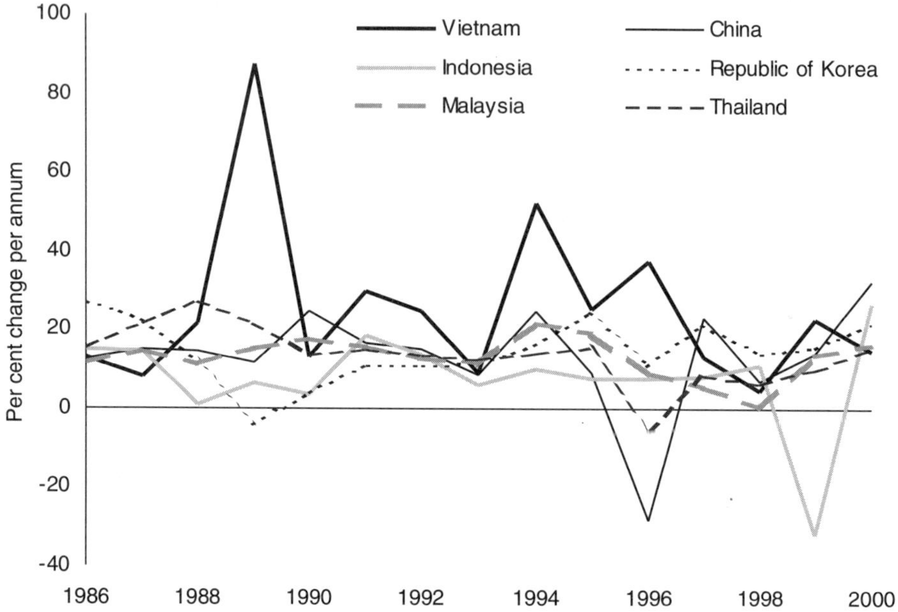

Sources: World Bank, 2002. *World Development Indicators*, World Bank, Washington, DC; General Statistical Office (for Viet Nam data, 1986–89).

from US$79 million in 1988, to US$756 million in 1992. By 1995, petroleum exports topped US$1 billion per annum, one-fifth of total exports (Table 12.2).

In the subsequent period (1996–97), petroleum exports continued to grow, but fell as a share of total exports, as agricultural and light industrial exports grew at high rates. 1998 saw a continuing increase in the quantity of oil exports, but a decline in their value as a result of sharp price declines, thus compounding the problem of generally flat export growth following the onset of the East Asian crisis. During 1999–2000, fast expansion in the quantity and value of oil exports contributed to the export growth of more than 20 per cent per annum.

In one sense, the presence of crude oil is an exogenous factor, although its exploitation did require complex negotiations with foreign partners and the encouragement of foreign private and state investment. However, while the gains from mineral exploitation can be interpreted as a windfall, the international record demonstrates that the uses made of such windfalls can vary quite widely—

Table 12.2 Export performance, by main commodity, 1988–2000 (US$ million)

	1988	1989	1990	1991	1992	1993	1994	1995	1996	1997	1998	1999	2000[a]
Selected items													
Crude oil	79	200	390	581	756	844	866	1,024	1,346	1,423	1,232	2,092	3,503
Rice	-	317	272	225	300	363	425	496	855	870	1,020	1,025	667
Marine products	124	133	220	285	302	427	551	431	551	762	858	974	1,479
Garments	..	..	..	..	190	239	476	431	1,150	1,503	1,450	1,746	1,892
Footwear	..	..	..	..	5	68	122	200	531	978	1,031	1,387	1,465
Rubber	17	27	29	50	54	74	133	159	163	191	127	146	166
Electronics	..	..	..	..	..	..	..	..	..	440	497	585	783
Total	733	1,320	1,731	2,042	2,475	2,985	4,054	5,198	7,337	9,145	9,365	11543	14,449

Note: [a] Estimate

Sources: For 1988–91, International Monetary Fund 1994. *Vietnam: recent economic developments*, International Monetary Fund, Washington, DC. For 1992–94, International Monetary Fund, 1998. *Vietnam: selected issues and statistical annex*, International Monetary Fund, Washington, DC. For 1995–2000, International Monetary Fund, 2002. *Vietnam: selected issues and statistical appendix*, International Monetary Fund, Washington, DC.

there are plenty of examples of mineral booms having little sustained development impact, or generating 'Dutch disease' problems.[3]

In the event, during the 1990s Viet Nam avoided 'Dutch disease' effects. Despite the usefulness of the oil revenues, the growth in oil production never resulted in the export economy becoming dominated by oil, at the expense of other exports. Non-oil exports expanded alongside the oil industry. This can be contrasted, for example, with the experience of Nigeria (with roughly the same per capita income level as Vietnam), where the rapid expansion in oil revenues was associated with a decline in the competitiveness and levels of traditional exports.

The surge in rice production, which resolved the national food security problem, also supported the swift growth of Viet Nam to the front ranks of the international rice trade, making Viet Nam one of the big three rice exporters (along with the United States and Thailand). By 1999, rice exports peaked at 4.5 million tons. In the first half of the decade, grain production increased by about 1 million tons each year, with more than 3 million tons of rice becoming available for export by 1996, a significant contribution to the rapid growth in total exports. Efforts are currently being concentrated on improving the quality of rice exports.

In addition to the early success with rice exports, an important and sustained contribution also came from other agricultural and marine products. Although the collapse of the CMEA trading bloc in 1991 had a negative impact on exports of industrial ('cash') crops, Viet Nam quickly developed other markets for such crops as coffee, cashews, rubber and tea, and more recently fruit and vegetables.

Successful expansion of agricultural exports was a direct benefit of *Doi Moi*. Policy reforms had strengthened incentives. Production of food, industrial crops, livestock, fishing, and aquaculture products all grew at very high rates, responding to price and land reforms, investment of time in accessing new ideas and seeds, investment in terms of income foregone while coffee plants were maturing, and limited investments in post-harvest facilities.

Expansion in some tree crops (particularly rubber) also initially reflected a return from state farm investments in the 1980s, and then was increasingly supported by the fast growth in private (smallholder) production. In minor export crops, such as cashews and pepper, Viet Nam has moved from negligible production to being a major player in world markets. Exports of marine and aquatic products (for example, shrimp, fish, cuttlefish and crab) have also grown at a very high rate, topping US$1 billion for the first time in 2000.

During the 1990s, Viet Nam was particularly successful in expanding coffee production, displacing Indonesia as the world's third largest producer in 1999 (after Brazil and Colombia) and then overtaking Colombia in 2001 with coffee exports totalling 931,200 tons.

Viet Nam's experience with coffee has also demonstrated the potential risks involved in primary commodity exporting. Starting as a small producer, Viet Nam was initially a price-taker, responding to prices determined in international markets, to which its own contribution was still minor. While a small supplier, Viet Nam was subject to the fluctuations in the international coffee market, but could still expand production without having to take into account the impact of its own output on prices. That changed, however, as Viet Nam became a big enough player in the world coffee market for its own contribution to have a significant impact on world supply and as such contribute to price instability. As a result, benefits from the dramatic increase in coffee production have been offset by the fall in coffee prices on international markets to historic lows in real terms. As a result, coffee production and exports are expected to fall in 2002.

The key to ongoing export success is to move on to new products when Viet Nam's share in a given world product rises to a level at which it cannot expect to expand its sales by further increasing market share. This has been possible to some degree by diversification within the agricultural export sector, but further expansion will increasingly have to be based on growth in industrial exports.

In this regard, an important feature of Viet Nam's export performance has been the diversification into industrial exports. As Western and Asian markets replaced traditional trade with the CMEA at the beginning of the 1990s, light manufacturing exports expanded, reflecting the re-orientation of existing state-owned light manufacturing firms to the requirements of new markets and the increasing contribution of private foreign direct investment. Clothing and textile exports topped US$1 billion in 1996 and footwear did likewise in 1998. Contributions to this growth came from adjustment to new market opportunities by existing state enterprises and direct foreign investment (including joint ventures with state firms). There was a good deal of regional interest in the possibilities for using Viet Nam, with its low labour costs, as an export platform at a time when boom conditions in other East Asian economies were pushing them into other stages of the export product cycle. Many buyers from the region came to Viet Nam and, sensing opportunities, provided basic inputs (raw materials), know-how and equipment in return for future production. Much of this indirect foreign investment never appeared in official statistics as foreign investment.

Despite the strong export diversification and growth, the IMF (1999:59), citing 'pervasive NTBs and relatively high tariffs', judged Viet Nam's trade system as 'one of the most restrictive of Fund members' at the end of the 1990s. Other external observers have argued that Viet Nam has adopted import substitution policies that place undue emphasis on protecting capital-intensive industry (and state enterprises) and have restricted trade in areas where the country has greatest comparative advantage.[4] The private sector has, until recently, has been restricted in directly engaging in trade (other than for goods produced by that firm).

Nevertheless, export growth has been extraordinarily high and, with the exception of oil, most of this has involved the export of labour-intensive agricultural and light manufacturing products. Jenkins (2002) reports that the share of manufactured industrial goods increased from 14 per cent of exports in 1991 to 37 per cent in 1999 and that, if processed agriculture products are included, 'manufacturing accounts for two-thirds of exports in 1999'. Jenkins estimated that the employment impacts of recent trade developments have been positive and that, while there 'were some industries where import substitution occurred, most notably motor vehicles and other transport equipment...in most industries the share of imports in domestic demand increased'.[5] He estimated that the share of imports in domestic demand for manufactured goods increased from 56 per cent in 1995 to 61 per cent in 1999.

The degree to which the Vietnamese economy opened up during the 1990s is illustrated in Figure 12.3, which shows comparative data for trade turnover as a percentage of GDP for selected Asian economies. Viet Nam has transformed from a closed economy, with a very low ratio of trade to GDP, to an economy with total trade turnover greater than annual GDP. This ratio is high compared with the Philippines or Indonesia, is on a par with Thailand, but is considerably lower than that of Malaysia.[6]

Figure 12.3   **Total trade turnover in selected Asian economies, 1986–2000 (per cent of GDP)**

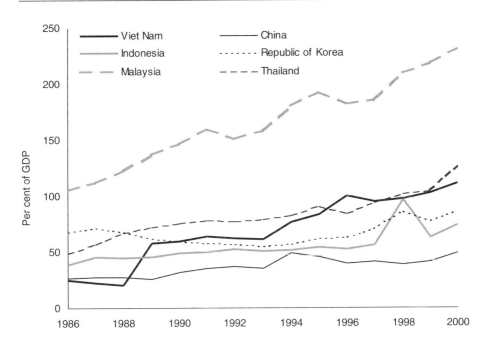

Source: World Bank, 2002. *World Development Indicators*, World Bank, Washington, DC; General Statistical Office.

GROWTH FOLLOWING THE EAST ASIAN CRISIS OF 1997

The reverse side of the benefits flowing from successful integration into the global economy is vulnerability to external shocks. Given the role played by the fast growth of foreign investment and exports in fuelling the 1993–97 expansion, it was inevitable that Viet Nam would be vulnerable to downturns in the regional and global economies. With the onset of the East Asian economic crisis, growth in the economy slowed and foreign direct investment declined sharply.

Nevertheless, the economy exhibited a degree of resilience in the face of the East Asian crisis of 1997. Viet Nam performed better than many other economies in the region (Korea, Malaysia, Indonesia, Thailand, Philippines and Singapore have all experienced one or more years of output decline since 1997) and better than most observers (including the government) expected.

The Vietnamese economy weathered the East Asian crisis rather well, and per capita incomes continued to increase, albeit at a reduced rate. The downturn in the world economy in 2001 has had an additional negative impact, resulting in low export growth and overall economic growth lower than long-term plan targets.

A number of factors contributed to the resilience of the Vietnamese economy. The diversified export base helped. Although export growth fell to less than 3 per cent in 1998, exports returned to double digit growth rates in 1999 and 2000. This was partly the result of the buoyancy of petroleum exports, but also because of the fast expansion of footwear, garments and marine products, as capacity created in the earlier period came into use.

One way the East Asian crisis seriously impacted on Viet Nam was through the sharp decline in foreign investment. Regional investors had played a leading role in the build-up of foreign direct investment. After 1997, foreign direct investment declined and the government slowed down planned public investment. The downward pressures on capital formation were partly offset by increased domestic private investment, which became increasingly important in the post-1997 economy. There was a rise in the domestic rates of savings and investment, and foreign aid flows continued to accumulate, reflecting with a lag the rapid growth of commitments following the ending of the US embargo in 1993.

Somewhat ironically, Viet Nam also benefited from the slow pace of reform of the financial sector. Foreign banks had been allowed to open branches, but domestic capital markets were only at a very early stage of development. Most international private financial flows were to finance foreign direct investment. There was little portfolio investment or external flows into the banking system or local financial markets. Although there was an element of speculative boom before 1998 (particularly in relation to foreign investments in the real estate sector), there had been no financial bubble fuelled by international financial flows and expansion in bank credit, as experienced elsewhere in the region, and by the same token there was no speculative shock as the bubble burst.

In general, the play of market forces has the maximum positive impact in periods of international economic expansion. During periods of economic crisis, the political case for moderating the effects of the market becomes more

Figure 12.4   Growth rates in selected Asian countries, 1986–2001

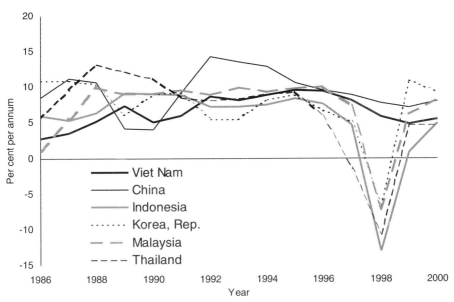

Source: World Bank, 2002. *World Development Indicators*, World Bank, Washington, DC.

Table 12.3   Growth rates in selected Asian economies, 1996–2001

	1996	1997	1998	1999	2000	2001
China	7.7	7.0	1.8	7.6	8.3	3.9
Hong Kong	9.6	8.8	7.8	7.1	8.0	7.3
South Korea	6.8	5.0	−5.3	3.0	10.5	0.1
Taiwan	6.1	6.7	4.6	5.4	5.9	−1.9
Indonesia	3.5	3.7	1.5	6.9	5.4	5.3
Malaysia	10.0	7.3	−7.4	6.1	8.3	0.4
Philippines	5.8	5.2	−0.6	3.4	4.0	3.4
Singapore	7.7	8.5	0.0	6.9	10.3	−2.0
Thailand	5.9	−1.4	−10.8	4.4	4.6	1.8

Note: Asian Development Bank, World Bank and Government of Vietnam estimates of growth are not always consistent.

Source: Asian Development Bank, 2002. *Asian Development Outlook*, Asian Development Bank, Manila.

persuasive. In some cases (for example, contemporary United States), this may strengthen the case of domestic interest groups arguing for trade protection. In the case of Viet Nam, it could be argued that the continued importance of the state investment, and the measured pace of enterprise and financial reforms, may have provided an element of countercyclical stability in a period of international economic difficulty. However, the slowdown in the international economy did not result in any lessening of the pace of reform. Indeed, the slowing of the pace of foreign investment appears to have contributed to an increasing focus on the importance of the domestic private sector.

SECTORAL DEVELOPMENTS: AGRICULTURAL POLICIES AND AGRICULTURAL GROWTH

The importance of agricultural growth

A central pillar of Viet Nam's success in the late 1980s and 1990s was the sustained high rate of agricultural growth. This was of crucial importance for a number of reasons. Growth in agricultural exports made an important contribution to export growth. In 1995, agricultural, forest and aquatic products accounted for 46 per cent of total exports. Although that figure dropped to 33 per cent by 1999, over that period the increase in agricultural, forest and aquatic exports of US$1,253 billion accounted for one-fifth of total export increase,

In the simplest statistical terms, given the relative importance of agriculture, the achievement of high rates of overall growth would have been unlikely without a buoyant agricultural sector. Buoyant agricultural growth has also generated non-agricultural rural employment opportunities in services, input supply and food processing industries.

Even more important, the successes in reducing poverty were only possible with significant growth in rural incomes. Rice is not only the main product of Vietnamese agriculture and the dominant food staple, but also provides the basic income source for a large segment of the population of poorer farmers. Data from the 1992–93 and 1997–98 Viet Nam Living Standards Surveys indicate that four-fifths of households in the lowest income quintile were occupied in agriculture, a proportion that has remained stable. For the highest quintile of households, 34 per cent were engaged in agriculture in 1992–93, a figure that dropped to 19 per cent in 1997–98. The 1992–93 survey also indicated that almost three-fifths of the per capita income of people in the

Figure 12.5 **FDI inflows in selected Asian countries, 1986–2000 (per cent of GDP)**

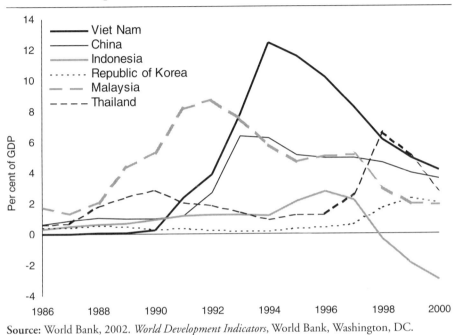

Source: World Bank, 2002. *World Development Indicators*, World Bank, Washington, DC.

lowest expenditure quintile were generated by agricultural activities, compared to less than one-fourth for the highest quintile.[7] The reverse was true for income generated through non-agricultural self-employment activities. These activities accounted for 15 per cent and 52 per cent of total per capita income for the lowest and highest quintiles, respectively. For all quintiles, the income from wage labour activities was around 20 per cent.

Nutritional standards were low in the 1980s, and output increases of nearly 2 per cent per annum were necessary just to match population growth. The growth in food production was therefore an essential condition for economic and social progress for the mass of the population. The boost in rural incomes meant that despite a widening gap between urban and rural incomes, which could be expected to act to pull population from rural to urban areas, the push factor encouraging people to leave the countryside was limited and migration was as much from one rural area to another as from countryside to city. That limited the pressure for heavy expenditures on urban development.

Perhaps most important, the success of the agricultural sector relaxed the pressures and anxieties of ensuring national food security. In the mid 1980s, Viet Nam had been faced with the need to import substantial quantities of food. Fluctuations in the rice harvest, at a time when the external financial situation was precarious, had placed national food security in question, resulting in incidents of widespread near-famine. The growth in rice output was therefore a key component of Viet Nam's economic success. In the 1980s, food shortages resulted in widespread suffering and national food security was a leading preoccupation. The shift from food shortages to being a leading grain exporter was important both economically and politically.

Total rice production did not meet domestic demand up to 1988, necessitating imports of 700,000 to 1,600,000 tonnes annually. From being a net importer of rice, Viet Nam became self-sufficient and then a net exporter of rice. By 1992, staple food production was 24.2 million tonnes (paddy equivalent), of which paddy was 21.6 million tonnes, while 1.95 million tonnes of rice were exported. Food output continued to grow, and total grain production rose to 26.2 million tonnes paddy equivalent in 1994 and an estimated 27.4 million tonnes in 1995. Rice exports were an estimated 2 million tonnes in 1994 and 1995. The growth in food production was sustained throughout the decade. In 2000, despite floods in the southern and central regions and drought in the north, food output reached 35.6 million tonnes (paddy equivalent), up 1.4 million tonnes from 1999, including 32.6 million tonnes of paddy.

Over the longer term the existence of a large exportable rice surplus provides a cushion whereby the impact of fluctuations in production on domestic supply can be limited.

Determinants of agricultural growth

The Vietnamese reform process began with reforms in the agricultural sector in 1985. The process of change since then has involved continuous modification to polices and institutional arrangements, which often involved the government acting to accommodate spontaneous changes in grassroots activities. Given the timing of the reforms and the subsequent acceleration in growth there can be no question that the move to a more decentralised, market orientated system of agricultural production was a decisive factor in promoting agricultural growth. McCarty (2001) shows the impact of key policy changes on food grain output (and the ratio of paddy to other cereals) since 1975.

Figure 12.6   **Per capita food production in Viet Nam, 1975–88**

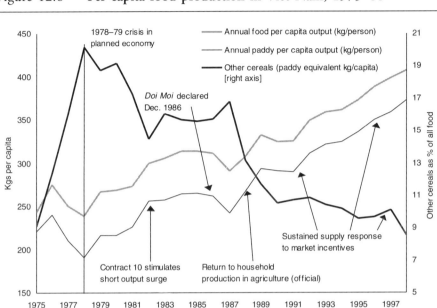

Source: McCarty, A., 2001. Governance Institutions and Incentive Structures in Vietnam, paper presented at Building Institutional Capacity in Asia (BICA) conference, Jakarta, 12 March 2001. Available at www.riap.usyd.edu.au/bica/2001/confpaper.htm.

The basic unit for agricultural production in Viet Nam is the family farm. There are some 10 million agricultural households. State farms are restricted to about 4 per cent of Viet Nam's agricultural land and concentrate on the production of industrial crops, such as rubber, and food crops, such as sugar, where there are considerable economies of scale in production.

Even during the period of tight state control of agriculture, the family holding had remained at the base of the system, although subject to considerable control from the cooperative. Following the reforms of the 1980s, the family farm became even more important as the basic production unit. Cooperatives continued to control access to land and water and the farmer bartered a portion of the farm output with the cooperative for input and services supplied.

The role of the cooperative declined particularly rapidly in the south, but in some areas (particularly in the north and centre of the country) the cooperatives were able to retain a strong position as a supplier of inputs to individual households. The household controlled production decisions and the surplus left after meeting various obligations to the cooperatives and to local authorities (which can be onerous). The private sector has become increasingly involved in the marketing and transport of agricultural output. [8]

Reforms affected all aspects of rural economic life. The development of the household farming unit as the core of rural production determined the nature of the rural economic system. The growth of the private trading and transport system has resulted in a competitive, low cost and innovative rural trading system in most parts of the country.

The land area used for paddy production increased through the extension of multiple rice cropping. Although the wet season paddy area declined marginally (4 per cent) between 1987–92, the area planted for the winter–spring crop increased by 24 per cent, and the summer–autumn crop by 59 per cent, over the same period (World Bank 1994b). Che (1997) provided estimates of factors contributing to increased rice output (Table 12.4).

After the initial gains achieved following the agricultural reforms and the resulting increase in farmer incentives, many external observers were somewhat pessimistic about the potential for continued output growth.[9] Typical of international opinion was the conclusion of the World Bank 1994 study of agricultural marketing that

> …in the absence of substantial new investments in irrigation and drainage, in the mid 1990s yields are likely to peak at 3.4 tonnes per hectare, multiple cropping increases will slow, and total production of paddy will level off at around 23 million tonnes. Even with new investments (given the time required to complete systems), for the next years, production growth may decelerate to average 1.9 per cent per annum over the decade (World Bank 1994a:23).

Table 12.4 **Average annual growth rates in paddy output and inputs, 1976–94**

Period	Output	Labour	Land	Materials	Capital	TFP[a]
1976–80	0.4	0.4	-0.8	-1.1	2.2	0.6
1981–87	4.2	0.3	-1.2	3.3	1.7	3.3
1988–94	6.1	1.3	-0.5	5.6	10.6	3.1

Note: [a] TFP is total factor productivity calculated as Solow Residuals.
Source: Che, Nhu, 1997. The Effects of Internal and External Trade Liberalisation on Agriculture Growth: a case study of Viet Nam, PhD Dissertation, The Australian National University, Canberra.

However, it was not solely the 'magic of the market' that resulted in sustained agricultural growth. No doubt the flexibility and improved incentives resulting from market reforms was the most important force in the growth process, but sustained growth in smallholder agriculture also required the support of effective infrastructure and services, particularly in the provision of irrigation and transport, the promotion of new crops and the supply of improved inputs.

An important component of success was that, alongside the market reforms, the state organisations responsible for infrastructure have operated effectively, and state-owned enterprises responsible for servicing the agricultural sector have in many instances adjusted to the complexities of the new economic environment. Although private firms are now playing an increasingly important role in promoting innovation (for example, introduction of hybrid maize and horticulture seeds), state organisations also played an important role in promoting new crops and cultivation methods, for example, by introducing such crops as cashew in the 1980s, promoting the massive development of coffee in the Central Highlands and supporting the introduction of new varieties of paddy. With the introduction of new varieties and improved cultivation methods, yields have risen significantly

The state was also important in maintaining and expanding infrastructure. Important investments included rehabilitation of the storm protection system and rehabilitation of the transport network. Investments in irrigation have facilitated multiple cropping. The Vietnamese government has also repeatedly demonstrated a high level of commitment and effectiveness in disaster management—Viet Nam is subject to frequent climatic disasters, but often manages relief efforts with only modest international support.

It is not entirely clear how the combination of state support, development of private marketing and processing and household agriculture has worked. In a general sense, the basis of success seems to be that market liberalisation has been accompanied by a reasonable level of state capacity in providing the support required by farmers. There is merit in criticisms that the system is sub-optimal, there is plenty of evidence that many state organisations are not very efficient, and no doubt that further reforms in state-owned and run rural delivery systems are needed. The achievement of sustained agricultural growth nevertheless suggests that a reasonable level of effectiveness was achieved. In particular, continued output growth beyond the initial gains from market reform confounded the predictions of knowledgeable observers that growth was expected to slow in the early 1990s.

During the reform period many state research and service institutions suffered from financial distress, sometimes resulting in a diversion of energies from their main task. The references in consulting reports—and in official government and Party pronouncements—to the inefficiency of state enterprises are legion. Nevertheless, the system has worked well enough, often through a mixture of pragmatic response by state institutions in competition with each other, accommodating newly emerging private firms, cooperating with foreign businesses and, in some notable cases, demonstrating a continuing professional commitment to research and advisory work

One distinguishing characteristic of the system is the high degree to which all organisations generate revenues from cash transactions, even government departments funded by the state budget. This means that, even when the state budget is unable to fund activities or pay reasonable salaries, agencies often take initiative in seeking cash through the sale of their services. The pervasive practice of boosting incomes through one form or another of fringe payment is obviously open to abuse, but as a transitional mechanism it has worked well enough in keeping many institutions in operation despite stringencies in official budget allocations.

Thus Vietnamese agricultural growth has succeeded both as a result of market reforms providing incentives to the farmer and through continued public provision of infrastructure, including extensive efforts to rehabilitate irrigation systems and improve the transport network, and a pragmatic and rather *ad hoc* approach to the reform of the system of input provision and technical support.

One area in particular which requires better documentation is the process whereby innovations in rural production are introduced. Observed performance suggests that in the agriculture sector there has been a successful combination of state-sponsored change and farmer response, but a more detailed analysis is required.

In the longer term, sustained agricultural growth will require large infrastructure investment, especially in water management and transport infrastructure, the strengthening of research, extension and other agricultural support services and encouragement of competition in the agricultural trading system. And, as successful export growth has increased the integration of

Box 12.1   **The seed sub-sector**

An example of the mixture of public service and private provision supporting agricultural growth can be drawn from the seed sub-sector. Improvements in seed varieties and seed quality have accounted for an estimated 15–20 per cent of the increases in crop yields. Before *Doi Moi*, the seed sector was in principle tightly organised into four distinct administrative levels

- the central level (research, production of pre-basic seed—national seed companies)
- the provincial level (production of basic seed—provincial seed agencies)
- the district level (production of first generation certified seed by seed stations)
- the local level (multiplication of seeds by specialised brigades in the cooperatives).

Since the introduction of *Doi Moi*, the whole process of seed multiplication and distribution has been liberalised *de facto*, so that all economic sectors, including state-owned enterprises, private companies, farmers' groups and farmer households participate actively. The resulting system is somewhat chaotic but has distinctly positive characteristics. The industry now comprises a large number of different agencies. At the base, the farm household has a choice as to which seed will be used, while the cooperatives are no longer organised to produce seed in the same way as under the pre-reform system.

Formal agencies include two state-owned national seed companies, one each in the North and South, under the umbrella of the Ministry of Agriculture and Rural Development Provincial Seed Agencies (PSA) comprising Provincial Seed Companies (in the North and Central regions) and Seed Centres (in the Southern region) owned by the provincial governments; a number of government research and breeding institutions, responsible for research and development, which also produce and sell seed directly to farmers and a few private companies, mainly based on foreign direct investment, which produce and/or import and sell hybrid cereal seed and vegetable seed to farmers.

Competition in the seed market has increased. A PSA typically faces competition for its open pollinated varieties from seed companies in the neighbouring provinces, one or both of the national seed companies, the agents of government research and breeding institutions, cooperatives and farmers' groups. In the market for vegetable and hybrid maize seed, there is competition from other state-owned enterprises, private seed producing companies and importers. In a number of cases, the PSA cooperates with private companies and serve as their 'sales agents', buying and selling hybrid and vegetable seed with an attractive margin. The formal seed industry only supplies a small fraction of the open pollinated varieties used for paddy production, but hybrid seed, mainly promoted in the North,[10] is necessarily produced through the formal system.

The market for hybrid grain seed is increasing rapidly, even in the formal sector the emerging institutional structure seems quite complex. Almost all the higher level research, university and breeding institutions, which might have been expected to specialise in the pre-basic and prior levels of activity, engage in some activities supplying seed directly to the market. While this provides the higher level research and breeding facilities with income to support their activities and keeps them directly in touch with the needs of farmers, it is probably sub-optimal because by-passing the intermediate stages results in pre-basic seed not being reproduced through the seed production chain to extend the benefits of improved seed more widely.

Vietnamese agriculture into international markets, fluctuations and downward trends in export prices will have an impact in terms of changing product mixes, increasing export quality, opening up new markets and introducing new crops.

INDUSTRIAL GROWTH

As may be expected at this stage of Viet Nam's development, the industrial sector has grown much more rapidly than agriculture. Despite the high rate of agricultural growth, agriculture's share of total economic activity has been declining over the last ten years. This is a typical feature of successful growth, whereby somewhat paradoxically agricultural expansion helps sustain a high rate of overall growth, which in turn results in a declining share of agriculture in total production. Thus, although the great success in food production and agricultural exports were key factors in Vietnam's successful growth performance, agriculture's contribution (including forestry) to GDP fell to an estimated 25.4 per cent of GDP in 1999, down from 38.7 per cent in 1990. The high rate of industrial growth achieved during the 1990s was another key factor contributing to the overall growth achievement.

Industrial value added (GDP at constant prices) declined in the difficult transitional year of 1989. The recovery was fast, however, and industry and construction achieved 13 per cent growth in 1992 and subsequently sustained growth at above 10 per cent per annum (except for 1998 and 1999, when, under the impact of the East Asian crisis, industrial growth fell back to 8 per cent per annum). Although the structure of GDP has shifted towards industry, the proportion of the labour force working in industry and construction has not increased, remaining in the range of 12–13 per cent of the labour force.

Developments in the industrial sector have been complex. The larger (mainly national level) state enterprises continued to make substantial investments in heavy industries, such as cement and steel, often as a joint partner with foreign firms. Government rhetoric remained committed to the idea of a heavy industrialisation strategy as being essential to development. Arguably this had led to over-investment in some sectors (for example, over-investment in coal and cement during the 1995–2000 Five-Year Plan) and output expansion in some activities which may be difficult to sustain in the context of commitments to open trade under the the ASEAN Free Trade Area (AFTA) Common Effective Preferential Trade scheme and the US–Viet Nam bilateral trade agreement.

Table 12.5   **Industrial output, 1985–2001 (VND billion)**

Year	Total output	Domestic	FDI[a]	Growth rate in total output[b]
Constant 1982 prices				
1985	103.3	..	..	109.9
1986	109.6	..	..	106.1
1987	120.6	..	..	110.0
1988	137.8	..	..	114.3
1989	133.4	..	..	96.8
1990	137.5	..	..	103.1
Constant 1989 prices				
1990	15,361	14,011	1,350	103.1
1991	17,437	15,471	1,966	110.4
1992	20,876	18,117	2,759	117.1
1993	23,547	20,412	3,135	112.7
1994	26,751	23,214	3,537	113.7
1995	30,431	26,584	3,847	114.5
Constant 1994 prices				
1995	103,375	77,442	25,933	114.5
1996	118,097	86,535	31,562	114.2
1997	134,420	95,542	38,878	113.8
1998	151,223	102,865	48,358	112.5
1999	168,749	110,235	58,514	111.6
2000	198,326	125,910	71,285	117.5
2001 (prel.)	226,406	125,910	79,908	114.2

Note: [a] FDI output is output by 'foreign invested firms' which includes output by joint enterprises.
[b] Previous year=100.
Source: General Statistics Office, 2001. *Statistical Yearbook 2001*, Statistical Publishing House, Hanoi, General Statistics Office, 2000. *Statistical Data of Viet Nam Socio-Economy 1975–2000*, Statistical Publishing House, Hanoi.

An important part of state-owned industry is made up of light industry and small and medium-sized enterprises. Some have decayed under pressure from increased competition and reduced subsidisation, but a number were successful in finding new export markets, particularly in cooperation with foreign investors.

Implementation of the state investment program contributed to the high rate of industrial growth. While some state industrial investments resulted in the production of goods that were able to compete in home and export markets, it also resulted in a significant element of over-investment in some industries and pressures to protect inefficient domestic producers from low-cost imports (for example, sugar).

There was also some foreign investment in excess capacity in classic import substitution activities, such as vehicle assembly, but that was a small part of the total investment in the industrial sector. There was no across-the-board emphasis on import substitution of consumer goods behind tariff barriers.

The trend in protection has been downwards. A wide range of cheap imported goods has been available in Vietnam, even in the early stages of the *Doi Moi* process. Quite apart from adjustments to the tariff regime which have been implemented under *Doi Moi*, the efficiency of Vietnamese smugglers places a limit on the degree of protection that can be offered to domestic industry. For many consumer goods it is difficult if not impossible to suppress smuggling, because of the long borders and the proximity of low cost producers (most notably China).

Industrial production therefore was under pressure to compete with imported goods, and in many areas there was lively competition between domestic producers even within the state-owned sector. In key areas of continuing public monopoly, the picture has been more mixed. In telecommunications, for example, great strides were made in the early 1990s in transforming the external telecommunications system, which had been dependent on antiquated lines of communication through Moscow. Considerable progress was also made in increasing the coverage and density of the internal telecommunications system. Despite the considerable technical improvements, however, international services remained expensive by international comparative standards, with the benefits of technical improvements only being slowly passed on to customers through price reductions. High communications costs act as a brake on Viet Nam's ambitions to increase its participation in the information technology market in the next stage of its development.

Likewise, although there have been large investments to ensure that power provision has kept up with the demand generated by the rapid economic growth, power rates have risen because of the need to generate substantial cash flows to contribute to the investment costs of further expansion.[11]

Industry was also a focus of interest for expanding private foreign investment.[12] A Foreign Investment Law had been promulgated as early as 1987, opening up opportunities for foreign direct investment. A major part of the foreign investment was through the vehicle of joint ventures with state-owned enterprises.[13]

Output from foreign-invested enterprises increased from negligible levels to more than one-quarter of total industrial output by 1995, and continues to grow more quickly than state sector ouput, accounting for 35.5 per cent of total industrial production in 2000 (preliminary estimate). The first major foreign investments were concentrated in the petroleum sector, so that in 1995 about 42 per cent of the output of foreign-invested enterprises was in the mining (mostly oil) sector. The foreign sector still only accounted for about 17 per cent of manufacturing output. By 2000, however, mining activities accounted for only 32 per cent of 'foreign-invested' industrial output, while the foreign sector had grown to account for 30 per cent of total manufacturing output.

An important impetus, particularly for regional investors (notably Singapore, Taiwan, Korea and Malaysia), was to make use of Vietnam's low-wage but reasonably educated workforce, in a period in which the success of their development efforts at home had resulted in increasing wage costs as labour markets tightened and their workforces began to benefit from their growing national incomes. This was particularly so in the boom years before the regional financial crisis in 1997.

Over the 1995–2000 period, foreign-invested firms expanded exports from US$440 million (1995) to US$3,320 million (2000 preliminary), or from 8 per cent to 23 per cent of total exports (32.5 per cent of the increase in total exports came from foreign-invested firms). Thus foreign investment made a significant contribution to the expansion of Vietnamese exports, but did not play the major role. The major component of industrial and export growth was the domestic sector.

To sustain its successful export performance, Viet Nam will have to go on meeting competition from export platforms in the region and further afield. In the short term, if there is a revival in the world economy and a resulting acceleration in international trade, this should not present great difficulties. But, over the longer run, if the Vietnamese labour force is to enjoy the rising incomes which are the objective of development, then the same agility shown in the past decade in adjusting to international market opportunities will have to be applied to raising labour productivity and adjusting the product and export mix to more sophisticated exports, capable of accommodating higher income levels.

NOTES

1. The extent to which administrative constraints were relaxed varied considerably throughout the country depending on the actions of local level administrative authorities.

2. As mentioned in Chapter 7, the program included positive real interest rates, drastic exchange rate adjustment and efforts to contain the state budget.

3. The term 'Dutch disease' was coined to describe the negative consequences of the North Sea natural gas boom for the Netherlands economy. The dangers are that a mineral boom can lead to an exchange rate that is overvalued in relation to the needs of other export sectors and to a 'soft' government budget, with increases in public welfare spending discouraging more productive economic activity.

4. For example, Kokko and Zejan (1996) argued that, 'in spite of the impressive export growth recorded during the first half of the 1990s, it is still appropriate to characterise Viet Nam's development strategy as import substitution'. Kokko et al. (2001) argued that 'lagging growth…was caused by weaknesses in the import substituting parts of the economy'. CIE (1999) cautioned that 'the problem at the moment is that the general thrust of policies is to encourage *inefficient* import substitution'.

5. Rhys Jenkins (2002) argues that '[i]t is clearly not the case that import substitution was a significant factor contributing to slow employment growth in Viet Nam in the second half of the 1990s'.

6. Countries with smaller populations, like Malaysia and Singapore, will typically have a higher ratio of trade turnover to GDP because their smaller scale means they are likely to have a comparative advantage in a more limited range of products. Larger countries, like China, the United States and Indonesia will typically have lower ratios of trade turnover to GDP.

7. Using the 1992–93 survey, a very basic measure of severe poverty was based on the income level estimated to be necessary to sustain consumption of 2,100 calories per day (which was estimated to be the case for incomes equivalent to VND 1.07 million per person per year at 1992–93 prices to cover food and non-food consumption). The poverty line of 2,100 calories for total consumption expenditures, of which 65 per cent was food expenditures, included rice consumption of 171.5 kilograms per person per year, or 263.8 kilograms of paddy (using a conversion factor of 1:0.65). Using that measure, households with incomes below the poverty line (that is, subject to severe poverty) accounted for 51 per cent of the population.

8. In describing a system subject to a continuing process of change, it is difficult to pinpoint the precise nature of the system at any given point in time. This account therefore emphasises the process of change over time without attempting a precise description of the speed and extent of change at any one moment.

9   In personal exchanges with senior agricultural advisers in the early 1990s, the view was expressed that the gains from reform having been reaped, deceleration in growth could be expected.

10 Hybrid rice seed is being introduced from China. The Vietnamese seed industry has begun to develop its own capacity in the complex process of producing hybrid rice seed.

11 In relation to infrastructure investment, many Western commentators, aware of the risks of over-design and excess capacity, and advisors have emphasised caution. Japanese commentators, however, have tended to be much more ambitious in their estimates of investment requirements. By and large, the Japanese advice has proved more appropriate, as the pace of economic growth has been such that lower investment in infrastructure would have resulted in constraints on industrial growth.

12 Initially the biggest concentration of foreign investment was in petroleum; there was also substantial investment in real estate development, including hotels.

13 Which means that the statistical breakdown in earlier statistical series between state and private industrial output (which shows growth in state industrial production outstripping private production) has to be interpreted with some care. In the series now in use, output by the so-called foreign invested sector includes the production of joint enterprises.

13

CAPITAL FORMATION AND EXTERNAL ASSISTANCE

THE ROLE OF INVESTMENT

The role of investment in the Vietnamese growth process may be interpreted as follows. Increases in the rate of capital formation did not initiate the acceleration in growth, and the high rates of growth achieved are not to be explained by the rate of capital formation. Nevertheless, rising rates of capital formation played an important role in the growth process in two important ways.

Once the pace of growth accelerated, increased levels of capital formation were necessary to accommodate the growth in output. For example, without an expanded program of infrastructural investment, output growth would eventually have been constrained by bottlenecks in the transport system, power supply, and so forth.

The inflow of foreign investment was also important as a vehicle for the transfer of technology to Viet Nam, in particular providing the basis for the establishment of a number of new exports. It would be a mistake, however, to interpret growth in the rate of capital formation as leading the overall growth process, as is implied by 'capital–output ratio' type growth models, which assume that an increase in the rate of capital formation will be sufficient to raise the rate of output growth. Moreover, at the critical period for growth acceleration, the factors that increased the productivity of capital were more important than increases in capital formation in contributing to growth.

INVESTMENT PERFORMANCE

After 1992, there was an increase in recorded investment. The ratio of gross capital formation to GDP is estimated to have risen from 15 per cent in 1991 to 25 per cent in 1993–95, continuing in the range of 25–27 per cent in subsequent years (Table 13.1). While this represented a significant acceleration, the investment rate remained well below the very high levels achieved by the East Asian Tigers in their periods of high growth and, for reasons argued in the previous section, does not in itself explain the output growth performance. However, it should also be noted that, even by conventional definitions, official series may underestimate capital formation. Given the rural structure of the economy and the growing importance of household and small enterprise activity, a significant amount of investment was probably not fully recorded.

In addition, aggregate investment figures miss important intangible capital investments. Parente and Prescott (2000) develop a powerful argument that conventional measures of investment greatly underestimate the level of capital formation, even in economies with fairly complete statistical coverage. They argue that the conventional measure of investment in terms of expenditures on new structures and equipment and inventories is misleading, particularly in underestimating the importance of intangible investments (for example, research

Table 13.1 **Gross fixed capital formation, 1991–2001 (per cent of GDP)**

Year	Investment
1991	15.4
1992	18.8
1993	24.5
1994	24.6
1995	25.4
1997	26.7
1998	27.0
1999	25.7
2000	27.7
2001 (preliminary)	28.9

Sources: Ministry of Planning and Investment, 1996. *Public Investment Program 1995–2000*, Ministry of Planning and Investment, Hanoi; and General Statistics Office, 2001. *Statistical Yearbook 2001*, Statistical Publishing House, Hanoi.

and development and software, the organisational capital of firms, investments in individual human and social capital).[1] They conclude that if such factors are taken into account as a general rule 'unmeasured investment is big and could be as much as 50 per cent of GDP and is surely at least 30 per cent of GDP' (Parente and Prescott 2000:47). Increased competition and openness to international information and technology flows can help accelerate growth in such intangible investments (Rodrigo 2000).

This is particularly important in a changing international economic environment where investments in information and know-how are becoming increasingly more important relative to investments in fixed capital. Examples include operations and maintenance (in Viet Nam many resources for the operation and maintenance of public infrastructure are mobilised at a local level and do not even appear in expenditure data). The average life of much physical capital in Viet Nam can be very high because of investments in maintenance and in adapting capital goods to local needs (the long life and wide variety of uses made of small tractors in rural villages is a case in point).

It is estimated that investment during the period 1991–95 totalled VND 206,000 billion, equivalent to US$16–17 billion, of which the state sector accounted for VND 96,000 billion (46.6 per cent).

The sources of investment activity in the period 1995–2000 are shown in Table 13.2. The figures suggest that foreign direct investment made a critical contribution to the surge in investment activity in 1995–97, but was of declining importance following the onset of the East Asian crisis. The period of high rates of foreign direct investment was associated with the period of the highest export growth.

When the relative contribution of foreign investment fell in 1998, state investment accounted for the major share in investment activity. This expansion of state investment is explained by the build up of official development assistance, reflected in the item 'credit' under the state investment category.

By contrast, the figures for domestic non-state investment suggest that the relative importance of the non-state sector is declining, a surprising finding given the evident growth in importance of non-state economic activity followng the *Doi Moi* reforms. There are a number of possible explanations.

One possibility is simply undercounting of non-state investment, particularly by households and small enterprises.[2] It is also likely that investment data exaggerate the relative productive impact of public investment, as it is strongly

Table 13.2 **Investment, by ownership, 1995–2001 (per cent of total investment)**

	1995	1996	1997	1998	1999	2000	2001[a]
State investment	42.0	49.1	49.4	55.5	58.7	57.5	58.1
Domestic non-state investment	27.6	24.9	22.6	23.7	24.0	23.8	23.6
Foreign direct investment	30.4	26.0	28.0	20.8	17.3	18.7	18.3

Note: [a] Preliminary estimate.
Source: General Statistical Office, 2001. *Statistical Yearbook 2001*, Statistical Publishing House, Hanoi.

Table 13.3 **Allocation of state investment, 1995–2001 (per cent of total investment)**

	1995	1996	1997	1998	1999	2000	2001[a]
State budget	44.6	45.6	44.0	40.4	41.3	41.3	42.5
Credit	19.9	19.9	19.3	23.7	28.3	32.1	32.2
Equity in state enterprises	12.2	14.8	16.8	17.7	17.4	16.9	17.9
Other	23.3	19.7	19.9	18.2	13.0	9.7	7.4

Note: [a] Preliminary estimate
Source: General Statistical Office, 2001. *Statistical Yearbook 2001*, Statistical Publishing House, Hanoi.

weighted with highly capital-intensive projects. Investments in the private sector have generated higher output and much more employment in proportion to outlay than state sector investments. This, however, would not explain the trend increase in the relative importance of recorded state investment.

Another factor may be the increasing importance of official development assistance in the state investment budget. By and large, aided projects are more expensive per unit of output than domestically financed activities, certainly compared with those in the non-state sector, but even in relation to state investments.

The data also reflect the reality that the government of Viet Nam throughout the 1990s tended to be more sympathetic to foreign direct investment than to domestic private investment and, until the implementation of the new enterprise law in 2000, persisted with a regulatory regime which was not encouraging to formal private business activity. The result was that much non-state activity was implemented by unregistered firms and appeared statistically, if at all, under the amorphous category of 'household' economic activity.

The investment strategy adopted by government in the Public Investment Program 1995–2000 and in the 1995–2000 Five-Year Plan was to focus public investment on economic and social infrastructure, particularly on critical economic infrastructure needs, such as transport, electricity, telecommunications, and water resources, and on investment in human capital through education and health programs.

The government also committed public investment funds to such basic industries such as cement, steel, mining and oil and gas processing, and provided loan finance from state credits, funded from domestic and foreign sources, for such activities. The main weakness in the government investment strategy was over-investment in some of the basic industries (for example, cement and coal) and some other state enterprise activities (for example, sugar refining). The government committed resources to stimulate investment in other industries by establishing industrial parks and by providing the infrastructural requirements of focal economic zones.

While it is difficult to draw firm conclusions from the investment data, they are consistent with the view that a strong role for state investment was not inimical to vigorous export led growth. This suggests that, at least in the Vietnamese case, an active public investment program can support the development of other sectors, rather than 'crowd out' their efforts.

Examination of the government investment program (not including investment in state-owned enterprises) indicates that a great deal of emphasis was put on investment in infrastructure—a rather traditional approach to development. Generally, government investment reflected the established doctrine that government investment priorities in supporting the growth process should be to ensure the supply of those resources which have a strong 'public goods' component, primarily infrastructure which cannot be readily funded by commercial mechanisms. Segments of economic activity which should be treated as public goods at this stage of Viet Nam's development, such as roads, flood control and major irrigation works, and water supply and sanitation (which have an important public health element), placed great demands on the government capital budget.

The priorities for public investment at the beginning of the 1990s were fairly obvious. The major component was the rehabilitation of basic infrastructure that had been damaged in the war years, a challenging task that had only been partly dealt with in the difficult years following unification.[3]

The flow of foreign direct investment following the opening up of the economy was mobilised for a number of different reasons. One strong impetus was regional investors seeking platforms for low cost labour-intensive exports. Another element was the attraction of investment in the oil industry (the major share of UK investment was made by British Petroleum in the oil industry). Such investments were important in helping finance the export boom.

Some of the investment to meet the needs of the domestic market was more problematic (for example, the over-investment in property development[4] and vehicle assembly), and the downturn in foreign direct investment in 1998 not only reflected the regional crisis, but also specific problems facing investors supplying the domestic market who had made over-optimistic assessments of the Vietnamese market.

Following the 1997 crisis, although government postponed a number of public investments and reduced the level of public investment below levels that had been planned, the relative importance of public investment in total capital formation increased sharply. State investment grew from 48 per cent of total investment in 1997 to an estimated 62 per cent in 2000. The expansion of state investment was fuelled partly by the increased flows of official development assistance, which fortuitously played a countercyclical role in coming on stream just as regional foreign investment flows were falling sharply.

In relation to non-state domestic investment, more work is required to increase understanding of the structure of the sector. Surveys undertaken on the private sector suggest that the growth of the sector has been more vigorous than the statistics suggest. Existing official data suggest that domestic non-state investment has consistently accounted for one-fifth of total investment annually over 1997/–2000. The rapid registration of new enterprises under the new enterprise law may increase the information available.

One macroeconomic weakness identified by some observers was the modest domestic savings target set in the 1995–2000 Five-Year Plan. Although the GDP data suggest that savings have risen significantly, the savings rate still falls short of the very high rates achieved in other successful economies in the region, and may be too low to sustain very high growth rates in output over the longer term. As noted above, however, the data on private investment and savings is inadequate, so that actual savings performance may have been better than targets and available data indicate.

This is suggested by the macroeconomic data for recent years. IMF data indicate that gross national savings rose from 13.6 per cent of GDP in 1995 to 26.5 per cent of GDP by 1999. This also reflected the declining relative importance of foreign direct investment after 1997.

THE ROLE OF EXTERNAL FINANCE

Private foreign investment

In the period before 1994, the key foreign direct investment in Viet Nam was in the oil and gas sector, with peak investment in 1993. In the period until 1996, the growth in crude oil exports was the leading component of total export growth. The next two most important contributors to export growth in the first half of the decade, rice and marine products, were not areas that received much attention from foreign investors.

Figure 13.1   **Savings ratios in selected Asian countries, 1986–2000 (per cent of GDP)**

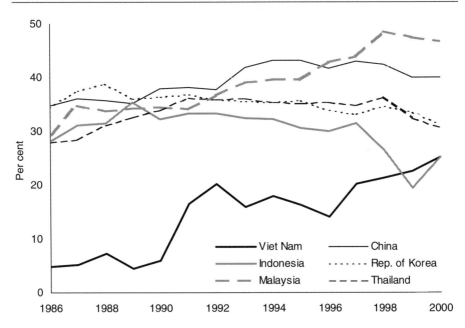

Source: World Bank, 2002. *World Development Indicators*, World Bank, Washington, DC.

In the second half of the decade, foreign investment became influential in a range of new activities. It was important not only in providing finance, but in introducing new ideas, processes, management skills and know-how, in providing models that have been copied by domestic investors and in facilitating access to export markets. Increased competition from foreign firms helped generate innovation.

Foreign investment in industry made an important contribution in the second half of the decade, when industrial exports took over the leading role in export growth,. The foreign role in the industrial sector was important not only, or primarily, because of its financial contribution, but because of the catalytic role it often played in joint ventures, typically with state enterprises, in providing technology, designs and trademarks necessary for access to international markets. In addition to the impact of capital equipment introduced through foreign investment, the interaction with people with different ideas, skills and work practices has influenced domestic productivity (for example, transformation of service quality in many areas, such as domestic banking services).

Table 13.4 **Savings–investment balance, 1995–2000 (per cent of GDP)**

	1995	1996	1997	1998	1999	2000
Gross national savings	13.6	17.6	21.4	19.1	26.5	27.3
Gross capital formation	27.1	28.1	28.3	23.7	22.4	25.6
Savings–investment balance	-13.5	-10.5	-6.9	-4.6	4.1	1.7

Note: These data are taken from an IMF source which gives a somewhat different picture about the timing and magnitude of the change in national savings than presented in Vietnamese national accounts. A recent publication by the General Statistics Office (2002a) includes a detailed discussion of difference between government estimates and IMF figures , including a reasoned case for the validity of the Vietnamese figures. In particular, the IMF has estimated growth in the services sector at a somewhat lower rate than official estimates in recent years; the Vietnamese volume argues that on the basis of available employment and productivity data their own estimates are more plausible. Also, the IMF data show a sharper decline in capital formation after 1997. Both sources show a substantial rise in gross national savings, although the timing and magnitude of the changes varies between the two sources.

Source: International Monetary Fund, 2002. *Vietnam: selected issues and statistical appendix*, IMF Country Report 02/5, International Monetary Fund, Washington, DC.

Table 13.5   **Foreign direct investment: disbursement by economic sector, 1988–2000 (US$ million)**

(a) 1988–95

	1988–91	1992	1993	1994	1995
Industry	150	40	239	435	641
Oil and gas	68	62	369	304	353
Construction	39	6	43	35	113
Transport and communication	46	28	23	67	88
Real estate and tourism	143	51	106	157	458
Agriculture ,forestry and fishing	54	11	27	30	107
Other[a]	70	97	62	20	21
Total	620	295	869	1,048	1,780

(b) 1995–2000

	1995	1996	1997	1998	1999	2000
Industry	801	1,141	1,326	922	835	910
Oil and gas	567	337	261	375	345	205
Construction	133	261	407	198	152	221
Transport and communications	155	82	101	80	106	28
Real estate and tourism	433	421	488	471	340	299
Agriculture, forestry and fishing	130	113	234	124	192	208
Services	120	95	61	77	71	87
Total						
Government estimates	2,341	2,490	2,878	2,246	2,041	1,959
IMF staff estimates	2.276	1,813	2,074	800	700	800

Note: [a] Includes banking and finance.

Data on foreign direct investment are somewhat inconsistent and unreliable. The two series, both taken from IMF documents, show differing totals for overlapping years. For the series for 1995–2000, there are substantial differences between official estimates from the Ministry of Planning and Investment and IMF staff estimates, particularly for the years 1998–2000. The official series is total reported disbursements less equity contribution by domestic partners and therefore includes domestic borrowing by joint ventures. This gives an indication of the actual importance of foreign enterprises, but exaggerates the external inflow. The IMF Staff estimates are based on reported foreign equity inflows plus foreign borrowings by joint ventures, an appropriate measure for balance of payments estimates.

Source: International Monetary Fund, 1998. *Vietnam: selected issues and statistical annex*, International Monetary Fund, Washington, DC; International Monetary Fund, 2002. *Vietnam: selected issues and statistical appendix*, International Monetary Fund, Washington, DC.

What is striking about the Vietnamese experience with foreign investment (in comparison, for example, with the history of foreign investment in Latin America or Africa, but in line with regional experience) is the degree to which it has helped promote new exporting activities, rather than producing import substitutes for the domestic market. This is partly because of the importance of investors from the region, whose main strategic interest is to produce for exporting to world markets. Thus, one powerful stimulus to foreign direct investment, particularly in the period 1990–97, was the conditions facing successful neighbours. In the boom preceding the crash of 1997 in Asia, rising labour costs meant that exporters of labour-intensive commodities in Taiwan, Korea, Singapore, Malaysia and Thailand were seeking out new locations for their production. Viet Nam proved an attractive location, particularly in clothing and footwear and more recently in electronic assembly.

The need to improve the environment for foreign investment has been a continuing topic for dialogue between the government and the international business and diplomatic community and has centred on such issues as dual pricing policies (steadily being reduced), restrictions on rights to invest in property and in areas of continued state monopoly. However, the investment regime was sufficiently conducive to attract considerable foreign investment between 1993 and 1997.[5] Evidently, the attractions of low labour costs, a relatively skilled and educable labour force and reasonable infrastructure outweighed the disincentives of a sometimes cumbersome, often opaque and restrictive regulatory environment.

Despite the rhetoric of international commentators, the downturn in investment spending in 1998–99 can be largely explained by the impact of the East Asian economic crisis, and the break in the Vietnamese property boom, which had involved unsustainable speculative foreign investment in property. In 1996, 58 per cent of FDI commitments were from regional investors (in order of importance—Singapore, Korea, Taiwan, Hong Kong, Thailand and Malaysia). The financial crisis and investment downturns in those economies explain most of the sharp decline in foreign direct investment in Viet Nam from 1998 onwards.

Nevertheless, it is evident that the difficult regional investment climate prevailing since the onset of the East Asian crisis increases the need to improve conditions for investment in Viet Nam if Viet Nam is to compete successfully for the diminished flows of investment funds.

Table 13.6 **Manufacturing output by foreign-invested sector, total and selected sub-sectors, 1995 and 2000 (1994 prices)**

Product group	Gross output of foreign-invested manufacturing sector	
	1995	2000[a]
Total	15,084	47,438
Of which		
Food products and beverages	5,158	8,256
Textiles and wearing apparel	1,606	3,211
Leather and leather products	1,274	3,817
Chemicals and chemical products	742	3,148
Non-metallic mineral products	450	3,288
Basic metals	1,014	2,619
Office, accounting and computing machinery	1	5,058
Radio and communication equipment	948	3,840
Motor vehicles and other transport equipment	1,884	6,827

Note: [a] Preliminary estimate.
Source: General Statistical Office, 2000. *Statistical Yearbook 2000*. Statistical Publishing House, Hanoi.

The impact of foreign investment was not all positive, particularly in relation to investments in production for the domestic market. The market mechanism did not prove very effective in coordinating real estate investment. Over-investment in urban construction (particularly in relation to investment in hotels) led to persistent overcapacity. The volatility of this sector might suggest that the government should use its access to licensing information to provide an indicative basis on which private investors could make more realistic judgments of project viability. It is unlikely, however, that the bureaucracy would show any better foresight in this regard than property speculators.

Another area in which investment mistakes were made which reproduced the earlier experience of many other developing economies was in relation to investment in vehicle assembly, where international firms wishing to gain a foothold in the Vietnamese market created great overcapacity.

While under-the-table payments are not uncommon in domestic business, the rapid growth in foreign direct assistance also increased domestic concerns about the wealth acquired by some public officials associated with foreign-invested projects, especially in the property sector.

External assistance: official capital flows

The Vietnamese authorities have shown self-confidence in handling the aid relationship, avoiding excessive aid dependence. Indeed, in the critical period of growth acceleration (1989–93), the Vietnamese economy experienced a sharp decline in official development assistance inflows as aid flows from the former Soviet Union and East Europe effectively ceased in 1990. During the first three years of the 1991–95 Five-Year Plan, Viet Nam received only limited development assistance. Sources of assistance were limited to the few established bilateral donors, with UN organisations and non-governmental organisations providing mainly technical and humanitarian assistance.

The implementation of the *Doi Moi* policies was welcomed by the international community, but aid commitments did not really grow significantly until 1993 when the US embargo was lifted. Aid from the multilateral agencies and from a number of development assistance community members resumed in 1993. A new pattern of relations between Viet Nam and the international donor community was established through the Donors' Conference for Viet Nam held in Paris in November 1993. The first Consultative Group Meeting was held in Paris in November 1994. Official development assistance and foreign direct investment inflows expanded significantly during 1994–95. Official development assistance commitments of US$1.8 billion were made in 1993, and annual commitments went on growing until 1996, when annual new commitments were estimated to have peaked at over US$2.4 billion.

In the mid 1990s, Japan, the World Bank and the Asian Development Bank became the leading sources of external assistance. Between November 1994 and August 1995 donors signed agreements on programs and projects with the total value of US$1,500 million, of which Japan accounted for 43 per cent, the World Bank for 18 per cent, the Asian Development Bank for 17 per cent and other donors for 22 per cent. A large number of bilateral donors and the European Union also expanded their programs in Viet Nam.

Disbursement, however, built up only slowly.[6] A great part of the initial growth in disbursements came from structural adjustment lending, budget support, and quick disbursing sector program loans such as the Structural Adjustment Credit (SAC) provided by the World Bank and the Enhanced Structural Adjustment Program (ESAP) run by the IMF, Japanese-funded commodity aid projects, and an agricultural sector loan from the Asian Development Bank.

Capital construction projects were concentrated in the sectors of energy, transport, and water resources, which together accounted for more than 70 per cent of the total value of donor commitments by 1995.

While the aid total has built up, foreign aid has played a relatively minor role in the Vietnamese development financing picture. Before 1998, private investment flows were well in excess of aid disbursements, and, despite the decline since 1998 FDI levels remain ahead of official development assistance according to official government estimates (IMF estimates suggest that since 1998 ODA has exceeded private investment flows). Moreover, remittances from Vietnamese people based overseas exceed flows of official development assistance.[7] Viet Nam has been able to avoid aid dependency because its exports have grown more rapidly than its aid flows; aid flows remain around 12 per cent of export earnings.

This does not mean that has not been effective because aid is at its most productive when playing a supporting role in the development process. There are no examples of successful development where aid has played the major financing role.

In practice, the aid provided in the 1990s was quite successful because the priorities were so clear. Decades of war and enforced economic isolation had left a large backlog of requirements in terms of rehabilitating basic infrastructure and investing in basic services. The government was realistic in its expectations about the level of aid and sought to fund mainly public infrastructure, social services and public support for rural development with the aid it did receive.

Thus, within the framework provided by the Five-Year Plan and the Public Investment Plan, the government aimed to mobilise official development assistance resources of US$7–8 billion over the period 1996–2000. Support was sought for the following main areas of the 1996–2000 Five-Year Plan
- infrastructure in the focal economic zones, industrial parks, and processing zones.
- expansion of major airports and seaports
- expansion of the main road and rail networks
- investment in electrical power production
- rehabilitation and extension of the water supply system
- improvements to the irrigation system
- support for animal husbandry, development and protection of forests, and key projects for ecosystem protection

- development of the telecommunications system
- upgrading and equipping medical facilities, including upgrading the two national health centres in Hanoi and Ho Chi Minh City
- upgrading and extending key education and training facilities.

It is difficult to make the case that financial assistance from the multilateral financial institutions and development assistance community members was a crucial factor in the initiation of successful growth in Viet Nam. Capital assistance only built up after the end of the US embargo in 1993, and with the usual lags between commitments and disbursements, it was only in 1997 that disbursements topped US$1 billion. As the acceleration in growth began even before the renewal of aid from the multilateral financial institutions in 1993, the decisive improvement in economic growth performance cannot be attributed to the subsequent expansion in aid flows. Indeed, given the initial sluggish growth in disbursements and the normal gestation period between the initiation of investment and productive results, little of the boom in growth 1992–97 can be explained by the expansion in aid from 1993 onwards.

Although it can be argued that donor finance lent support to the *Doi Moi* process, that process was not initiated by donors and was not, at its crucial early stages, influenced by aid conditionality. It was designed and led by the

Table 13.7 **Annual ODA commitments and disbursements, 1993–2001 (US$million)**

Year	New commitments	Disbursements
1993	1,810	413
1994	1,940	725
1995	2,260	737
1996	2,430	900
1997	2,400	1,000
1998	2,200[a]	1,242
1999	2,210[b]	1,350
2000	2,400	1,650
2001	2,400	1,711[c]
Total	17,540	9,728

Notes: [a] Excluding US$0.5 billion budget support for economic reforms.
[b] Excluding US$0.7 billion support for economic reforms.
[c] Estimate.
Source: Ministry of Planning and Investment

national authorities. When multilateral financial institutions resumed their programs in 1993, the reform process had already been carried far enough to have real credibility. Difficult reforms had been carried through with minimal external assistance, and the economy was already substantially market based.

The donor programs initiated following the lifting of the embargo in 1993 were important, however, in providing the support needed for Viet Nam to reap the full benefits of the earlier reforms, as well as lending support to the later stages of the reform process.

In particular, aid made a particularly useful contribution to the rehabilitation and expansion of basic economic infrastructure, ensuring that infrastructure bottlenecks have not acted as a constraint on growth. The emphasis on the finance of investment in physical infrastructure meant that the profile of the aid program in the 1990s was somewhat 'old-fashioned' in appearance, but was probably not the worse for that.

With the development of the aid program, the aid agencies (notably the multilateral financial institutions) have actively tried to introduce policy conditionality, attached long lists of conditions to loan agreements.[8] There is an extensive literature debating the effectiveness of such assistance, and it increasingly recognised that programs to support reform should not be seen as just a matter of rapidly implementing a standardised set of optimal market-based rules.[9] Senior World Bank staff have recognised that

> [o]n average market-oriented reforms worked, but not in a reliable fashion. Our reading of the 1990s is that the reform process too often neglected the institutional foundations necessary for markets to be effective for poverty reduction. It is not enough to focus on 'getting prices right', public action is needed to 'get the markets right' (Collier, Dollar and Stern 2000:2).

Stiglitz (1999) notes the importance of 'knowing when you don't know what you are doing'. There is also often an implicit assumption that everything is urgent, and that substantive change can be realised by a new regulation or policy document.[10] There is no evidence that policy-based lending has been instrumental in accelerating the reform process in Vietnam. In practice, much of the apparent conditionality is window-dressing by the staff of the agencies to convince their own managements that they are 'buying' sufficient reforms to justify the financing.[11] The Vietnamese government will probably continue to prove shrewd enough to avoid the consequences of dependency and the erosion in national policymaking capacity that have occurred in many other countries.

As flows have grown, questions have been raised regarding the effectiveness of the program, both on the donor and the Vietnamese side. At the National Assembly meeting in November–December 1999, questions were raised about the efficiency of foreign aid, and particularly its effectiveness in public administration reform and infrastructure construction projects (for example, roads, bridges, irrigation and rural water systems). Concerns were also expressed about the cost of some projects (particularly distortions resulting from donor practices such as tying procurement) and about the burden of debt arising from the development assistance program.

A number of donors have also expressed reservations about the effectiveness of capacity building activities. At the Seventh Consultative Group meeting in December 1999 the need to avoid the 'debt trap' and heavy aid dependency was raised, as was the need to give more attention to the efficient use of aid.

The quality of aid needs as much attention as the quantity. With the build up of support, efforts of various donors have often overlapped. The government has made considerable efforts to improve its aid management capacity in the face of the fast increase in aid commitments, but it has limited capacity to coordinate programs effectively, particularly in light of the shared interest of donors and particular beneficiary agencies to push 'their' projects.

Concern is expressed on both the donor and the government side that the identification and formulation of projects is too often 'donor driven', sometimes resulting in weak 'national ownership' of projects and limited commitment, concerns familiar in the donor world internationally. Despite this verbal recognition of the problem, pressures remain on both sides to push projects and to short-cut coordination.

One interesting feature of aid flows in the 1990s was the emphasis placed on investment in infrastructure and program aid to support the reform process and growth, and the relatively minor attention to poverty alleviation, which is now becoming a focus of donor attention. Despite this, the record of poverty reduction was exemplary during these years. This was because, under Vietnamese conditions, the achievement of high growth rates had a big impact on poverty. Now that donors are devoting a great deal more attention to poverty alleviation, it will be interesting to see if there is any improvement in performance in that regard. There is a danger that the channelling of investment to areas which are poor because of their low economic potential may be less effective in reducing poverty than a growth-oriented strategy.

EXTERNAL ASSISTANCE: TECHNICAL COOPERATION

Technical assistance made a more valuable contribution to policy and institutional development than capital assistance, particularly in the period prior to the re-entry of the multilateral financial institutions in 1993. At that stage, the UN system was particularly important as a source of useful advice to the Vietnamese. Even the involvement of Bretton Woods institutions at that time was mainly through UNDP support, with the Bretton Woods institutions acting as executing agencies for UN projects. Indeed, one of the interesting aspects of Vietnamese experience is the light it throws on the efficacy of technical assistance and the redundancy of policy conditionality (at least in Viet Nam). It is difficult to find tangible evidence that the effectiveness of external advice has increased as institutions such as the World Bank have become active in promoting their view of reform requirements through conditions attached to structural adjustment and program loans.

In the years before the end of the US embargo, Viet Nam sought assistance from the international community for training and for policy advice. Much of this assistance was channelled through the UNDP and other UN agencies, although the Swedish International Development Agency also played an active role. It is widely recognised that training and advice offered in that period was highly effective in aiding the Vietnamese in the development of their reform policies.[12] The Vietnamese government was able to select from the advice offered based on their own priorities and understanding of the local reality. Moreover, playing a purely advisory role, the various agencies avoided the arrogance that sometimes accompanies the allocation of large amounts of financial assistance.

A recent evaluation of donor technical assistance to Viet Nam concluded that

> ...the TC program in Viet Nam has been successful overall, particularly when compared to the problems experienced with TC in many other countries. Areas of success include

> strong human resource development (HRD) through many kinds of training, including on-the-job training, short-term courses, training of trainers, and post-graduate training programs in Viet Nam and abroad.

> Policy advice supported changes in key areas, including: fiscal and banking reform, drafting laws essential to the transitional economy, rationalising the regulations relating to key ministries (MPI, MOJ, MOFI, National Assembly Office, the Judiciary Office, the Public Prosecutor

Office etc.), assisting with development plans and the Public Investment Program, assisting in regional and international integration, and public administration reform.

Assisting in many social aspects of development: including rural development linked to poverty alleviation, environment and natural resource protection, gender issues, HIV control and drug control, etc.

Assisting in a number of important surveys and statistical development (e.g. population census, Living Standards Measurement Survey of household incomes, national income data, etc.), greatly improving the availability of reliable information for planning and policymaking.

With the help of TC programs, many agencies at different levels—ministerial, provincial, sub-provincial levels—have developed their capacity (e.g. through skill upgrading and organisational strengthening) (Van Arkadie et al. 2000:5).

Although the contribution of technical assistance to Viet Nam development is evident, the greatest contribution came in the early years of reform, when flows were quite modest. The fast increase in technical aid in the 1990s was not reflected by anything like a proportionate increase in impact—diminishing returns set in and in some areas may have even reached negative returns at the margin. Disbursements on technical aid grew from US$76.7 million (12.9 per cent of total development assistance) in 1992 to US$209.4 million (34.2 per cent of total development assistance) in 1995, falling to 24.4 per cent in 1998, when US$287 million was disbursed for technical aid. Disbursements reached a peak in 1997 of US$ 294.8 million, equal to 31.4 per cent of total development assistance in that year.

From the Vietnamese point of view, too much of the typical project budget goes on costs for foreign experts (often seen as not more competent than local experts) and too little on local costs and non-personnel items, while the practice of some agencies leaves the selection of, and control over, consultants in donor hands.

Donors and Vietnamese also express concerns regarding the sustainability of projects over the longer term (that is the continued operation of facilities and flow of benefits after the project is 'completed' and external funding ceases).

Expressions of concern about aspects of utilisation of development assistance in Viet Nam are a healthy recognition of the risks of aid dependence. Viet Nam could still benefit from being a late participant in the aid game by studying the experience of other aid recipients.

A recent report on technical cooperation concluded that weaknesses in the aid system 'need to be addressed with some urgency' (Van Arkadie et al. 2000:17). However, there is a good deal of inertia in the international aid system, and the Vietnamese experience demonstrates how quickly a pattern of vested interests build up on both sides of the aid relationship (on the donor side, among the aid bureaucracies, suppliers, consulting firms and individual consultants, on the recipient side among the beneficiary agencies and officials who reap project benefits).

NOTES

[1] Human capital refers to investments in individuals, whereas social capital refers to investments in business organisations, institutions (political, financial, market and industrial relations) and the social environment.

[2] This is not special to Viet Nam, as it is often the case that national accounts data greatly underestimate the own account investment by farm households and in rural housing. This sort of activity has been of great importance to Viet Nam's development in the past 15 years. The figures included for 'non-state investment' in the official data is apparently a rough estimate, as there is no comprehensive survey of such investments.

[3] In practice, government has been ready to seek out private funding for public services where they are commercially viable (for example, telecommunications) and has sought to expand private funding through such innovations as build-operate-transfer schemes (for example, in the power sector). Where some degree of cost recovery is possible through user charges, the government has been quite willing to introduce such charges. Large government investments are necessary, however, to prevent infrastructure becoming a bottle-neck that constrains growth in other sectors.

[4] Somewhat ironically, in light of advice the Vietnamese received suggesting that it was likely that private investors would not make the same sort of investment errors as state enterprises, the inflow of foreign investment before the 1997 regional crisis included heavy over-investment in the hotel sector greatly in excess of any plausible market growth, resulting in persistent over-capacity in hotel space, leading to strong downward pressure on prices. At least the costs were borne by the investors (and their workers) and not the state.

[5] The timing of the downturn in foreign investment can either be located in 1996, when approvals for new investment proposals peaked, or in 1997, when expenditures on foreign investments peaked.

6 The report of the Government of Viet Nam at the Consultative Group Meeting organised in 1994 indicated the main reasons for delays in the disbursement of projects funded by development assistance. Bottlenecks occurred in project preparation, administrative procedures for the consideration and approval of projects; and issues of compensation and resettlement.

7 A news item in Hanoi on 26 December recorded that '[r]emittances by overseas Vietnamese are expected to reach US$2 billion in 2001, US$300 million more than 2000, according to the State Bank of Viet Nam. Some 60 per cent of remittances were channelled through banks. General Director of the Eastern Asia Bank in Viet Nam, Tran Phuong Binh, said that remittances channelled through his bank were expected to reach US$260 million in 2001, a year-on-year increase of 50 per cent. It is estimated that there are more than 2.5 million overseas Vietnamese, mostly in the United States, France, Australia and Canada.

8 Dollar and Svensson (1998) concluded that multiple tranches—and a large number of other design variables—play no role in effectiveness.

9 Recent internal critiques of policy-based lending include Paul Collier (1998, 1999, 2000), Dollar and Svensson (1998) and Asian Development Bank (2001).

10 Stiglitz, in reference to transition economies, noted that it is easy to 'make the facile recommendation that everything is important and everything should be done at once. But real choices are always necessary given the real limitations of any government's time, focus and resources' (1999:19).

11 Such problems are recognised by the multilateral financial institutions. A World Bank report written by Paul Collier refers to the 'fig leaf' theory that policy change is costly and that aid finances upfront adjustment costs (Collier 2000; see also Asian Development Bank 2001).

12 Dollar, who was in that period lead economist for the World Bank and played an active role in advisory work and in participating in policy workshops, was also lead author of a World Bank study of aid effectiveness, *Assessing Aid* (World Bank 1998c). The book includes a case study of experience in Viet Nam. The study records the successes of the *Doi Moi* process in promoting growth and in poverty alleviation, but notes that in the important reform period, 1989–93, Viet Nam was receiving only a small amount of aid. In that period, ideas were more important than money. One key role of external agencies was to help the Vietnamese access relevant regional and international experiences with economic policy.

14

POVERTY ALLEVIATION

POVERTY ALLEVIATION ISSUES

The performance of the Vietnamese economy in relation to alleviation of poverty in the past decade has been exemplary. This is of considerable interest in the context of the international concern for poverty alleviation throughout the developing world. Donor agencies now place a high priority on poverty reduction, and poverty reduction programs have been enthusiastically adopted in many countries. However, the commitment to poverty alleviation as a goal has not yet been matched by plausible programs or very much success in most of the countries that have adopted poverty reduction as a key policy goal. The Vietnamese success in the 1990s is therefore of more general interest.

Understanding the reasons for past success may also be of importance for future policy in Vietnam. Through 2002, the Vietnamese government continued formulating a comprehensive poverty reduction strategy that was likely to influence the allocation of substantial national and donor resources. The nature of the past achievement might provide some insights into the viability of the new strategy.

However, the lessons are not obvious. One set of issues relates to the balance to be struck between growth and poverty alleviation. The Vietnamese poverty reduction achievement was not the result of focused efforts to reduce poverty. The significant alleviation of poverty during the 1990s happened despite (or perhaps because of) the lack of an explicit poverty alleviation strategy or program.

Poverty alleviation came as a result of the successful pursuit of growth in the context of an economic and social structure that was conducive to the spread of the benefits of growth. Will the new emphasis on focused interventions to tackle poverty improve the link between growth and poverty alleviation, or will it reduce the growth performance by emphasising low productivity investments, and in so doing reduce the rate of poverty alleviation?

One difficulty in interpreting the record is that even if there was some success in achieving growth plus poverty alleviation during the 1990s, it may not be replicable in the future. Although the growth of the Vietnamese economy lifted large numbers of people out of poverty, the reduction in poverty was accompanied by a tendency towards increased inequality between the better-off and the poor and between urban and rural areas. Is increasing inequality a necessary facet of fast market-based growth? Will the tendency to increasing inequality reduce the tendency for the benefits of growth to be diffused, so that future growth could be less rewarding to the poor (and justify the new emphasis on focused poverty reduction programs)?

The discussion in this chapter cannot provide definitive answers to these questions. But examination of the record can provide some pointers to the policy issues that need to be considered in formulating future poverty eradication programs.

POVERTY ALLEVIATION PERFORMANCE

Definitive evidence is now available on the impact of the high rates of growth on the income of the poor in Vietnam.[1] Before looking at the detailed evidence it might be useful to note how poverty has been defined in the Vietnamese literature. The basic data in use to analyse trends in poverty are those derived from the Living Standards Measurement Surveys (LSMS) conducted in 1992/93 and 1997/98.[2] The results of the 1997/98 LSMS provide a solid basis for judging what happened to absolute poverty and income distribution over the 1992–98 period. This covers the period of dramatic acceleration in Vietnamese growth

The government also uses the concepts of 'poor areas and poor communes' to identify the places where the percentage of poor households is much higher and living standards are much lower than the national average level, areas typically characterised by unfavourable natural conditions (poor land, frequent natural disasters) and underdeveloped infrastructure.

In interpreting the LSMS data, the government of Vietnam has used two poverty lines.[3] 'Poverty' is defined in terms of incomes below the minimum level required to cover basic needs for food, clothes, residence, health care, education, travel and communications. A lower level is defined as a 'hunger' line (or food poverty), in order to distinguish what is described as the 'very poor' population from the 'poor' population.

'Hunger', or food poverty, is defined as a situation in which incomes are below the minimum level required to provide food to eat, enough clothes to wear and enough income to sustain their lives. This lower 'hunger' line is intended to identify the proportion of population that lacks food for several months in a year and who typically have to borrow to survive and lack repayment capacity.

The food poverty line is set at an average of 2,100 kilocalories per person per day, in line with the definition used by most international organisations and developing countries. People whose expenditures are not sufficient to attain this level are considered poor in terms of food.[4]

To define the total poverty line, the cost of minimum necessary non-food items is added to the minimum food expenditures.[5] The 1993 expenditure-based total poverty line was VND1,160,000 and the 1998 line was VND1,789,700.

Based on these poverty lines, the Vietnamese General Statistics Office and the World Bank estimated that the total poverty incidence in Vietnam in 1993 and 1998 was 58 per cent and 37 per cent respectively, while that of food poverty was 25 per cent and 15 per cent respectively. The data were extrapolated by the government to estimate levels for the year 2000 as 32 per cent and 13 per cent respectively.

The evidence provided by the LSMS data is clear. Whatever poverty line is used, poverty decreased substantially between 1992/93 and 1997/98. Poverty declined more rapidly in urban areas than in rural areas. Urban poverty fell from 25 per cent to 9 per cent whereas rural poverty rates dropped from 66 per cent to 46 per cent. Rural poverty therefore remains a critical challenge.

The regional pattern of poverty reduction was quite varied. Poverty levels declined in all seven economic regions, but not at the same pace. The largest decline in overall poverty was in the Red River delta, where poverty dropped from 63 per cent to 29 per cent. In 1992–93, this area had ranked fourth out of the seven regions in terms of the extent of poverty, but by 1997–98 it had moved to second in the rankings (the only region with less poverty was the Southeast, which includes Ho Chi Minh City). The Southeast, already the least poor region in 1992/93, enjoyed a further significant reduction from 33 per cent to 8 per cent. Central Coast and the Mekong delta had only moderate declines in overall poverty. The poor performance of the Mekong delta probably reflected the impact of Typhoon Linda, which struck the area in November 1997.

Analysis of the distribution of poverty across ethnic groups reveals that the Chinese, who constitute 2 per cent of the population, and are in general better off than the majority Kinh, who constitute 84 per cent of the population. All the other ethnic groups (mostly located in remote and mountainous areas) are much worse off than the Kinh. The incidence of poverty among the Kinh dropped from 55 per cent to 32 per cent from 1992/93 to 1997/98. For all other groups taken together (not including the Chinese), the incidence of poverty was 75.2 per cent in 1997/98, some improvement over 1992/93, when the poverty rate for this group was 86.4 per cent. The survey found poverty levels increasing for some minority groups.

Data on the regional incidence of poverty need to be interpreted with some care. The three regions which have the highest poverty incidence are the Northern and Central Uplands regions (which have a concentration of ethnic minorities), and the North Central Coast, which suffers from an inhospitable environment. As a result, these areas are the focus of government and donor poverty alleviation efforts. It should also be noted, however, that in 1997/98 over one-third of all poor people were residing in the Red River and Mekong deltas.

Some general comments to illustrate the options in tackling poverty alleviation can be drawn from this.

- Remote and mountainous areas (particularly the Northern Uplands,[6] which contains 28 per cent of the poor), where ethnic minorities are concentrated, experience difficult economic conditions because of physical isolation and mountainous terrain. Within these areas, a distinction can be made between those areas that would have economic potential if binding infrastructural constraints could be relaxed (for example, through the improvement in communications opening up access to national markets) and new income possibilities could be developed (for example, high-value tree crops) and those areas with a very poor natural resource base, where straightforward infrastructure improvement investment may not be very productive in increasing household incomes. It is in these areas that the complex issues related to the development of ethnic minorities must be addressed.

- Many Central Coast areas have poor soils and a negative climate which hold back agricultural development (that is, some disaster management is required to reduce economic risks). Nonetheless, these areas have reasonable access to markets and a well-educated population that could benefit from exploitation of niche markets in agriculture (for example, pepper) and from the promotion of non-agricultural employment opportunities.
- The Red River delta still has many poor people, even though large numbers of others have been lifted out of poverty by fast economic growth. Land scarcity is one critical factor limiting household livelihood options. In the Red River delta, household livelihoods are likely to be improved by further growth in productivity through sophisticated innovations in the

Table 14.1 **Food poverty and overall poverty headcounts in Viet Nam, 1993 and 1998 (per cent)**

	Food poverty		Overall poverty	
	1993	1998	1993	1998
All Vietnam	24.9	15.0	58.1	37.4
Urban	7.9	2.3	25.1	9.0
Rural	29.1	18.3	66.4	44.9
Region				
Northern Uplands	..	..	78.6	58.6
Red River delta	..	..	62.9	28.7
North Central	..	..	74.5	48.0
Central Coast	..	..	49.6	35.2
Central Highlands	..	..	70.0	52.2
Southeast	..	..	32.7	7.6
Mekong River	..	..	47.1	36.9

Source: Food poverty figures are from World Bank, 1999. *Vietnam Development Report 2000: Vietnam attacking poverty*, Joint Report of the Government–Donor–NGO Working Group, Hanoi. Overall poverty figures are from Glewwe et al., 2000. *Who Gained from Vietnam's Boom in the 1990s: the analysis of poverty and inequality trends*, World Bank, Washington, DC.

already highly intensive agricultural systems and from the expansion in off-farm employment opportunities (for example, further development of successful rural and small-town industries).

- The Mekong delta has undergone a less rapid reduction in poverty than the Red River delta despite high agricultural potential. The success of some Mekong households in moving out of poverty has been significantly offset by the incidence of households falling into poverty between the two surveys (see Justino and Litchfield 2002). In the Mekong, there is potential for agricultural expansion both at the extensive margin and from more intensive land use, but difficult issues of environmental and natural disaster (particularly flood) management need to be overcome if large and sustainable increases in household income are to be achieved.

The importance of this distinction between poverty in regions which are 'backward' and poverty in the more 'highly developed' areas is two-fold. First, it would be a mistake to see poverty reduction as mainly a matter of dealing with backward areas. Second, this distinction has implications for policy approaches in different areas. Poverty which results from residence in a poor area will demand a different approach than that appropriate for poverty that results from households failing to participate in the benefits of growth in areas with a high growth performance.

The government, in introducing its poverty eradication strategy in early 2002, noted that living standards improved greatly during the 1990s and that social indicators confirmed a broad improvement in standards of welfare. For example, the under-five child mortality rate and the maternal mortality rate halved between 1990 and 2000. The proportion of the rural population with access to safe water doubled. The net level of enrolment in primary education increased to 95 per cent. Life expectancy rose from 64 in 1990 to 68 in 2000.

By 2000, 88 per cent of communes had access to electricity and 95 per cent of communes were accessible by vehicle. Viet Nam's Human Development Index (HDI) and social service accessibility showed continuing improvement, indicating that Viet Nam's social development was well ahead of what was typical of countries with similar income levels. In 1999, Viet Nam was ranked 167 in the world in terms of per capita GDP, but 101 in terms of its Human Development Index.

GROWTH AND POVERTY ALLEVIATION

The Vietnamese record of high growth combined with poverty alleviation can be interpreted in many ways, each of which suggest a different approach to poverty reduction.

One possible interpretation is that promoting growth is an effective poverty alleviation strategy. Certainly, during the 1990s the main emphases of Vietnamese policy were economic growth and 'modernisation'. Continuing concern was expressed for the plight of poor people, particularly in mountainous and backward areas, but the main thrust of government investment and incentives was the development of the three growth poles, in the north, centre and south of the country. Growth was achieved, and the evidence set out above demonstrated that substantial segments of the population were lifted out of extreme poverty.

This view is certainly partly correct, and hardly surprising in the sense that, in a country with pervasive poverty of the kind prevalent in Viet Nam in the 1980s, economic growth must be a necessary pre-condition to widespread poverty reduction, and at that stage of growth it does not make sense to divert resources from high growth potential investments to low potential investments on distributional grounds. This suggests that, at very low levels of average income, poverty alleviation should be about the development of productive capacity, rather than redistributive welfare measures. Despite the substantial growth gains during the 1990s Vietnam remains a poor country, with an average income per capita of around US$400. Given the success of growth in lowering poverty in the 1990s, it is possible that the move to a focused poverty alleviation program may be premature.

At Vietnam's level of development in the 1980s, raising the income levels of a significant segment of the poor was not feasible without high rates of growth in national income. In an economy which was so poor that the average income was not much above the poverty line and more than half the households were classified as poor, there was little scope for poverty alleviation through redistribution, so that economic growth was a necessary condition for poverty alleviation.

However, the composition of aggregate growth will influence the impact on poverty. In the case of Vietnam, the high growth performance included high rates of agricultural growth, resulting in growing rural incomes. Although rural incomes grew much more slowly than urban incomes, large segments of the

Table 14.2 **Poverty gap and poverty severity level headcounts for Viet Nam, 1993 and 1998 (per cent)**

	1993	1998
Ethnic group		
Kinh	55.1	31.7
Tay	81.3	63.8
Thai	82.3	71.1
Chinese	11.8	8.4
Khome	75.4	57.5
Moung	89.6	80.6
Nung	91.8	72.0
H'mong	100	91.8
Dao	88.5	100
Other	90.0	75.8
Education of the household head		
No schooling	69.9	57.3
Primary	58.2	42.1
Low secondary	63.8	38.1
Upper secondary	45.9	24.9
Technical/vocational	47.7	19.2
University	13.4	4.5
Occupation of the household head		
White collar	24.1	10.1
Sales	27.7	13.2
Agriculture	69.0	48.1
Production	44.5	25.8
Other/no work	59.0	26.3
Sex of the household head		
Male	61.0	39.8
Female	48.3	28.2

Source: Glewwe et al., 2000. *Who Gained from Vietnam's Boom in the 1990s: the analysis of poverty and inequality trends*, World Bank, Washington, DC.

rural population enjoyed increases in absolute income, and a significant portion of the rural population was raised out of poverty as the benefits of growth were spread beyond the urban growth poles. An emphasis on rural development was consistent with both high growth and poverty alleviation.

The distribution of benefits within the rural economy is also important in determining the poverty impact of growth. In Viet Nam, there was a significant diffusion of the benefits of growth because of the egalitarian social relations in rural areas. Viet Nam does not suffer from the kind of semi-feudal landlord–

tenant relations which has checked the spread of the benefits of growth in other parts of the world (for example, in the Indian sub-continent).

Another possible interpretation of the 'growth and poverty reduction' record is that market liberalisation is supportive of fast poverty alleviation. Again, in this period it was part of the truth in Viet Nam. Market reforms were a key input into the acceleration of agricultural growth, much of it based on the household farm, which has been a critical factor in reducing rural poverty. Moreover, the fast growth of the small and medium-sized enterprise in the liberalised urban economy generated widespread income opportunities and underpinned the fast growth of urban incomes, despite declines in public sector employment.

Against this view, it should also be noted that some aspects of the market-led growth strategy may create difficulties for poverty alleviation in the future. Some indicators suggest that some aspects of wellbeing among the poorest sections of the population are being eroded, for example as a result of reduced access to some public services. Moreover, despite the improvements in rural incomes, the absolute gap between urban and rural incomes is widening persistently and substantially. Although economic growth has contributed to a great reduction in poverty, there has also been an increase in inequality as measured by the gaps between the top and bottom income levels (for example, the top and bottom quintiles) and between town and country.[7]

The government's own analysis notes that the income of the poor has grown at a lower rate than that of the middle-income group, who in turn have experienced lower growth than the high-income group. The gap between the richest and poorest quintiles is widening (from 7.3 times in 1996 to 8.9 times in 1999). Between the two living standard surveys (from 1993 to 1998), the richest 10 per cent of the population increased their spending by 53.3 per cent compared to a 23.3 per cent spending increase by the poorest 10 per cent. So, although poverty has been reduced, the rate of income improvement among the poor is slower than the average rate. Also, the gap in living standards between urban and rural areas remains very large and is growing.

Some increase in income and wealth inequality is a virtually inevitable result of fast growth at the current level of development. The challenge is how to prevent such inequalities from being consolidated generation to generation— that is, from becoming the basis for an entrenched class society. To do this, conscious and specific efforts will be required to ensure that access to public services is available to the poor, so that there is a reasonable degree of equality of opportunity. At the moment, there are some tendencies pushing the economy in the opposite direction.[8]

Both the 'growing out of poverty' and 'liberalisation as a poverty reduction strategy' have to be tempered by the argument, developed in various places in this volume, that the initial conditions inherited from the pre-reform period were important determinants of the inclusive character of the Vietnamese performance. The sustained commitment to investment in human capital, the lack of great inequalities in the access to rural assets and modest differentials in employment incomes were particularly important.

NOTES

[1] World Bank research staff undertook a detailed statistical analysis of the results of the 1998 LSMS and of the lessons to be learnt regarding the changes between 1992 and 1998 (see Glewwe et al. 2000).

[2] The surveys covered 4,800 and 6,000 households respectively.

[3] In addition to these poverty lines based on LSMS data on poverty, the Ministry of Labour, Invalids and Social Affairs developed a national poverty line to identify who are the poor, with specific numbers and addresses in order to develop a list of poor households at the hamlet and commune levels and to identify poor communes eligible for support from the National Target Poverty Reduction Programme. In 1997, Vietnam set a poverty line under the national programme (the old poverty line) to apply to poverty measurement in the 1996–2000 period as follows—hungry households: households with average per capita monthly income in rice equivalence of less than 13 kilograms or less than VND 45,000 (in 1997 prices, applied to all regions); poor households: criteria set for different areas/regions. For rural mountainous and island areas, less than 15 kilograms per person per month (equivalent to VND 55,000). For rural plain and midland areas, less than 20 kilograms per person per month (equivalent to VND 70,000). For urban areas, less than 25 kilograms per person per month (equivalent to VND90,000); poor communes: communes with poverty incidence of 40 per cent and above and lack of infrastructure (roads, schools, clinics, electricity and water for livelihood needs, small irrigation works and markets). A new poverty line was published in 2001 to be applied to poverty measurement in the 2001–05 period. The new poverty line was set at VND80,000 per month for people in island areas and rural mountainous areas (or VND960,000 per year), VND100,000 per

month for people in rural plain areas (or VND1,200,000 per year) and VND150,000 per month for people in urban areas (or VND1,800,000 per year). Localities estimate poor households as a percentage of total households based on these poverty criteria. Provinces and cities are allowed to apply higher poverty standards than the stipulated levels.

4　When the 1992/93 survey was conducted, the calculation of minimum expenditures needed to buy the food basket to provide the minimum calorie intake was made using January 1993 prices. The result was VND749,000, which was defined as the food poverty line (US$65 at 1993 exchange rates). In the 1997/98 survey, the food poverty line was calculated by multiplying the amount of goods in the food basket that was used to calculate the 1992/93 food poverty line by January 1998 prices. The resulting poverty line for 1997/98 was set at VND1,286,000 (equivalent to US$123).

5　This was done by observing the non-food expenditures of those households whose food expenditures just allowed them to purchase the 2,100 calorie food basket.

6　The Central Highlands also had more than 50 per cent poor, but it is sparsely populated, so only accounts for 5 per cent of the total poor.

7　The social consequences of an increase in inequality may be influenced by the degree of mobility between income groups. A given degree of inequality may in some sense be more acceptable if there is great household mobility. In a paper analysing economic mobility on the basis of the survey data, Glewwe and Nguyen (2002:19) conclude that, although a simple analysis of the data suggests a high degree of mobility, when adjustments are made for measurement error, a much lower degree of mobility is suggested, implying that 'Vietnam's worries about increasing inequality cannot be dismissed by pointing to high economic mobility'.

8　See Van de Walle (1998) which highlights the problems of unequal gains from growth and the erosion of social safety nets.

15

CAUSES OF CONTINUING POVERTY

PERSISTENCE OF POVERTY AND CONTINUING VULNERABILITY

The Vietnamese government estimated that almost one-third of the population is still receiving an income below the poverty line, highlighting the critical challenge posed by remaining poverty in Vietnam.

In one sense, as in all developing countries, it is not difficult to explain widespread poverty—it reflects the low level of average income. Despite a period of successful growth, Vietnam's average income is still low and the income of a large segment of the population lies just above the poverty line. Even a small adjustment in the position of the line or a modest decline in household income would put many more households below the poverty line. With low average incomes, changes in definition and small changes in average incomes can have a great effect on the numbers identified as poor. For example, the definitions chosen in the surveys conducted by the Ministry of Labour, Invalids and Social Affairs identify a much smaller proportion of the population as being poor than the norms applied in analysing the Living Standards Measurement Study (LSMS) (11 per cent in 2000 as compared to just under one-third using the LSMS analysis and definitions).

As economic growth continues, and average incomes rise, it will become of increasing interest to analyse why some groups are falling behind, benefiting

235

little from the general increase in prosperity. The government's analysis of the poverty problem has identified a number of factors that are associated with continuing poverty and relative exclusion from the benefits of economic growth.

POVERTY AND RURAL CONDITIONS

The government places a good deal of emphasis on the many poor who live in areas that have very few natural resources and harsh natural conditions such as mountainous, remote and isolated areas. Also, the poor are often subject to the effects of natural disasters. Over 90 per cent of the poor live in rural areas and most of their income comes from agriculture. Agricultural income is unstable and vulnerable to climatic uncertainty and natural shocks. The income level of many rural households is close enough to the poverty line that natural calamities can easily push them back into poverty. The Mekong River delta region and the Central region are particularly subject to climatic uncertainty (typhoons, floods). This means that, while many families escape from poverty each year, that progress is offset to a significant extent by families falling back into poverty.

Differentials in the development of infrastructure also cause widening income gaps because inability to access to markets holds back the development of many poor areas.

Although Vietnam does not have a highly skewed land distribution, rural groups with relatively poor access to land or who have access to land of a poor quality or geographic location, find it difficult to achieve food security and invest in productivity improvements. Poor people also have limited access to various sources of credit despite the government's attempts to raise credit access and availability through the expansion of formal credit to agricultural areas.

URBAN POVERTY

The poverty rate is lower in urban areas, but within urban areas there has been a great deal of inequality in the distribution of the benefits of growth, with those working in the state and foreign-invested sectors doing better than for those working in the domestic non-state sector. Many of those who were made redundant as a result of state enterprise restructuring and other reductions in public employment have suffered a loss of income. Incomes are low in the growing urban informal sector, where the labour force is swollen by the influx of unregistered migrants from rural areas. Many migrants usually do not secure permanent registration and have no stable jobs; consequently their income is unstable and they are unable to gain access to basic public social services (health care, education) and may also be excluded from social surveys used for poverty targeting.

POVERTY AND ACCESS TO SOCIAL SERVICE PROVISION

One reason why the benefits of economic growth have been diffused is the broad spread of education and literacy. While education cannot ensure increases in income, illiteracy and lack of basic education can exclude the uneducated from economic opportunities.

While there was some deterioration in some aspects of education provision[1] the overall educational profile remained strong for a country with Viet Nam's income level. Programs to abolish illiteracy and to promote universal primary education contributed to the achievement of an adult literacy rate to 93 per cent by 1995, and an increase in the share of children of primary school age attending school from 75 per cent in 1991 to 99.9 per cent in 1997, with 55 per cent of the secondary level age group also attending school (UNDP 2001). Viet Nam's literacy and school attendance rates are on a par with economies that have per capita income levels ten times higher.

Not only have the number of pupils and students attending school increased, but there has also been some qualitative improvement, with repetition and drop-out rates and the number of three-shift classes declining. Vocational schools and classes have expanded.

There has been considerable progress in most aspects of education, but some aspects of the change in the delivery of education deserve careful monitoring, particularly in relation to the identification of poverty and gender issues. Almost daily reporting in the press suggests that the lack of funds to meet school fees and other costs is reducing access by the poor to education.

Increased schooling costs could have a negative impact on girls' access to higher education. The gender imbalance is already worse at the higher levels of the educational system. This may reflect prejudice but may also reflect a rational response to investment in human capital in the face of a job market which, while not subject to extreme imbalance, tends to provide more lucrative job opportunities to men. This imbalance could be reinforced if the government proceeds vigorously with plans for the 'socialisation' of social service provision.[2]

Poverty is associated with poor access to education both as cause and effect. Low educational attainment limits access to jobs and higher household incomes which are key to greater access to education. The results of the LSMS demonstrated the strong correlation between poverty and education, with the poverty rate declining as the level of education rises. Low educational attainment among parents also affects the economic prospects for the next generation, influencing decisions about education, child delivery and child rearing.

Large family size is also both a cause and the effect of poverty. In 1998, the average number of children per woman in the poorest quintile was 3.5 compared to 2.1 in the richest quintile. As a result, the dependency level among the poorest quintile was 0.95 compared to 0.37 among the richest quintile.

Poor health is also a factor pushing families into poverty, because of both the loss of income and the medical costs. Preventative health has improved through programs to expand immunisation, eradicate polio and also blindness caused by Vitamin A deficiency (dry eye blindness), increase malaria protection, prevent goitre, increase the proportion of the population with access to clean water, and improve access to health services in rural areas. The health insurance system has been expanded and partial cost recovery in hospitals has contributed to the financial viability of health centre operations.

However, despite remarkable improvements in health standards over the past decade, health inequality has widened. The 1998 Household LSMS found that the annual average number of sick days of the poorest quintile is 3.07, compared to about 2.4 for the richest quintile. Over the period 1993–97, the sickness status of the richest quintile was reduced by 30 per cent while that of the poor remained unchanged.

NOTES

[1] For example, the erosion of the communal resource base at the village level, as a result of the reduction in the role of the cooperatives in rural production, resulted in a reduction in the provision of pre-school facilities at the early stages of the reform process.

[2] The government has adopted this somewhat strange choice of terminology to describe proposals to increase user charges for social services.

16

POVERTY, LOCATION AND INTERNAL MIGRATION

POVERTY AND LOCATION

As noted above, one long-term poverty issue concerns what is to be done with the upland, remote and isolated areas and ethnic minority areas where many of the poor are concentrated.[1] In some cases, limited development may be largely a matter of physical isolation, which will be reduced as the transport system is strengthened. But some areas have inherently harsh natural conditions, with a high propensity to natural disaster and a poor natural resource base. This is especially important for ethnic minorities, the majority of whom live in remote and isolated areas. Ethnic minority communities make up around 29 per cent of the poor even though they form only about 14 per cent of the total national population.

Current approaches to poverty alleviation place a good deal of emphasis on targeting poor areas. Such an approach has the obvious merit of providing a straightforward way of targeting the poor. If poverty results from an infrastructural constraint (for example, poor transport access) that can readily relaxed through a focused investment program, poverty may be reduced by enhancing productivity, contributing both a reduction in poverty and growth in output. This, however, will not work in all instances. Where natural conditions are not propitious to growth, there may be little or no productive return from investment. In that case, geographically focused investment will neither increase output nor have a lasting effect on poverty reduction.

From the perspective of economic history, one response to persistent poverty in regions with basically poor conditions for productive investment has been migration. Historically, migration in Viet Nam has been a response to poverty.[2] Considerable migration continues in modern Vietnam, both from the countryside to the urban centres and from one rural area to another. A critical resource allocation choice may be whether to tackle the problems of the poor *in situ*, or to provide more economic opportunities in the areas where investment is most productive, and encourage the poor to move to take them up.[3]

This suggests a potential flaw in emphasising poverty alleviation through area-focused programs. Accelerated growth in an area may be associated with a reduction in the proportion of poor without necessarily benefiting the target group. Thus, high growth in the Central Highlands has been associated an influx of people seeking to benefit for example from the fast growth in tree crop production. This may result in an increase in the proportion of better-off households without necessarily reducing the poverty of the initial residents.

In the long run, reductions in poverty will involve both increases in rural income and the movement of population from the countryside to urban areas. Rural–urban shift can allow migrants to benefit from the better income opportunities in urban areas and improve rural incomes by tightening rural labour markets. An overview of the factors influencing poverty therefore needs to consider the potential rural–urban population movement. The discussion in the remaining parts of this chapter addresses that issue.

CONFLICTING EVIDENCE ON RURAL–URBAN TRANSITION[4]

Viet Nam is experiencing urbanisation, but there has been a good deal of uncertainty regarding the rapidity of this process.

In the mid 1990s, the government assumed that the pace of urbanisation would accelerate and had projected urban growth at 5 per cent for the period 1995–2000 and at 5.5 per cent for 2000–10. The Urban Strategy Team reporting at that time took the government projections as representing an 'high growth scenario', and also used as 'lower growth scenario' based on extrapolation of apparent existing trends, projecting 2.5 per cent per annum growth between 1993 and 2000 and 4.0 per cent per annum for 2000–10. The difference between these two scenarios was not trivial. The lower projection forecast an increase in urban population as a proportion of the total population to 29 per cent in 2000 and 35 per cent in 2010, whereas the government projection was of 34 per cent and 48 per cent respectively. That is, the different projections established a range for the urban population of between 35 and 47 million people.

Differences of this magnitude reflect more than a statistical quirk; they suggest that there is a basic lack of certainty and agreement regarding the expected speed of the rural–urban transition in Viet Nam, based upon whether expectations are derived from the apparently slow pace of transition in recent years, or from the likely impact of the accelerated growth. The differences may be moot, however, because the recorded rate of urbanisation has so far apparently been significantly lower than predicted by either of the projections. The 1999 Census recorded the urban population as still being only 23.6 per cent of the total (compared to 19.4 per cent in 1989).

The available evidence has been confusing regarding to the momentum of urbanisation, ranging from official data in the mid 1990s that suggested that there was very little movement to the cities to unofficial estimates that as many as 700,000 people were migrating to urban areas each year.

A difficulty was raised when a number of rural communes were reclassified as urban in 1997, causing the official urban population to jump 9 per cent. Furthermore, the Viet Nam Urban Sector Strategy Study (Ministry of Construction 1995) noted that the Vietnamese definition of urban residence did not conform to international practice because rural areas within cities and municipalities were excluded from the urban totals. The study team estimated that, using the more inclusive definition, about 8 per cent more of the population resided in urban areas than suggested by official estimates at that time.

Another difficulty arises from unauthorised urban migration. The Urban Sector Strategy Study (Ministry of Construction 1995:53) estimated that there were almost 200,000 unregistered immigrants in Ho Chi Minh City in the period 1986–94 (however, some of these would have become registered by the end of that period). Unregistered migration of that magnitude would have resulted in annual urban growth rates greater than 3 per cent (as compared with official estimates around 2 per cent). Apart from the issue of bureaucratic definitions of residence, there is always an element of ambiguity about migration in the urbanisation process. There will always be temporary migrants seeking employment, many of whom will eventually become residents.

Critical aspects of the urbanisation expected to take place in Viet Nam over the coming generation are already inherent in existing trends. The likely rate of urban growth will be around 2.5–3.0 per cent per annum, based on interpretation of the various somewhat conflicting data, implying that the urban population will double in 25–30 years.

THE DEVELOPMENT OF URBAN GROWTH POLES

Urbanisation will inevitably lead to the concentration of industry and many services in a few areas. Government has accepted this likelihood by emphasising the development of three focal economic zones where infrastructure and other facilities are being developed on a priority basis to attract both domestic and foreign investment.

The two key urban growth poles which have emerged are around Ho Chi Minh City and the corridor to Vung Tau in the Southeast region, and around Hanoi and the Hanoi–Hai Phong corridor in the Red River region.

Ho Chi Minh City and its neighbouring area is already the major centre for commercial and industrial development and is set to become one of the strategic urban growth poles of Southeast Asia. Not only is this virtually inevitable, given existing trends, but is also desirable—a dynamic and fast growing commercial centre will make a crucial contribution to the growth of the economy of Viet Nam. As the main focal point for commercial links with the rest of Southeast Asia and the rest of the world, the character and pace of its development will be strongly influenced by foreign investment.

The growth of Ho Chi Minh City is fed by the in-migration of large numbers of Vietnamese and also of foreign business people and professionals. Vietnamese migration into the city has a bi-modal character: the city attracts unskilled workers with only basic education, but acts as a magnet for the highly educated, who can take advantage of the most sophisticated job opportunities that the development of the city generates (Centre for Population and Human Resources Studies, 1995).

The development of Ho Chi Minh City to become a metropolis of more than five million people has necessitated substantial investment in infrastructure. Its international role demands a high level of services and a cosmopolitan urban environment. The government will have to steer between two dangers—that underinvestment in infrastructure chokes off the desired commercial development of the area and the danger that the demands of a fast growing and (relatively) high income urban area monopolise scarce resources, holding back the development of other areas. Ho Chi Minh City will have income levels, and will therefore demand service levels, out of line with conditions in the rest of the country. This suggests the need for careful programming of urban infrastructure and the search for imaginative solutions to potential problems before they arise (for example, transport modes to minimise urban congestion, land and credit policies which encourage household investment in low cost housing).

Since the mid 1990s, there has been an acceleration in urban growth in the northern 'focal zone' (Hanoi–Hai Phong), with industrial growth rates overtaking those of the southern zone.[5] Investment is drawn to Hanoi because of its facilities as the national capital. The trends now suggest that Viet Nam will have two large metropolitan growth poles. The pace of change in Ho Chi Minh City and Hanoi is already dramatically changing the character of the urban environment. Highrise development, funded by foreign investment, sprawling-small scale construction by the domestic private sector, and booming spending on motorised transport, have already changed the face of Vietnamese cities. The future path of urban development may be being chosen already, which means that some options may be closing without being given proper consideration (for example, in relation to transport modes).

There is less evidence of an integrated pole developing around the Quang Nam–Da Nang–Quang Ngai focal area in the central part of the country. In 1999, the population of Da Nang city, the fourth largest city in Viet Nam, was only 540,000. The share of manufacturing in GDP in this area is only slightly lower than in the Red River delta and irrigation in the region is the second highest in the country. Yet yields per capita in agriculture and per capita GDP are lower than the national average.

The emerging Vietnamese industrial economy can therefore be viewed as consisting of three regional sub-economies. The south has a well integrated, dynamic and rapidly growing economy. The Hanoi–Hai Phong corridor is now consolidating as the centre of a potentially powerful core–periphery economy in the north. The three regions along the central spine of the country have not yet been drawn into a core–periphery relationship with the focal economic area around Da Nang.

The first period of accelerated growth benefited the Southeast more than the other regions, particularly as most of the initial foreign investment was directed there. As growth has accelerated, the Hanoi–Hai Phong corridor has increasingly benefited.

A number of second and third-level towns are developing as significant urban centres (for example, Hue, Can Tho, Bien Hoa, and Nha Trang, all towns of more than 200,000 population) and serve as centres to stimulate rural development in their hinterlands. This de-concentration of urban development is a positive factor in supporting the geographical diffusion of the benefits of growth.

THE IMPLICATIONS OF RURAL–URBAN TRANSITION— ALTERNATIVE SCENARIOS

The nature of the future rural–urban transition could be crucial for the future pattern of income distribution and for poverty alleviation. A rural–urban shift can be associated with high growth but can also be associated with economic stagnation. While data on recent rates of urbanisation suggest that the rate of urbanisation is still quite modest, sustained economic growth will shift the centre of gravity of the economy from rural, agricultural activities to urban industry and services. As a consequence, the population will likely be attracted into urban areas by higher income opportunities.

Rural economic stagnation can also promote a rural–urban shift as deteriorating rural conditions push people to move to the cities. The desirable rate of urbanisation depends on the interplay of two concerns. On the one hand, the expansion of urban infrastructure is expensive, suggesting that a low pace of urbanisation would be more manageable. On the other hand, a low rate of growth of urban employment is likely to result in a widening of the gap between urban and rural incomes.

A healthy pattern of urbanisation is more likely to emerge from movements resulting from the attractions (pull factors) of expanding urban livelihood opportunities than from rural stagnation (pushing people out of rural areas). So far, the government of Viet Nam has avoided extreme urban bias.

Available evidence indicates that, while there are significant differences between rural and urban areas in the delivery of social services, the basic education and health outcomes do not vary dramatically. Thus, the literacy rate for people 10 years old and over in rural and urban areas is about 85 per cent and 94 per cent respectively. Similarly, indicators of morbidity show that 39 per cent of the population reported sick in the previous 12 months in rural areas as compared to 33 per cent in urban areas.

The incentive to migrate to urban areas could be moderated if social services are maintained at reasonable levels in rural areas and income opportunities in rural non-agricultural activities are expanded.

Nevertheless, although healthy development requires attention to rural development, it is also the case that urbanisation will be an inevitable outcome of economic growth, and expanding urban employment will play a key role in long-term poverty reduction. High rates of growth in the industrial and service sectors will be associated with increases both in the numbers employed in those activities and with increasing labour productivity. For a given increase in urban GDP, if the balance is struck more in the direction of increasing employment levels rather than raising average urban incomes, the widening in the gap between levels of urban and rural productivity (and incomes) can be restrained. That is, high rates of growth in urban population are not only an unavoidable side product of industrialisation, but are in one respect a desirable consequence.

The international experience of urbanisation has varied. The phenomenon of rapid urbanisation has been associated with successful development, but in many developing countries it has also been associated with economic stagnation and negative social consequences. Even where rapid urbanisation has been associated with national economic success, the poor social outcomes in terms of the condition of the urban poor and the stress of middle-class urban life are still apparent in some developing economies.

In a number of countries, the allocation of resources to support over-concentrated patterns of urban growth has been associated with rural stagnation, with the lack of economic opportunities in the countryside pushing the rural population to migrate to the cities, where many are recruited to an urban underclass. Investment rushes to an urban core, followed by a rush of migrants in search of better jobs, while the peripheral areas are left to stagnate. The incidence of poverty in the periphery is then matched by festering and crammed shanty towns in the ill-prepared urban cores. Crime, stress, pollution, congestion and overloaded transport and communication systems come to dominate the life of the city, while the vast majority eke out a living in the informal sector. The result has been unmanageable urban environments and increasing rural and urban poverty. Also, the resulting imbalances in urban and rural development have in many instances generated constraints on growth, which at the extreme have resulted in a vicious circle of high rates of urban population growth associated with low rates of economic growth.

In a more positive scenario, urban growth contributes to the development of the rural periphery through the expanding market for rural products, the spread of improved infrastructure and social services, and the withdrawal of surplus labour from rural areas, all of which lead to rising prosperity in the rural hinterland.

While high economic growth will result inevitably in urbanisation, the consequences of that transition will vary, depending on whether urban growth is combined with continued improvements in rural incomes, or whether it is associated with rural stagnation. Rural stagnation not only creates problems for rural areas, but makes urban development more difficult to manage, as the rural poor are forced into the cities as a survival strategy. A more virtuous scenario is one where accelerated urban growth is linked to expansion in rural economic opportunities.

So far, development in Viet Nam has achieved a reasonably virtuous urbanisation pattern because rural households have enjoyed increasing income levels notwithstanding the widening gap between urban and rural incomes. Certain features of Viet Nam suggest that the prospects of the virtuous process of rural–urban transition continuing are reasonable.

- With its long coastline and two areas of dense population (the Red River delta and the Mekong delta), the underlying geography (and history) does not provide the conditions which would give rise to one growth pole, resulting in a single megalopolis (such as Mexico City or Manila).
- The two highest potential agricultural areas (the Red River and Mekong deltas) are adjacent to the two leading urban growth poles (Hanoi–Hai Phong and Ho Chi Minh City) creating good possibilities for linkages between urban and rural development.
- While the growth in the industrial and service industries has been much higher than that of agriculture, the growth of the agricultural sector has been lively—in some areas high enough to generate labour scarcities and local wages higher than unskilled wages in the major urban areas.
- Although the evidence is not conclusive, data suggest that an explosion in the urban growth rate has not yet happened.

- In some parts of country, there has been a lively growth in rural industry, and the potential for further development of rural non-agricultural activities is high.

PATTERNS OF MIGRATION

Migration patterns revealed in the 1992–93 VLSS and the Census of 1999 indicate some acceleration of urbanisation in Viet Nam. Data from the VLSS indicated that most rural migration (75 per cent) was to other rural areas, with 25 per cent of rural migrants moving to urban areas and 40 per cent of urban migrants moving to other urban areas. Data from the 1999 census show a substantial increase in these figures with 42 per cent of rural migrants now moving to urban areas and 72 per cent of urban migrants moving to other urban areas. However, migration to rural areas remains important. The Central Highlands has continued to attract a large amount of rural in-migration as has the Red River delta and Southeast area. Ho Chi Minh City and the Vung Tau corridor has seen the highest level of in-migration taking 43 per cent of migrants according to 1999 Census, and Hanoi has increased its in-migration, now taking 12 per cent. Despite these obvious urban core areas pulling migrants from surrounding areas as well as from further afield, the Central Highlands has continued to be an important destination for migrants, accounting for 25 per cent of in-migration between 1994 and 1999 (compared to 44 per cent between 1984–89).

In the Southeastern region the share of manufacturing in GDP was already as high at 25 per cent in the mid 1990s. It was only half that or less in all other regions except the Red River delta, where it was around 14 per cent. Per capita GDP in the Southeast was about double the national average at VND5,275 in 1994. Every other region was below the national average. Moreover, GDP was growing at 11 per cent in this region as compared to 7 per cent or less in most other regions.[6] The fairly high population density of the region is mainly a reflection of the concentration of population in Ho Chi Minh City and along the corridor to Vung Tau. An economic growth pole is clearly emerging along this corridor, its periphery lying in the Southeast region itself and the adjoining provinces of the Mekong Delta region. The latter is one of the country's most dynamic agricultural regions, with paddy yields of over 3 tonnes per hectare and the highest per capita value of agricultural output in the country. The return to land is also reflected in the rental value of land, which is also the highest in the country.[7] In the mid 1990s the region grew at an annual rate of 6–7 per cent, and had the highest GDP per capita after the Southeast and the Red River Delta.

The Red River delta is the second largest region after the Mekong delta in terms of population, with over 14 million people. It has the second highest manufacturing share of GDP after the Southeast at 14 per cent and has received large in-migrations from the Northern Mountain region as well as the North Central Coast region. The region's population density is the highest in the country (1,142 per square kilometre), about three times that of the Southeast and the Mekong Delta. Ninety per cent of the region's cropped area is irrigated, the highest proportion in the country and more than double that of the Mekong delta. Paddy yield at 3.8 tons per hectare is the highest in the country.[8] Per capita GDP is higher than in the Mekong Delta and the growth rate is second only to that of the Southeast. However, the Red River delta region also has one of the largest concentrations of people in poverty in the country because of the high density of population. In this region, more than anywhere else, labour needs to be drawn into non-agricultural activities in order to reduce the intense pressure of population on land.

As noted earlier, the response of a number of donors and the government to the dangers of unequal development has been to focus special attention to the poorest groups and poorest districts. The government has placed particular emphasis on the needs of 'mountainous and remote areas', as the poorest and most problematic. The World Bank Poverty Assessment and Strategy projections of regional incidence of poverty under alternative growth scenarios suggest that poverty is likely to be particularly intractable in the Northern Uplands and North Central regions (World Bank 1995b).

Poverty alleviation should be about tackling the problems of poor people rather than poor areas—in the development of all countries, part of the poverty problem is resolved by the poor in areas of limited potential moving to high growth areas. In this regard, although policy should aim to manage the rural–urban transition to avoid rural stagnation pushing the migration rate to undesirable levels, there will be high levels of rural–urban and rural–rural migration.[9]

Although a 'poverty alleviation strategy' should involve attention to the poorest regions, that concentration should be tempered by the facts that resources are limited and the poor are many and are to be found in all regions. Although the VLSS and the World Bank correctly identified the Northern Uplands and North Central regions as having particularly high poverty problems, with 58.6 per cent and 48.0 per cent below the poverty line respectively, the absolute numbers of poor in the two densely populated deltas was also large. Choices must be made regarding which poor are targeted in the first instance. Given the scarce resources at Viet Nam's disposal, it might make good sense to alleviate poverty, at least in part, by supporting growth in areas where there are concentrations of poor people but which have a reasonable medium-term growth potential. It would be highly desirable to focus on those low income groups that, with some help, could raise their own incomes rapidly—thus achieving both growth and poverty alleviation. This may include encouraging the potential for highly dynamic small-scale development among those who are not so poor and in provinces which have already demonstrated growth potential.

Thus a possible regional focus for an accelerated rural development strategy which would both support high growth and achieve a reasonably wide diffusion of benefits in the specific circumstances of Viet Nam would be to target the 'middle sectors'—the viable and growing small business sector, rural areas which have already demonstrated good development potential and areas which can be provided with reasonable access to the main growth centres with relative ease (that is, a strategy to promote linkages between the three focal development zones and their immediate hinterlands).

Judgment will be required about the existing or potential comparative advantage of the three focal economic zones and their hinterlands, both for the home market as well as for exports. The characteristics of the three zones vary in relation to existing economic activities, land–labour ratios and their natural resource base. Analysis of potential constraints that might limit the realisation of the potential comparative advantage can provide insights into the required government interventions. It should also be noted, however, that the detailed characteristics of a dynamic process of small-scale industrial growth are inherently difficult to predict because they depend on local-level responses to market opportunities.

The government has committed itself to the development of a third economic zone in Quang Nam–Da Nang–Quang Ngai. This strategy seeks to develop the central coast, so that the development of the country is not focused entirely on the two more highly developed areas to the north and south of the country. But the development of this zone is problematic because it does not extrapolate established patterns of urban growth. Although Da Nang is the fourth-largest city in Viet Nam, it has less than a half million urban population and has not yet attracted foreign investors in numbers that would suggest that it about to become a key centre. Quang Ngai has a population of just over 100,000 and is not even among Viet Nam's top 40 towns.

Public investment will have to play a far more prominent role in the central regions and the Quang Nam–Da Nang–Quang Ngai focal area than it has elsewhere. Though the area is yet to pick up the momentum of growth, it has longer-term economic possibilities because of its strategic location. Highway No.1, connecting the northern and southern parts of the country, is being restored and a bold scheme has been proposed under the Greater Mekong sub-regional initiative to build a transnational highway from the eastern seaboard of this area, through Laos, to Bangkok and beyond. To complete the link, the region will also have to be provided with an improved deep water port. Once these projects are implemented, the focal economic area located at the crossing of these two major transport corridors would re-emerge as a great commercial hub, as it used to be in the distant past. It could then draw all the contiguous regions into its periphery, providing them with convenient outlets not only to the national market but also to the rest of the world.

NOTES

[1] Van de Walle and Gunewardena (2000) examine this in some detail.

[2] Hardy (2000:27) discusses the phenomenon of 'two white hands people' (*dan hai ban tay trang*) or the movement of poor landless peasants within Vietnam looking for work and eventually settling.

[3] Post-war population redistribution programs had questionable outcomes but surely established a vanguard that was the basis for future cash crop expansion and diversification and established the infrastructure allowing future migration.

[4] Parts of this section are based on Van Arkadie and Mundle (1996).

[5] In 1994 Hanoi overtook Ho Chi Minh City as the favoured location for foreign investment, as measured by the total value of newly licensed projects in that year (although Ho Chi Minh City remained the clear leader in terms of the accumulated total of licensed projects).

[6] The reported growth rate for the Central Highlands is 8 per cent in the VLSS. However, the reported paddy yield of 4.2 tonnes for this region is clearly inaccurate and distorts other derivative estimates for this region.

[7] This is barring the reported rental value of almost VND 6,000 for the Central Coastal region. This is completely out of line with the rental data for the rest of the country and is probably incorrect.

[8] This excludes the reported yield for the Central Highlands, which is probably inaccurate.

[9] The Central Highlands region has enjoyed a particularly high rate of growth of rural GDP compared to the national average (11.34 per cent in 1993 compared to 4.60 per cent for the Red River delta and 7.5 per cent for Viet Nam overall. See World Bank 1995b:Table 2.1). Economic growth in the Central Highlands has been associated with movement into the region. Continued growth at that rate would not only reduce the poverty of those currently resident in the Central Highlands, but would also sustain further in-migration from other rural areas.

17

ACHIEVEMENTS OF *DOI MOI* AND FUTURE CHALLENGES

One objective in writing this book was to provide a comprehensive review of developments in the economy and the evolution of economic policy since the mid 1980s. Hopefully, the preceding chapters have described salient features of economic change in Viet Nam, helped illustrate the complexities of the economic policymaking process and highlighted some of the ambiguities in explaining Viet Nam's performance. It is hoped that, at a minimum, this information will be useful to some readers in making their own assessment of Viet Nam's performance and the major factors affecting it.

A more ambitious objective was to interpret and explain some key factors driving Vietnamese economic growth, and to assess any implications for development planning elsewhere. At the beginning of this book, a warning was offered about the care needed in drawing lessons from national experience for more general application. Certainly, this account has identified a number of characteristics of Viet Nam which were quite special to the country, including its specific history, geographical location and natural resource endowment. Moreover, the acceleration of Vietnamese growth happened when the East Asian economic boom was at its height and the world economy was in an upswing. Nevertheless, there are a number of aspects of the Vietnamese experience that may be useful in thinking about development policy issues more generally.

THE ROLE OF THE STATE

The Vietnamese experience offers some evidence regarding the role of the state in development. The lessons are not simple and are certainly subject to alternative interpretations.

It was possible to view the Vietnamese state as being a 'weak state' in terms of its economic management capability, as has been argued by some commentators (for example, Fforde and de Vylder (1996), who identified the state as weak because of failures to implement stated policy intentions effectively during the pre-reform period). An alternative approach sees the measured nature, continuity and national ownership of the policymaking process as characteristics of a strong state. The differences in interpretation partly reflect the gap that often exists between the definition of objectives and policies at the national level and the pragmatic accommodation of the decentralised decisions of individual actors in the economy, even when these are in apparent conflict with stated policies. The arguments developed in this volume posit that this pragmatic willingness to accept change resulting from decentralised initiatives is indicative of the strength of the state.

The Vietnamese experience suggests the need for a balanced view about the appropriate role of government intervention in the economy. Viet Nam has combined a willingness to shift vigorously towards using market policy instruments and maintaining a fairly orthodox macroeconomic stance, while maintaining an active role for the state, particularly in investing in infrastructure and human resource development, and in providing strong planning and policy guidance regarding medium-term growth and equity goals.

In that broad sense, Viet Nam can be seen as yet another variation on the East Asian model of the developmental state. The approach has been both flexible in the use of market instruments and pragmatic about the requirements for active state intervention to develop infrastructure and market institutions and influence the allocation of resources to realise national social and economic development goals.

This study has not been about political goals or the merits of alternative political institutions. In recent years, however, issues of 'good governance' have played an important part in the development literature and the thinking of donors. Insofar as the governance agenda is about asserting a particular set of political values and Western political institutions, it lies outside the economic policy issues that are the focus of this study. A particular view of governance is currently being promoted which sees good governance not only as a set of desirable political values but also as an appropriate means of achieving economic development with equity (UK Department of International Development 2001). What light does the Vietnamese experience throw on the relationship between political institutions and growth with equity?

Viet Nam certainly does not conform to the model which is implicit (and sometimes explicit) in the donor literature on governance. It is a one-party state, there are definite limits on the role of autonomous institutions representative of what is called 'civil society' in the governance literature, and the system is perceived to be fairly corrupt. Yet Viet Nam has benefited from the continuity of political institutions, which has provided a stable environment and has enabled the Vietnamese authorities to make decisive macroeconomic policy decisions at times when there were strong economic reasons for action. The particular Vietnamese method of policymaking provided the basis for a pragmatic and gradual ('step-by-step' to use the Vietnamese term) process of institutional change. The continuity and stability of political institutions was underpinned by a complex consensus-building process that sometimes has resulted in a slow and opaque decision making process, which has had its frustrations, but which has also helped ensure ownership of the reform process by national institutions and facilitated profound institutional changes with minimal open conflict or tension. Despite the one-party system, the government eventually responded to domestic pressures to introduce reforms because of grassroots pressure for action to address the country's economic crisis in the mid 1980s and has in recent years been sensitive to local discontent.

Many external observers have trouble reconciling the fact that such far-reaching change and economic development has occurred under the aegis of an avowedly one-party Marxist-Leninist state. The successful implementation of *Doi Moi* suggests that implementation of political liberalisation is not a necessary initial condition for successful economic reform or the acceleration of economic growth and poverty alleviation.[1] Indeed, the counter-historical hypothesis might be that if abrupt political change had been attempted alongside the economic changes, growth could have been more difficult to achieve, as it could have led to instability, less coherent economic policies and uncertainties that would have increased investment risk and made it more difficult to protect property rights.

Of course the fact that Viet Nam has achieved a relatively strong development performance with a one-party system in no way suggests that a one-party political system is either a necessary or sufficient condition for successful development. Successful East Asian economies have achieved growth and poverty alleviation under various regimes, including various forms of multi-party system, and with varying degrees of authoritarian leadership. Under a one-party system, Viet Nam has experienced both economic stagnation relative to other East Asian economies (1976–88) and a period of relatively strong economic performance in the 1990s. Despite the one-party system, the government eventually acted decisively (in the late 1980s) to confront a mounting economic crisis and is responsive to the needs of the mass of the people. However, the nature of the domestic political processes that resulted in this change remains poorly understood.[2]

What the study does suggest is that relative stability in social and political institutions can be particularly important in generating investor confidence, entrepreneurial activity, and thus competition, in a situation where the formal legal and institutional framework for business and commercial activity remains weak. Moreover, such stability may facilitate a successful pragmatic process of innovation and shield the economy from reckless experiments in launching untried solutions. In practice, the stable system may provide a good foundation for the subsequent development of effective market institutions.

The conclusion therefore is that, although it is the normal stuff of politics to espouse one or another set of political values as desirable and to promote particular political institutions that reflect those values, it is questionable that any particular political model can be justified as a vehicle for economic growth.

The reality is that terms such as 'one-party' and 'multi-party' each encompass a wide range of factors and institutions important to economic actors. In some respects, the way the Vietnamese state operated in practice is not particularly consistent with what observers might expect of a Marxist-Leninist state. The state has managed to combine a degree of authority and legitimacy for national institutions with considerable autonomy in practice at the local level (both in local government and in state-owned business). On the other hand, the state continues to exercise tight control over direct criticism of the political system and stifles the work of national intellectuals and authors who offer alternative political views.

One by-product of the nature of the Vietnamese government system is that the policy process has remained under strong domestic control, with strong national ownership. At the most critical periods of reform in the late 1980s and early 1990s, access to external financial assistance was negligible. This meant that any external advice was largely judged on its merits rather than being accepted primarily as a means of unlocking donor coffers.[3] The national ownership of policy was unequivocal. When conditionality attached to large transfers of official development assistance emerged as a factor in the policymaking process, there is little evidence to suggest that this was effective in accelerating reform.

Political stability and orderly (albeit bureaucratic)[4] administration provided an adequately predictable context for economic decision making, despite the limited development of a formal legal system. Nevertheless, as the non-state sector expands and the economy grows in size and complexity the economic returns from more formal market institutions, including a transparent legal system, will also increase.

Through much of the reform period, the design of the business regulatory environment was not conducive to—and often discouraged—domestic private sector development. However, in practice, the system accommodated growth in small-scale private sector activity. No doubt the regulatory system imposed hidden costs on private business, both in the pecuniary sense of the 'envelopes' to be passed to officials and in terms of the time involved in handling bureaucratic processes. Furthermore, ambiguities regarding legal rights and obligations and in official attitudes towards private wealth left successful business people vulnerable, and encouraged secrecy and strategic alliances with state officials in conducting business. Nevertheless, the growth of the non-state sector has been lively. The extent of informal business activity was evidenced by the rapid registration of businesses when procedures were simplified, and costs reduced, under the new enterprise law.

One difficulty in drawing lessons from the Vietnamese experience is that it demonstrates that the informal characteristics of the institutions and understanding of the economic 'rules of the game' are quite as important as the formal institutions. At early stages of transition and development, having a reasonably predictable political environment and social stability may be more important than adopting a formal legal framework of the kind that underpins market economies in more developed countries. This has non-trivial implications for policy advisors, and for the design of programs to support institutional and policy reform in transition and developing economies.

AGRICULTURAL DEVELOPMENT

The Vietnamese experience confirms the importance of agricultural transformation as a component of successful growth in a low-income country with a predominantly rural population. This is, of course, not an original or surprising conclusion. But there are also lessons to be learnt about how transformation is to be achieved.

While a comprehensive analysis of the sources of agricultural growth in Viet Nam has not yet been made, salient characteristics included

- a fairly egalitarian system of land-holding which ensured access to land for rural households
- that the use of market instruments to coordinate and provide incentives to farm households, beginning with reforms in the early 1980s, stimulated growth. Efficient, functioning markets are especially important as an economic coordinating mechanism for small-holder agriculture
- that increasingly competitive commodity markets were supported by effective public provision of basic infrastructure (notably water and transport)
- that progress in human development has facilitated the transfer of ideas and improved technology, and has underpinned strong productivity growth
- that continued functioning of organisations responsible for research, extension and distribution of inputs (by a mix of private and public enterprise, the latter despite financial stress) has facilitated productivity growth. While the support system is sub-optimal, it has been sufficiently effective to help facilitate the transfer of new technology
- that opening up domestic and international markets has greatly expanded choices, increased value added per worker, and thus increased income
- fluid population movement can be conducive to both growth and poverty alleviation—for example, encouraging migration and investment to open up new areas for tree-crop production.

INVESTMENT IN HUMAN CAPITAL

A strong commitment was made to investment in human capital in the period before reform as well as during the reform period. This included a massive commitment to basic education which resulted in very high levels of literacy in rural as well as urban areas, and for women as well as men. Viet Nam, as a consequence, is a society with widespread adult literacy.

A good deal of effort was also devoted to technical and professional training, including technical training outside Viet Nam, as well as development of national technical training capacity. Viet Nam was successful initially in developing and utilising capabilities in intermediate technology, constructing buildings and other physical facilities and producing goods for the domestic market cheaply and of appropriate standard for a low income market, while more recently it has begun to adapt its technology to the more demanding standards required for export markets.

There has also been a strong commitment to basic health care, including children's health, which resulted in much better statistics for mortality and life expectancy than are usually found in a country with such a low per capita income level.

Broad-based investment in human capital paid off in terms of the receptivity to technical change and the economic opportunities emerging in the reform period.[5] Relatively strong education and health services have also contributed to the speedy demographic transition.

POVERTY ALLEVIATION

The successful Vietnamese performance over the past decade in alleviating poverty is capable of alternative interpretations, which can lend support to varying approaches to poverty reduction strategies.

One possible interpretation is that promoting growth is an effective poverty alleviation strategy. In a country with pervasive poverty, of the kind prevalent in Viet Nam in the 1980s, economic growth is a necessary condition for widespread poverty reduction, and at that stage of growth it did not make sense to divert resources from high growth potential investments to low potential investments on distributional grounds. To be sustainable, poverty alleviation should be about the development of productive capacity, rather than redistributive welfare measures.

Market liberalisation, because it promoted high growth, also supported rapid poverty alleviation. In particular, market reforms were a key input into the acceleration of agricultural growth, much of it based on the household farm, a critical factor in reducing rural poverty, while the fast growth of small and medium-sized enterprise generated widespread income opportunities.

However, some aspects of the market-led growth strategy may create difficulties for poverty alleviation in the future. Despite the improvements in rural incomes, the absolute gap between urban and rural incomes is widening persistently and substantially.

It must also be recognised that poverty alleviation in the 1990s was not simply the result of reforms. The liberalisation measures took effect in an economy with important features inherited from the pre-reform period which spread the benefits of growth, in particular the sustained commitment to investment in human capital, the lack of great inequalities in the access to assets (especially land) and modest differentials in employment incomes.

ENTERPRISE AND INDUSTRY POLICY

It is in the area of enterprise policy that the Vietnamese authorities have been most persistently criticised, notably in relation to the slow pace at which changes in ownership of state-owned enterprise have been introduced, the rather negative regulatory environment facing private domestic business and the cautious approach to providing incentives to foreign investors. And yet Viet Nam has achieved high growth, including rapid expansion in the private domestic sector and in private foreign investment.

One response of critics to this evidence of successful growth despite the slowness of enterprise reform is that growth would have been even faster with more conducive policies and that, in the current harsh international business climate, failure to reform more vigorously will hold up future development.

An alternative, and not particularly transferable, explanation is that, if the 'animal spirits' of business enterprise are sufficiently lively, the policy environment may not be of primary importance (aggressive entrepreneurs, public and private, domestic and foreign, may be able to get round unhelpful regulations). This is unhelpful to the economic policymaker because the supply of entrepreneurship is largely exogenous. It does suggest, however, the need for careful evaluation of underlying entrepreneurial capacities and investment opportunities when judging the potential efficacy of policies—there are surely countries that have implemented 'open door' policies only to discover the lack of applicants to enter.

By contrast, this study has also argued that Vietnamese policy towards the private sector has often been more accommodating in practice than in rhetoric (reversing a more normal situation). The accommodation of an emerging national private sector had a positive impact which is likely to become increasingly important.

In relation to state enterprises, interpretation is more controversial. While price and trading reforms, abolition of direct subsidies, and other reforms have fairly rapidly exposed state enterprises to much greater competition, ownership reform has been slow, with consolidation rather than privatisation. Slow movement in this area has been a particular focus of criticism from within the donor community. Nonetheless, slow state enterprise reform has not proved to be the drag on growth predicted by external commentators. While it is not difficult to come across horror stories of inefficiency, and of large monopoly rents (for example, in telecommunications), there are also many examples of successful joint ventures and of productive contributions made by the sector.

It may be that the competitive environment faced by many state enterprises stimulated improved performance, while a degree of decentralisation permitted innovation by state enterprise managers. This would suggest that a competitive environment may be a more important factor in determining performance than the nature of ownership—an outcome more consistent with the Lange–Lerner model of combining decentralised public ownership with efficient allocation, than with Kornai's view that a soft budget constraint, and its adverse consequences for efficiency, is the virtually inevitable outcome of widespread public ownership (for example, Kornai 1980).

THE ROLE OF PRIVATE FOREIGN INVESTMENT

Private foreign direct investment played a useful role mainly in two ways. Foreign investment, particularly from other economies in the region, was important in promoting the fast growth in labour-intensive industrial exports. Foreign investment was also important in providing know-how and finance for the fast growth in energy exports.

The impact of foreign investment in real estate development was more ambiguous in that it stimulated a property boom which led to severe excess capacity in some areas (notably hotels). Investment in import substitution industries also led to high-cost excess capacity in some industries (for example, car assembly) but this was not severe enough to undermine overall industrial performance.

The slow pace of financial reform and the limited development of financial and equity markets has meant that foreign portfolio investment has been insignificant. While that may have limited access to external funding, it also shielded the economy from speculative flows and limited the impact of the East Asian financial crisis.

REFORM PROCESSES AND PRESSURES FOR REFORM

Grassroots pressure to improve economic opportunities and increase living standards has been important in driving the reform process. After the euphoria of national reunification, the credibility of the government and the Party increasingly depended on improving living conditions. Periods of deteriorating external conditions increased pressure for change at both the grassroots and top level policymaking.

While much of the reform process remains opaque, several more visible features provide some lessons about the management of a reform process. First, most public policy decisions are only made after broad consensus is reached on policy directions within the system. The initiation of major policy and institutional change requires sustained effort in consensus building. This process, often time consuming, has to be nationally led. Opportunities for external input into these processes are mostly limited either to presentation of international experiences or to assistance in analysing the potential impacts of policy options.

Second, many formal regulatory changes are in effect formalising what is already happening in practice in some parts of the country. Other reform efforts were initially implemented on a pilot basis. In effect, 'learning by doing' has been an important feature of reform efforts. For example, the private sector began to emerge and small-scale private trading was widespread before it was formally legalised. Land-use rights were widely used as collateral for informal credit before such practices were sanctioned by formal legal provisions. More recently, domestic business associations have emerged even though the decree on their operations is still being drafted. Many of the smaller state-owned enterprises have responded rapidly to changing market circumstance, but not always in accordance with state regulations on corporate governance. Indeed, state-owned assets have at times been used for personal benefit. Where policy reforms have clearly been top-down (for example, the bankruptcy and state enterprise laws, and equitisation), implementation is often problematic. At the same time, the backing of Party and government leaders has been important in removing formal institutional barriers to business development.

While entrepreneurs emerged from a broad cross-section of society, contacts with the state apparatus are particularly valuable in periods of regulatory and institutional ambiguity. Many government and Party officials have family and friends engaged in business. Thus, officials were often personally aware of the bureaucratic and administrative constraints faced by entrepreneurs. This has facilitated and encouraged recent moves to more formal consultations between the state and the business community to reduce barriers to business growth.

Finally, unlike in some less developed economies, national policymakers in Viet Nam have rarely relied directly on external advisors in policy formulation. At times, changes promoted by donors and external advisors are adopted, but the process by which this policy change has occurred is difficult to identify or define. Few external advisors would claim to understand fully the policymaking process or to even know who the key players are in the process of developing policy.

In the contemporary setting, it is interesting to speculate whether difficulties in the international economy will be taken as a spur to intensified reform or as a call for greater caution. It could be argued that fast reform is needed in an increasingly competitive environment to attract limited international investment. But it could also be argued that further and more aggressive liberalisation might leave the economy excessively exposed to the consequences of international economic instability (as a corollary to the argument that the slow pace of financial sector reform insulated the economy from some of the worst impacts of the post-1997 East Asian downturn). Regardless, there is little doubt that the government sees continuing trade development and inflows of foreign direct investment as important for the achievement of the rapid increases in productivity, production and incomes needed to further reduce poverty and to reduce income gaps with other East Asian economies.

THE ROLE OF FOREIGN ASSISTANCE

Foreign official development assistance played little role in the acceleration of growth. In fact, the period in which reform was initiated with particular vigour and the acceleration in growth began was characterised by sharp declines in external assistance, as support from the CMEA countries collapsed but had not yet been replaced by flows from members of the development assistance community. Indeed, the sharp growth in foreign assistance flows coincided with a slackening of the growth rate (although a causal relationship is not be to inferred—it was also contemporary with the onset of the East Asian economic crisis).

A plausible case can be made that ideas provided by way of technical assistance activities provided a useful input into the reform process. However, such inputs were primarily of a technical advisory nature. There was little direct input in drafting policy, and such assistance was not associated with aid conditionality and therefore did not erode national ownership of policies.

There is no evidence that the contemporary attempt to introduce pervasive conditionality,[6] particularly by the Bretton Woods institutions, is accelerating or improving the reform process. Vietnamese institutions appear to have been strong enough, and accountable enough to their domestic constituents, to withstand any undue outside influence over national policymaking processes.

WHAT MIGHT HAVE BEEN DONE TO ACHIEVE HIGHER AND/OR MORE EQUITABLE GROWTH?

It trying to explain and interpret Vietnamese policy, we may give the impression that Viet Nam followed a near-optimal strategy. In reality this is never the case—it is always possible to identify areas where there was and is room for policy improvement however much success has been achieved.

Obviously, serious mistakes were made in the 1970s and 1980s. *Doi Moi* and stabilisation reforms could have come sooner.

Once the country moved along the path to reform, probably the key thing they could have been done better was to more quickly and more thoroughly to remove barriers that hinder the development of the domestic private sector. An earlier focus on removing the regulatory, administrative and other barriers to domestic private sector investment would have increased the contribution of the private sector to growth and employment, as is evidenced by the response in the last two years to the belated improvement in business legislation. If there had more focus on exploiting the potential of indigenous entrepreneurship, a considerable Vietnamese resource, rather than concentrating attention on foreign direct investment, growth probably would have been faster and more equitable because more non-farm employment would have been created. The issue is not one of an 'either/or' choice between domestic and foreign investment, but rather a more balanced approach throughout the 1990s and more of an effort to encourage joint foreign investor/domestic private initiatives. For example, income tax regimes that were heavily biased against national tax payers discouraged the development of local talent (especially by foreign investors).

On the other hand, the interpretation developed in this volume suggests that it is difficult to judge what impact accelerated ownership change in state enterprises would have had on growth. Greater effort to reduce monopoly power would have been helpful, both by encouraging competition within the state sector and opening up to competition from private domestic and foreign business. Maybe donors could have focused more on helping domestic agencies develop capacity to undertake substantive analysis of the distributional and efficiency consequences of some key national and provincial monopolies (for example, in agricultural processing and trade), and of continuing barriers to private sector development.

Apparently there was some initial deterioration in the social sector (education and health) during *Doi Moi*, both because of funding constraints and the unintended consequences of some institutional changes (for example, the deterioration of service delivery by rural cooperatives). Also, the move to implement user charges may have consequences in skewing access to social facilities in favour of the better off. Borje Lljunggren, a Swedish former ambassador who has followed developments in Viet Nam during the reform process, has challenged the Vietnamese authorities to make a greater effort to translate their stated commitment to socialism into a more systematic concern for maintaining equitable access to public services (Lljunggren 2001).

Continued attempts to control information flows also increase the costs of acquiring knowledge, market access and technology, and from a significant constraint on the development of knowledge-based industries and information technology.[7]

An area which will require increasing attention is the management of public funds. During the period of great financial stringency, the sheer scarcity of resources constrained budgetary waste. With the fast build-up of foreign aid, there is a grave risk of deterioration in resource use—not surprising given the tendency of donors to push the flow of aid with only limited access to local budgetary processes and information. On the Vietnamese side, the access to 'free' resources encourages a relaxation in budgetary discipline. In this regard, the strong questioning of the waste of aid funds in the National Assembly was a welcome development. Donors could help if they could establish a better connection between their own practices in project and program funding and their rhetoric about the need for improved public sector management.

One area where there is a widespread perception, both by the government leadership and outside observers, that progress has been much too slow is in relation to public administration reform. In parts of this study some of the virtues of the existing system, which may not be immediately apparent, have been identified. These include the real, if not always transparent, efforts to build consensus and the degree of flexibility in the system that results from the autonomous behaviour of many parts of the system.

However, the poor coordination within government (horizontally between departments and ministries, and vertically between national, provincial and local government) has also been noted. Difficulties arise when creative autonomy and flexibility phases into chaotic indiscipline and lack of coordination. As the economy gets more sophisticated and public management tasks more complex, a greater coherence will be required of government institutions.

Likewise, there has been no serious effort to raise the salary scales of public servants in line with growing income levels in the private sector, making it difficult to check the spread of corruption.

With the state still playing a leading role in the economy, ineffective public administration and poor public spending decisions could slow economic growth.

While much remains to be done, Viet Nam has, in its own way, been remarkably successful in implementing *Doi Moi* to move the economy to a high growth path and to reduce poverty dramatically.

NOTES

[1] This is consistent with international empirical studies. Sen argues that, based on empirical studies, the hypothesis that there is no relationship between political freedom and economic performance 'is hard to reject'. However, Sen argues that 'developing a democratic system is an essential component of the process of development' (1999:150). Interestingly, the need to improve democratic processes (especially grassroots democracy) is a recurring theme in the development strategy approved by the Vietnamese National Assembly. At the end of the July–August 2002 session of the National Assembly, the Chairman called on Vietnamese 'to uphold national unity, strength self-reliance to successfully implement the

industrialisation and modernisation process for a powerful country with wealthy people and an equal, democratic, and civilised society'.

2   Sen (1999) stresses the interconnections between political freedoms and the understanding and fulfilment of economic needs. He notes that 'political freedoms can have a major role in providing incentives and information in the solution of acute economic needs' (1999:147). While there were few political freedoms in Viet Nam in 1986, the state did respond to domestic concerns about economic needs.

3   Without large financial incentives, there was also greater incentive for external policy advisors to prepare arguments for policy reform carefully. In the absence of financial incentives, national policymakers were only likely to implement reforms if they were convinced of the benefits.

4   The Sixth Party Plenum (Ninth Congress) in August 2002 called for 'accelerated administrative reform to abolish intermediary agencies that are usually found to be beset with red-tape and complicated procedures' and the separation of state administrative functions from business operations.

5   Castello and Domenech (2002) argue that both the level and the distribution of education is important for economic growth. They find that greater equality in human capital development is associated with higher investment rates and income growth.

6   The World Bank IDA Poverty Reduction Support Credit of US$250 million, agreed in 2001, includes a policy matrix with over fifty policy actions to be implemented over the coming three years. Given the success of the Vietnamese without such support and policy conditionality, this sort of comprehensive donor guidance might seem gratuitous, if not arrogant. The explanation seems to lie in the internal process of the World Bank, where the management seems to require the purchase of a policy matrix commensurate with the size of a credit.

7   At a conference on information technology in September 2002, Nguyen Khoa Diem (Secretary of the Communist Party Central Committee and Politburo member) stressed the importance of the internet for social and economic development but complained that 'Internet and e-newspaper development remains slower than other regional countries and has not met the demand for national development and the needs of the people...Viet Nam's e-newspapers are not very informative and are not very attractive to readers while Internet costs remain so high'.

APPENDIX 1

STATISTICAL APPENDIX

Table A1.1 **GDP at current prices by economic sector, 1985–2001 (VND billion)**

	Total	Of which		
		Agriculture, forestry and fishing	Industry and construction	Services
1985	177	47	32	38
1986	599	228	173	198
1987	2,870	1,164	814	892
1988	15,420	7,139	3,695	4,586
1989	28,093	11,818	6,444	9,831
1990	41,955	16,252	9,513	16,190
1991	76,707	31,058	18,252	27,397
1992	110,532	37,513	30,135	42,884
1993	140,258	41,895	40,535	57,828
1994	178,534	48,985	51,540	78,026
1995	228,892	62,219	65,820	100,853
1996	272,036	75,514	80,876	115,646
1997	313,623	80,826	100,595	132,202
1998	361,017	93,073	117,299	150,645
1999	399,942	101,723	137,959	160,260
2000	441,646	108,356	162,220	171,070
2001 (prel.)	484,493	114,412	183,291	186,790

Source: General Statistics Office.

Table A1.2   **GDP at constant prices by economic sector, 1985–2001 (VND billion)**

	Total	Of which		
		Agriculture, forestry and fishing	Industry and construction	Services
At constant 1989 prices				
1985	23,875	10,455	5,231	8,189
1986	24,431	10,705	5,769	7,957
1987	25,321	10,649	6,297	8,375
1988	26,835	11,069	6,630	9,136
1989	28,093	11,818	6,444	9,831
1990	29,526	12,003	6,629	10,894
1991	31,286	12,264	7,228	11,794
1992	33,991	13,132	8,242	12,617
1993	36,735	13,634	9,324	13,777
1994	39,982	14,169	10,631	15,182
At constant 1994 prices				
1994	178,534	48,968	51,540	78,026
1995	195,567	51,319	58,550	85,698
1996	213,833	53,577	67,016	93,240
1997	231,264	55,895	75,474	99,895
1998	244,596	57,866	81,764	104,966
1999	256,272	60,895	88,047	107,330
2000	273,656	63,717	96,913	113,036
2001 (prel.)	292,376	65,497	106,914	119,965

Source: General Statistics Office

Table A1.3 **GDP growth at constant prices by economic sector, 1985–2001 (previous year=100)**

	Total	Of which		
		Agriculture, forestry and fishing	Industry and construction	Services
1985	100	100	100	100
1986	102.33	102.39	110.28	97.17
1987	103.64	99.48	109.15	105.25
1988	105.98	103.94	105.29	109.09
1989	104.69	106.77	97.19	107.61
1990	105.09	101.00	102.27	110.19
1991	105.81	102.18	107.71	107.38
1992	108.06	106.88	112.79	107.58
1993	108.08	103.28	112.62	108.64
1994	108.83	103.37	113.39	109.56
1995	109.54	104.80	113.60	109.83
1996	109.34	104.40	114.46	108.80
1997	108.15	104.33	112.62	107.14
1998	105.76	103.53	108.33	105.08
1999	104.77	105.23	107.68	102.25
2000	106.79	104.63	110.07	105.32
2001 (prel.)	106.84	102.79	110.32	106.13

Source: General Statistics Office.

Table A1.4   **Retail price inflation—consumer goods and services, 1986–2001 (previous December=100)**

Year	Price levels
December 1986	874.7
December 1987	323.1
December 1988	493.8
December 1989	134.7
December 1990	167.1
December 1991	167.5
December 1992	117.5
December 1993	105.2
December 1994	114.4
December 1995	112.7
December 1996	104.5
December 1997	103.6
December 1998	109.2
December 1999	100.1
December 2000	99.4
December 2001	100.8

Source: General Statistics Office.

Table A1.5 **Total values of exports and imports, 1990–2001 (US\$ million)**

	Total	Exports	Imports
1990	5,156.4	2,404.0	2,752.5
1991	4,425.2	2,087.1	2,338.1
1992	5,121.4	2,580.7	2,540.7
1993	6,909.2	2,985.2	3,924.0
1994	9,880.1	4,054.3	5,825.8
1995	13,604.3	5,448.9	8,155.4
1996	18,399.5	7,255.9	11,143.6
1997	20,777.3	9,185.0	11,592.3
1998	20,859.9	9,360.3	11,499.6
1999	23,283.5	11,541.4	11,742.1
2000	30,119.2	14,482.7	15,636.5
2001 (prel.)	31,189.0	15,027.0	16,162.0
Index (Previous year = 100)			
1990	114.3	123.5	107.3
1991	85.8	86.8	84.9
1992	115.7	123.7	108.7
1993	134.9	115.7	154.4
1994	143.0	135.8	148.5
1995	137.7	134.4	140.0
1996	135.2	133.2	136.6
1997	112.9	126.6	104.0
1998	100.4	101.9	99.2
1999	111.6	123.3	102.1
2000	129.4	125.5	133.2
2001 (prel.)	103.6	103.8	103.4

Source: General Statistics Office.

Table A1.6   Merchandise exports by major commodities, 1992–2000 (US$ million, unless otherwise specified)

	1992	1993	1994	1995	1996	1997	1998	1999	2000
Total exports f.o.b	2,475	2,985	4,054	5,198	7,337	9,145	9,365	11,540	14,449
(excluding oil)	1,719	2,141	3,188	4,174	5,991	7,722	8,133	9,448	10,946
Crude oil									
Value	756	844	866	1,024	1,346	1,423	1,232	2,092	3,503
Volume ('000 tonnes)	5,400	6,152	6,949	7,593	8,705	9,638	12,145	14,882	15,424
Unit value (US$/tonne)	140	137	125	135	154	148	101	141	227
Rice									
Value	300	363	425	496	855	870	1,020	1,025	667
Volume ('000 tonnes)	1,860	1,725	2,040	1,922	3,003	3,553	3,730	4,508	3,477
Unit value (US$/tonne)	161	210	208	258	285	245	273	227	192
Coal									
Value	47	70	75	90	155	111	102	96	94
Volume ('000 tonnes)	1,580	1,940	2,319	2,620	3,647	3,454	3,162	1,259	3,251
Unit value (US$/tonne)	30	36	32	34	32	32	32	29	39
Rubber									
Value	54	74	133	159	163	191	127	146	166
Volume ('000 tonnes)	68	97	129	132	122	195	191	263	273
Unit value (US$/tonne)	800	763	1,031	1,208	1,336	980	667	556	608
Coffee									
Value	86	110	328	565	337	498	594	585	501
Volume ('000 tonnes)	96	122	177	241	239	392	382	482	734
Unit value (US$/tonne)	900	902	1,853	2,348	1,410	1,271	1,554	1,213	683
Marine products									
Value	302	427	551	431	651	782	858	974	1 479
Garments									
Value	190	239	476	431	1,150	1,503	1,450	1,746	1,892
Footwear									
Value	5	68	122	200	531	978	1,031	1,387	1,465
Handicrafts									
Value	..	..	..	70	79	121	111	168	237
Electronic goods and components									
Value	..	..	..	..	..	440	492	585	783
Other	734	790	1,078	1,732	2,071	2,228	2,342	2,736	3,662

Sources: International Monetary Fund, from Ministry of Trade and Customs Office data.

Table A1.7 Balance of payments, 1992–2000 (in US$million)

	1992	1993	1994	1995	1996	1997	1998	1999	2000[a]
Current account balance	-8	-1,395	-1,872	-2,648	-2,431	-1,664	-1,067	1,285	642
(excluding official transfers)	-72	-1,589	-2,004	-2,801	-2,581	-1,839	-1,239	1,154	506
Trade balance	-60	-1,177	-1,865	-3,155	-3,143	-1,315	-981	1,080	378
Exports, f.o.b	2,475	2,985	4,054	5,198	7,337	9,145	9,365	11,540	14,449
Imports, f.o.b	2,535	4,162	5,919	8,253	10,480	10,460	10,346	10,460	14,071
Non-factor services (net)	311	78	19	159	-61	-623	-539	-547	-615
Receipts	724	772	1,516	2,409	2,709	2,530	2,604	2,493	2,695
Payments	413	694	1,497	2,250	2,770	3,153	3,143	3,040	3,310
Investment income (net)	-382	-560	-328	-279	-427	-611	-669	-429	-597
Receipts	43	30	27	96	140	136	133	142	185
Payments	425	590	355	375	567	747	802	571	782
Transfers (net)	123	264	302	627	1,200	885	1,122	1,181	1,476
Private transfers	59	70	170	474	1,050	710	950	1,050	1,340
Official transfers	64	194	132	153	150	175	172	131	136
Capital account	271	442	1,476	2,326	2,079	1,662	216	-334	-772
Gross foreign direct investment (FDI)	260	936	1,627	2,276	1,813	2,074	800	700	800
Equity	222	697	1,033	1,287	891	1,002	240	301	320
Loan disbursement	38	238	594	989	921	1,072	560	399	480
FDI loan repayment	0	0	0	8	55	174	372	603	601
Medium and long term loans (net)	52	-597	-275	-253	98	375	432	605	729
Disbursements	487	54	272	443	772	1,007	1,121	1,036	1,411
ODA Loans	..	..	..	189	336	550	796	970	1,361
Commercial Loans	..	..	..	254	436	457	326	66	50
Scheduled amortisation	435	651	547	696	674	632	690	431	682
Short term capital (net)	-41	117	124	311	224	-612	-644	-1,036	-1,700
Errors and omissions	-198	-103	9	284	1	-2	327	-183	247
Overall balance	66	-1,056	-387	-38	-351	-4	-524	768	116
Financing	-66	1,056	387	38	351	4	534	-768	-116
Change in net international reserve	-262	438	-19	-390	-190	-319	-15	-1,316	-116
Arrears	196	-265	406	428	541	323	126	548	-9,691
Debt relief	0	883	0	0	0	0	413	0	9,691

Note: [a] Estimate

Source: International Monetary Fund (various issues), *Vietnam: selected issues and statistical appendix*, International Monetary Fund, Washington, DC

REFERENCES

Amsden, A., 1989. *Asia's Next Giant: South Korea and late industrialization*, Oxford University Press, London.

——, 1971. *Southeast Asia's Economy in the 1970s*, Longman, London.

——, 1989. *Economic Report on the Socialist Republic of Viet Nam*, Asian Development Bank, Manila.

Asian Development Bank, 1997b. *Emerging Asia: changes and challenges*, Oxford University Press, Hong Kong.

——, 2001. *Special Report on Program Lending*, SST: STU 2001-16, Asian Development Bank, Manila.

——, various issues. *Asian Development Outlook*, Oxford University Press, Hong Kong.

——, various issues. *Key Indicators of Developing Asian and Pacific Countries*, Oxford University Press, Hong Kong.

—— and IFPRI, 1996. *Rice Market Monitoring and Policy Options Study*, Asian Development Bank, Hanoi.

Asian Development Bank, MPI and CIE, 1998. Policies for Industrial Development and Enterprise Reform, Unpublished Report, ADB/MPI/CIE, Hanoi.

Asian Development Bank, UNDP and World Bank, 2000. *Viet Nam Development Report 2001. Viet Nam 2010: entering the 21st century*, Asian Development Bank, UNDP and World Bank, Hanoi.

Bauer, P.T. and Yamey, B.S., 1957. *The Economics of Underdeveloped Countries*, Cambridge University Press, Cambridge.

Bentley, J., 1997. Promoting dynamic self-sustaining economic growth to reduce poverty in Viet Nam: the legal agenda, Report to Ministry of Justice under UNDP Project VIE/94/003, Hanoi.

Beresford, M., 1988. *Vietnam, Politics, Economics and Society*, Pinter Publishers, London.

Berkowitz, D., Pistor, K and Richard, J-F., 2000. *Economic development, legality and the transplant effect*, CID Working Paper 38, Center for International Development, Harvard University, Cambridge, Massachusetts.

Boom, D. and Williamson, J.G., 1998. 'Demographic transitions and economic miracles in emerging Asia', *World Bank Economic Review*, 12(3):419–56.

Castello, A. and Domenech, R., 2002. 'Human capital inequality and economic growth: some new evidence', *The Economic Journal*, 112(478):187–200.

Centre for International Economics, 1999. *Trade and Economic Policies for Economic Integration*, Centre for International Economics, Canberra.

Central Institute for Economic Management, 1998. Review of the current company law and key recommendations for its revision, Report prepared under UNDP-financed project VIE/97/016, Central Institute for Economic Management, Hanoi.

——, 2000. Regulatory environment for business: evaluation study, CIEM/UNDP Project VIE/97/016, Central Institute for Economic Management, Hanoi (unpublished).

——, 2001. Report to CIEM Workshop on Implementation of the Cooperative Law, Central Institute for Economic Management, Hanoi.

Centre for Population and Human Resources Studies, 1995. Analysis, evaluation of the relation between population, migration, human resources and employment, Abstract report, Centre for Population and Human Resources Studies, Hanoi.

Chang, Ha-Joon, 1999. Industrial policy and East Asia: the miracle, the crisis, and the future, Paper presented to World Bank workshop 'Re-thinking the East Asian Miracle', San Francisco, 16–17 February.

Che, Nhu, 1997. The effects of internal and external trade liberalization on agriculture growth: a case study of Viet Nam, PhD Dissertation, Research School of Pacific and Asian Studies, The Australian National University, Canberra.

Chinh, Truong, 1986. *In Preparation for the Sixth Party Congress*, Foreign Languages Publishing House, Hanoi.

Collier, P., 2000a. Consensus-building, Knowledge and Conditionality, Paper presented to the Annual Bank Conference on Development Economics, 18–20 April, Washington, DC. Available online at http://orion.forumone.com/ABCDE/files.fcgi/139_collier.pdf.

——, 2000b. *A New Relationship Between Donors and Recipients: the end of conditionality?*, World Bank, Washington, DC.

——, Dollar, D. and Stern, N., 2000. Fifty years of development, Paper presented at ABCDE Europe 2000, Paris, 26–28 June. Available online at www.worldbank.org/research/abcde/eu_2000.

Communist Party of Vietnam, 1977. *Political Report of the Fourth National Congress*, Su That Publishing House, Hanoi.

——, 1986a. *History of the Communist Party of Vietnam*, Foreign Languages Publishing House, Hanoi. Available online at http://www.cpv.org.vn/cpv/history/index.htm.

——, 1986b. *On the Eve of the Sixth Congress of the Communist Party of Vietnam*, Foreign Languages Publishing House, Hanoi.

——, 1987a. *Sixth National Congress of the Communist Party of Vietnam: documents*, The Gioi Publishers, Hanoi.

——, 1987b. *Political Report of the Sixth National Congress of the Communist Party of Vietnam*, Foreign Language Publishing House, Hanoi.

——, 1991a. *Seventh National Congress Documents*, Foreign Language Publishing House, Hanoi.

——, 1991b. *Political Report of the Seventh Party Congress*, Foreign Language Publishing House, Hanoi.

——, 1991c. *To Understand the Seventh National Congress of the Communist Party of Viet Nam*, Foreign Language Publishing House, Hanoi.

——, 1996a. 'Political Report of the Central Committee', in *Eighth National Congress Documents*, Foreign Language Publishing House, Hanoi.

——, 1996b. *Resolutions of the Fourth Plenum of the Eighth Party Congress*, Foreign Language Publishing House, Hanoi.

——, 1999. *Guidelines, Regulations, and Decisions on the Organization and Personnel Management of the Communist Party of Viet Nam*, Communist Party of Vietnam Publishing House, Hanoi.

——, 2001a. *Ninth National Congress: documents*, The Gioi Publishers, Hanoi

——, 2001b. *Vietnamese Land and People*, Communist Party of Vietnam, Hanoi. Available online at http://www.cpv.org.vn/vietnam_en/land_people.

——, 2002. *The Fifth Plenum of the Central Committee of the Communist Party of Vietnam*, Communist Party of Vietnam, Hanoi. Available online at http://www.cpv.org.vn/chuyende/fifthplenumcpv_2002/index.htm

Dam, Dang Duc, 1997. *Vietnam's Macro-economy and Types of Enterprises: the current position and future prospects*, The Gioi Publishers, Hanoi.

Development Economics Vice Presidency, 2002. The role and effectiveness of development assistance: lessons from World Bank assistance, Paper presented to the United Nations International Conference on Financing for Development, Monterrey, 18–22 March. Available online http://econ.worldbank.org/files/13080_Development_Effectiveness.pdf.

De Vylder, S. and Fforde, A., 1988. *Vietnam: an economy in transition*, SIDA, Stockholm.

Dao Huy Giam and Vu Quang Minh, 2000. *Identification of WTO Inconsistent Policies*, Viet Nam's Socio-Economic Development 23, Institute of Economics, Hanoi.

Doanh, Le Dang, 1991. Economic renovation in Vietnam: achievements and prospects, Paper presented at the conference Doi Moi: Vietnam's economic renovation, The Australian National University, 19–21 September (reprinted in Forbes et al. 1991. *Doi Moi: Vietnam's renovation and performance*, Political and Social Change Monograph 14, Research School of Pacific Studies, Australian National University, Canberra).

——, 1995. Equitisation of State Enterprises in Ho Chi Minh City: a positive contribution to the task of reforming state enterprises, Report to the Workshop on Equitisation, Ho Chi Minh City, 3 August.

—— and McCarty, A., 1995. 'Economic reform in Viet Nam, 1986–94', in M.Than and J.Tan (eds), *Asian Transitional Economies: challenges and prospects for reform and transformation*, Institute of South East Asian Studies, Singapore:99–153.

Dapice, David O., 1998. Facing the new reality: an the economic crisis become an advantage for Vietnam?, Harvard Institute for International Development, Harvard University, Cambridge, Massachusetts, 1 May (unpublished).

Dollar, D., 2001. Reform, Growth and Poverty in Viet Nam, Paper presented to a workshop on Economic Growth and Household Welfare: lessons for Viet Nam, Hanoi, 16–18 May.

—— and Ljunggren, B., 1995. Macroeconomic Adjustment and Structural Reform in and Open Transition Economy: the Case of Viet Nam, Paper prepared for a conference on Participation of Reforming Economies in the Global Trading and Financial System, Helsinki, 26–27 May.

Dollar, D. and Svensson, J., 1998. *What Explains the Success or Failure of Structural Adjustment Programs?*, Policy Research Working Paper 1938, World Bank, Washington, DC.

Drabek, Z., 1990. *A Case Study of a Gradual Approach to Economic Reform: the Viet Nam Experience of 1985–88*, Asia Regional Series Report IDP 74, World Bank, Washington DC.

Druiker, W., 2000. *Ho Chi Minh*, Allen and Unwin, Sydney.

Le Duan, 1970. 'Under the glorious banner of the Party, for the sake of independence, freedom and socialism, let us advance toward new successes', in Communist Party of Vietnam, 1986, *History of the Communist Party of Vietnam*, Foreign Languages Publishing House, Hanoi.

Easterly, W., 2001. 'The lost decades: developing countries' stagnation in spite of policy reform 1980–98', *Journal of Economic Growth*, 6(2):135–57.

Fforde, A., 1990. 'Major Policy Changes and Socio-Economic developments in Viet Nam since mid 1988', in P. Ronnas and O. Sjoberg (eds), *Doi Moi: economic reforms and development policies in Viet Nam*, SIDA, Stockholm:7–29.

—— (ed.), 1997. *Doi Moi: ten years after the 1986 Party Congress*, Political and Social Change Monograph 24, Department of Political and Social Change, The Australian National University, Canberra.

—— and de Vylder, S., 1996. *From Plan to Market: the economic transition in Vietnam*, Westview Press, Oxford.

Forbes, D.K., Hull, T.H., Marr, D.G. and Brogan, B. (eds), 1991. *Doi Moi: Vietnam's renovation and performance*, Political and Social Change Monograph 14, Research School of Pacific Studies, The Australian National University, Canberra.

General Statistics Office, 1989. *Statistical Yearbook 1989*, Statistical Publishing House, Hanoi.

——, 1992. *Statistical Yearbook 1992*, Statistical Publishing House, Hanoi.

——, 1994. *Estimating the Fertility and Mortality of Provinces and Ethnic Groups: Viet Nam, 1989.* Statistical Publishing House, Hanoi.

——, 1995. *Inter-censal Demographic Survey 1994: major findings*, Statistical Publishing House, Hanoi.

——, 1996. *Impetus and Present Situation of Viet Nam Society and Economy after Ten Years of Doi Moi*, Statistical Publishing House, Hanoi.

——, 2000a. *Statistical Data of Vietnam Socio-Economy 1975–2000*, Statistical Publishing House, Hanoi.

——, 2000b. *Statistical Yearbook 2000*, Statistical Publishing House, Hanoi.

——, 2000c. *Viet Nam Living Standards Survey 1997–1998*, Statistical Publishing House, Hanoi.

——, 2001. *Statistical Yearbook 2001*, Statistical Publishing House, Hanoi, and earlier versions of this yearbook.

——, 2002. *Viet Nam's Economy in the Years of Reform*, Statistical Publishing House, Hanoi.

——, various years. *Statistical Yearbook*, Statistical Publishing House, Hanoi.

Gillespie, J., 2001a. *Viet Nam: legal and judicial development*, AusAID Working Paper 3, Australian Agency for International Development, Canberra.

——, 2001b. 'Self interest and ideology: bureaucratic corruption in Vietnam', *Australian Journal of Asian Law*, 3(1):1–36.

——, 2002. 'Transplanted company law: an ideological and cultural analysis of market entry in Viet Nam', *International and Comparative Law Quarterly*, 51(3):641–72.

Glewwe, P., Gragnolati, M. and Zaman, H., 2000. *Who Gained from Vietnam's Boom in the 1990s? An analysis of poverty and inequality trends*, Working Paper 2275, World Bank, Washington, DC.

Glewwe, P. and Phong Nguyen, 2002. *Economic Mobility in Vietnam in the 1990s*, Working Paper 2838, World Bank, Washington, DC.

Goddard, D., 1997. Enterprise Reform: legal and regulatory issues, presentation to MPI/ADB Enterprise Reform Workshop, Hanoi, October 1997.

Government of Vietnam, 1992. *Constitution 1992*, Foreign Language Publishing House, Hanoi.

——, 1993. *Viet Nam: A Development Perspective,* Government Report to Consultative Group Meeting, Hanoi.

——, 1995. *The Constitutions of Viet Nam. National Assembly (1946, 1959, 1980, and 1992)*, The Gioi Publishers, Hanoi.

——, 1996. Development and Official Development Assistance in the Period of Strongly Promoting Industrialisation and Modernisation in Viet Nam, Government Report to Consultative Group Meeting, Hanoi.

——, 1998. *The National Assembly of the Socialist Republic of Viet Nam*, The Gioi Publishers, Hanoi.

——, 2001. *Policies and Measures to Strengthen Implementation of the Five-year Socio-economic Development Plan (2001–2005) Aimed at Achieving Sustainable Growth and Poverty Alleviation*, Government of Vietnam, Hanoi.

——, World Bank and other donors, 2000. *Vietnam Public Expenditure Review*, Government of Vietnam, World Bank and others, Hanoi

Hardy, A., 2000. 'Strategies of migration to upland areas in contemporary Vietnam', *Asia Pacific Viewpoint*, 41(1):23–34.

Heritage Foundation and Wall Street Journal, 2001. *The 2001 Index of Economic Freedom*, Heritage Foundation, Washington, DC and Wall Street Journal, New York.

Hiebert, M., 1996. *Chasing the Tiger*, Kodansha International, New York.

Hirschman, A.O., 1958. *The Strategy of Economic Development*, Yale University Press, New Haven.

International Monetary Fund, 1996. *Viet Nam: transition to a market economy*, International Monetary Fund, Washington, DC.

——, 1999. *Viet Nam: selected issues*, IMF Staff Country Report 99/55, International Monetary Fund, Washington, DC.

——, 2002. Second Review Under the Three-year Arrangement under the Poverty Reduction and Growth Facility, International Monetary Fund, Washington, DC.

——, various issues. *Vietnam—Recent Economic Developments*, IMF Staff Country Reports, International Monetary Fund, Washington, DC.

—— and World Bank, 1999. *Vietnam: towards fiscal transparency*, IMF and World Bank, Hanoi.

Irvin, G.W., 1996. 'Emerging issues in Viet Nam: privatisation, equity and sustainable growth' *European Journal of Development Research*, 2(8):178–99.

Islam, R. and Montenegro, C.E., 2002. 'What determines the quality of institutions?', Background Paper for World Bank, *World Development Report 2002: building institutions for markets*, World Bank, Washington, DC. Available online at http://info.worldbank.org/etools/docs.

Jamieson, N.L., 1993. *Understanding Vietnam*, University of California Press, Berkeley.

Japan Bank for International Cooperation, 2002. Business environment for Vietnam's private enterprise, Japan Bank for International Cooperation, Hanoi (unpublished).

Japan International Cooperation Agency, 2001. Study on economic development policy in the transition to a market-oriented economy in the Socialist Republic of Viet Nam (Phase 2): executive summary, Japan International Cooperation Agency, Hanoi (unpublished).

Jenkins, R., 2002. The labour market effects of globalisation in Viet Nam, draft paper prepared for the Workshop on Globalisation and Poverty, Hanoi.

Jomo K.S., 1997. *Southeast Asia's Misunderstood Miracle*, Westview Press, Colorado.

Justino, P. and Litchfield, J., 2002. Poverty dynamics in rural Vietnam: winners and losers during reform, paper prepared for the 27th. General Conference of the International Association for Research in Income and Wealth, Stockholm, 18–24 August.

Kolko, G., 1997. *Vietnam: anatomy of a peace*, Routledge, London.

Kokko, A. and Zejan, M., 1996. *Viet Nam 1996: approaching the next stage of reforms*, Swedish International Development Cooperation Agency (SIDA), Stockholm.

Kokko, A., Hakkala, K. and Kang, O., 2001. *Step by Step: economic reform and renovation in Viet Nam before the Ninth Party Congress*, Swedish International Development Cooperation Agency (SIDA), Stockholm.

Kornai, J., 1980. *Economics of Shortage*, North-Holland Publishing, Amsterdam.

——, 1992. *The Socialist System: the political economy of communism*, Norton, New York.

Krugman, P., 1994. 'The myth of East Asia's miracle', *Foreign Affairs*, 73(6):62–78.

Leung, S. (ed.), 1999. *Vietnam and the East Asian Crisis*, Edward Elgar, London.

Ljunggren, B., 1997. 'Vietnam's second decade under *Doi Moi*: emerging contradictions in the reform process', in B. Beckman, E. Hansson and L. Roman (eds), *Vietnam: Reform and Transition*, Centre for Pacific Asia Studies, Stockholm University, Stockholm:9–36.

——, 2001. 'Comments on the socio-economic development strategy', *Proceedings from the Second Roundtable Consultation on the Ten-Year Socio-economic Development Strategy 2001–10*, Ministry of Planning and Investment/UNDP, Hanoi.

Luoc, Vo Dai, 1994. *Viet Nam's Industrial Development Policy in the Course of Renovation*, Social Science Publishing House, Hanoi.

——, 1996. *Viet Nam's Industrialisation, Modernisation and Resources*, Social Science Publishing House, Hanoi.

Maddison, A., 2001. *The World Economy: a millennial perspective*, Organisation for Economic Cooperation and Development, Paris.

Mallon, R., 1993. 'Vietnam: image and reality', in J. Heath (ed.), *Revitalising Socialist Enterprise*, Routledge, London.

——, 1996. *State Enterprise Reform in Viet Nam: policy developments, achievements and remaining constraints*, Consultant Report to the Asian Development Bank, Manila.

——, 1997. '*Doi Moi* and economic development in Vietnam', in A. Fforde (ed.), *Doi Moi: ten years after the 1986 Party Congress*, The Australian National University, Canberra:2–24.

——, 1998a. Mapping the Playing Field: options for reducing private sector disincentives in Viet Nam, Report prepared for Swedish Embassy, Hanoi (unpublished).

——, 1998b. Enterprise restructuring to create more equitable opportunities for private and state enterprises in the industry sector, Background Paper for GOV/ADB Enterprise Reform Project, Hanoi (unpublished).

——, 1999. 'Experiences in the region and private sector incentives in Vietnam', in S. Leung (ed.), *Vietnam and the East Asian Crisis*, Edward Elgar, London:165–92.

—— and Irvin, G., 1997. *Is the Vietnamese Miracle in Trouble?*, ISS Working Paper Series 253, Institute for Social Science, The Hague.

——, 2001. 'Systemic change and economic reform in Vietnam', in J. Weeks and B. Claes (eds), *Globalization and Third World Socialism: Cuba and Vietnam*. Palgrave, London:153–67.

McCarty, A., 2000. 'The social impact of economic transition in Vietnam', in J.Weeks and B.Claes, *Globalization and Third World Socialism: Cuba and Vietnam*, Palgrave, London:237–54.

——, 2001. Governance Institutions and Incentive Structures in Vietnam, paper presented at Building Institutional Capacity in Asia (BICA) Conference, Jakarta, 12 March. Available online at http://www.riap.usyd.edu.au/bica/2001/

——, 2002. The policy making process in Viet Nam, Mekong Economics, Hanoi (unpublished).

McMillan, J. and Woodruff, C., 1999a. 'Dispute resolution without courts in Vietnam', *Journal of Law, Economics and Organization*, 15(3):637–58.

——, 1999b. 'Interfirm relations and informal credit in Vietnam', *Quarterly Journal of Economics*, 114(4):1,285–320.

McNicholl, G., 2002. Demographic Factors in East Asian Regional Transition, Policy Research Division Working Paper 158, Population Council, New York.

Megginson, W.L. and Netter, J.M., 2001. 'From state to market: a survey of empirical studies on privatization', *Journal of Economic Literature*, 39(2):321–89.

Messick, R.E., 1999. 'Judicial reform and economic development: a survey of the issues', *World Bank Research Observer*, 14(1):117–36.

Do Muoi, 1995. 'Problems of agriculture, the countryside and the peasantry in the renovation of the countryside', in Do Muoi, *Viet Nam: new challenges and new opportunities*, The Gioi Publishers, Hanoi:43–70.

Ministry of Construction, 1995. Viet Nam urban sector strategy study—Final report, Ministry of Construction (with the assistance of ADB, UNDP, UNCHS), Hanoi (unpublished).

Nelson, R.R. and Pack, H., 1999. 'The Asian Miracle and modern growth theory', *The Economic Journal*, 109(457):416–36.

Tran Ngoc Trang, 1994. Re-registration of state enterprises, paper presented to a UNDP/World Bank workshop on State Enterprise Reform, Hanoi, 8–9 March.

Nguyen Ngoc Tuan et al., 1995. Situation and tendencies regarding the restructuring of state enterprises towards industrialisation and modernisation in Viet Nam, Hanoi (unpublished).

Nga Nguyen Nguyet and Wagstaff, A., 2002. *Poverty and Survival Prospects of Vietnamese Children under Doi Moi*, World Bank Working Paper 2832, World Bank, Washington, DC.

Nguyen Van Chi, 2000. *Tariff Policies and Trade Liberalization*, Viet Nam's Socio-Economic Development 23, Institute of Economics, Hanoi.

Nguyen Van Dang, 2001. 'Vietnam's economic renovation in retrospect', unpublished paper, January 2001.

North, D.C., 1994. 'Economic performance through time', *American Economic Review*, 84(3):359–68.

——, 2000. *Poverty in the Midst of Plenty*, Hoover Institution Weekly Essays, Hoover Institution Stanford University, Stanford. Available online at http://www-hoover.stanford.edu/pubaffairs/we/current/north_1000.html.

Parente, S.L. and Prescott, E.C., 2000. *Barriers to Riches*, MIT Press, Cambridge.

Pistor, K., 1999, The evolution of legal institutions and economic regime change, paper presented to Annual Bank Conference on Development Economics–Europe, Paris, 21–23 June.

—— and Wellons, P., 1999. *The Role of Law and Legal Institutions in Asian Economic Development*. Oxford University Press, Hong Kong.

Posner, R.A., 1998. 'Creating a legal framework for economic development', *World Bank Research Observer*, 13(1):1–11.

Reidel, J. and Chuong S. Tran, 1997. *The Emerging Private Sector and Industrialization of Viet Nam*, Report to the International Finance Corporation, International Finance Corporation, Hanoi.

RIAS, 2001. *Public Sector Challenges and Government Reforms in South East Asia*, Report Commissioned by the Ministry of Finance of Japan, Ministry of Finance, Tokyo.

Rodrigo, C.G., 2000. 'East Asia's growth: technology or accumulation?', *Contemporary Economic Policy*, 18(2):215–27.

Rodrik, D., 1996. 'Economic growth in East Asia: accumulation versus assimilation', *Brookings Papers on Economic Activity*, 2:135–209.

Ronnas, P., 1992. *Employment Generation Through Private Entrepreneurship in Vietnam*, International Labour Organization, Geneva.

—— and Ramamurthy, B. (ed.), 2001. *Entrepreneurship in Vietnam: transformation and dynamics*, Institute for South East Asian Studies, Singapore.

Ronnas, P. and Sjoberg, O. (eds), 1991. *Socio-economic Development in Vietnam: the agenda for the 1990s*, SIDA, Stockholm.

Schumpeter, J., 1936. *The Theory of Economic Development*, Harvard Univesrity Press, Cambridge, Massachusetts.

Sen, A., 1999. *Development as Freedom*, Oxford University Press, Oxford.

Stiglitz, J., 1999a. Wither reform: ten years of the transition, Keynote Presentation to the World Bank Annual Conference on Development Economics, Washington, DC, 18–20 April.

——, 1999b. Corporate Governance Failures in Transition, paper presented at the Annual World Bank Conference on Development Economics, Paris, 21–23 June. Available online at http://www.worldbank.org/research/abcde/eu/stiglitz.pdf.

Tan Teng Lang. 1994. *Economic Debates in Vietnam: issues and problems in reconstruction and development*, Institute for Southeast Asian Studies. Singapore.

Le Trang, 1989. 'Renewal of industrial management policy and organization', in Per Ronnas and Orjan Sjoberg (eds), *Socio-economic Development in Vietnam: the agenda for the 1990s*, SIDA, Stockholm:153–92.

Tri Vo Nhan, 1990. *Vietnam's Economic Policy Since 1975*, Institute of South East Asian Studies, Singapore

Tuong Lai, 1999. 'The role of small and medium scale business in the renovation process of Vietnam', in T. Heberer, A. Kohl, Tuong Lai and Nguyen Duc Vinh, *Aspects of Private Sector Development in Vietnam,* Duisberg Working Papers on East Asian Studies No. 24, Institute for East Asian Studies, Gerhard-Mercator-Universität, Duisberg:3–14.

UK Department for International Development, 2001. *Making Government Work for Poor People: building state capability*, Department for International Development, London.

United Nations, 1998. *Expanding Choices for the Rural Poor*, United Nations, Hanoi.

United Nations Development Programme, 2001. *Human Development Report 2001*, Oxford University Press, Oxford.

—— and SPC, 1990. *Report on the Economy of Viet Nam*, United Nations Development Programme, Hanoi

United Nations Development Programme, UNFPA and UNICEF, 1996. *Catching Up: capacity building for poverty alleviation in Viet Nam*, United Nations Development Programme, Hanoi.

Upham, F., 2001. Ideology, Experience and the Rule of Law in Developing Societies, presentation to the Roundtable on the Rule of Law, Carnegie Endowment for International Peace, Washington, DC. Available online at http://www.ceip.org/files/events/events.asp?p=1&EventID=380.

US Department of State, 2000. *Background Notes: Vietnam*, Bureau of East Asian and Pacific Affairs, US Department of State, Washington, DC. Available online at http://www.state.gov/www/background_notes.

Van Arkadie, B., 1990. 'The role of institutions in development', in *Proceedings of the First Annual World Conference on Development Economics*, World Bank, Washington, DC:153–75.

—— and Mundle, S., 1996. *Rural–urban Transition in Viet Nam: an exploration of policy options*, Occasional Paper 15, Economic and Development Resource Center, Asian Development Bank, Manila.

Van Arkadie, B. and Vu Tat Boi, 1992. Managing the Renewal Process: the case of Viet Nam, paper presented to UNDP/ODI Conference, London.

—— and Trang Dung Tien, 2000. Review of Technical Co-operation Support to Viet Nam, report prepared for United Nations Development Programme, Hanoi.

van Brabant, J., 1990. 'Reforming a socialist developing country: the case of Vietnam', *Economics of Planning*, 23(3):209–29.

Van de Walle, D., 1998. *Protecting the poor in Vietnam's Emerging Market Economy*, Working Paper 1969, World Bank, Washington, DC.

—— and Gunewardena, D., 2000. 'Sources of ethnic inequality in Viet Nam', *Journal of Development Economics*, 65(1):177–207.

Vijverberg, W.P.M. and Haughton, J., 2002. *Household Enterprises in Vietnam: survival, growth and living standards*, World Bank Working Paper 2773, World Bank, Washington, DC.

Wade, R., 1990. *Governing the Market: economic theory and the role of government in East Asian industrialization*, Princeton University Press, Princeton.

Wood, A., 1989. 'Deceleration of inflation with acceleration of price reform: Vietnam's remarkable recent experience', *Cambridge Journal of Economics*, 13(4):563–71.

World Bank, 1990. *Vietnam: stabilization and structural reforms*, World Bank, Washington, DC.

——, 1993a. *The East Asian Miracle: economic growth and public policy*, Oxford University Press, Oxford.

——, 1993b. *Vietnam: transition to the market*, World Bank, Washington, DC.

——, 1994a. *Vietnam: public sector management and private sector incentives*, World Bank, Hanoi.

——, 1994b. *Viet Nam Agricultural Marketing Study*, Country Office, World Bank, Hanoi.

——, 1995a. *Viet Nam: economic report on industrialisation and industrial policy*, Country Office, World Bank, Hanoi.

——, 1995b. *Viet Nam: poverty assessment and strategy*, World Bank, Washington, DC.

——, 1996. *Viet Nam: fiscal decentralisation and the delivery of rural services*, Country Office, World Bank, Hanoi.

——, 1997. *Viet Nam: deepening reform for growth,* World Bank, Washington DC.

——, 1998a. *Viet Nam: attacking poverty*, Country Office, World Bank, Hanoi.

——, 1998b. *Viet Nam: rising to the challenge*, Country Office, World Bank, Hanoi.

——, 1998c. *Assessing Aid*, World Bank Policy Research Report, Oxford University Press, Oxford.

——, 2000. *Viet Nam 2010: entering the 21st century*, Country Office, World Bank, Hanoi.

——, 2001a. *Viet Nam Development Report 2001: implementing reforms for faster growth and poverty reduction*, Country Office, World Bank, Hanoi.

——, 2001b. *World Development Report 2002: building institutions for markets*, Oxford University Press, Oxford.

——, 2002. *Transition, The First Ten Years: analysis and lessons for Eastern Europe and the former Soviet Union*, World Bank, Washington, DC.

——, various issues. *World Development Indicators*, World Bank, Washington, DC. Available online at https://publications.worldbank.org/subscriptions/WDI/.

Young, A., 1995, 'The tyranny of numbers: confronting the statistical realities of the East Asian growth experience', *Quarterly Journal of Economics*, 100(3):641–80.

INDEX

mining sector *116*, 118, 201, *272* (*see also* coal; petroleum sector)
modernisation, objective of 76, 96, 265–66*n*1
monetary management 58
monetary policy 90, 92–94, 95
monopolisation 133–34, 136, 150*n*38
mortality rates 17, 25*n*1, *52*, 55*n*22, 229, 258
mortgages 101, 102*n*7–8, 157, 174*n*6

National Assembly 56, 59–60, 63*n*1, 64*n*7, 265–66*n*1
national characteristics, evaluation of 35
national development objective 96
nationalisation, Constitutional guarantees against 107
national poverty line 226, 233*n*3
national—provincial relationship 60–62, 63*n*1
National Target Poverty Reduction Programme 233*n*3
National Tax Collection Office 94
National Treasury system 94
natural resources 8, 11, 13–16
neo-Stalinist model 78*n*15
Netherlands 202*n*3
Nguyen Khoa Diem 266*n*7
Nguyen Phong 234*n*7
Nguyen Van Dang 158–59
Nguyen Van Linh 65
Nigeria 184
Ninth Party Congress (2001) 64*n*8, 74, 146, 166, 266*n*4
non-state sector (*see* private sector)
North Central Coast region
    agricultural sector *23*
    GDP share *22*
    gross regional product per capita *22*
    industrial sector *24*, 25
    location map *12*
    population distribution *19*
    poverty incidence 227, *228*, 248, 249
    regional overview 20

Northeast region (*see also* Northern Uplands)
    agricultural sector *23*
    GDP share *22*
    gross regional product per capita *22*
    industrial sector *24*, 25
    location map *12*
    population distribution *19*
    regional overview 20
Northern Uplands *12*, 227–28, *228*, 248, 249 (*see also* Northeast region; Northwest region)
North Korea 76
North Viet Nam 38–42, 53*n*1, 54*n*7, 54*n*12
Northwest region (*see also* Northern Uplands)
    agricultural sector *23*
    GDP share *22*
    gross regional product per capita *22*
    industrial sector *24*, 25
    location map *12*
    per capita income 23
    population distribution *19*
    regional overview 20
nutrition
    1980s standards 191
    poverty line calorific value 202*n*7, 226, 233–34*n*3–5

occupation, poverty severity and *231*
official development assistance (ODA) (*see* external development assistance)
oil (*see* petroleum sector)
'open door policy' 84, 85
'opinion collecting' 57–58
Organisation for Economic Cooperation and Development (OECD) 110, 177
Osaka 26*n*8
output contract system (*see* contract system)
ownership rights 69–70, 78*n*10

paddy production 41, 176, 192, 194, *194*, 195
Pakistan 53